God Stories

VOLUME FIVE

The Regional Church of Lancaster County
www.theregionalchurch.com

Dedication

This book is dedicated to the people of South Central Pennsylvania.

Acknowledgments

Thank you to the many contributing authors who made this book possible.

Edited by Karen Boyd, Lisa Dorr, Lou Ann Good, Sharon Neal, Kim Wittel and Keith Yoder.

House To House Publications Team: Brenda Boll, Karen Ruiz and Sarah Sauder.

Proofreaders: Jan Dorward, Lisa Hosler, Sharon Neal, Denise Sensenig and Carolyn Sprauge

Cover photos: Mark Van Scyoc

Contact an author

If a particular devotional has encouraged you and you want to tell the author, please email Lisa Dorr (lisadorr@juno.com) who will endeavor to pass on your message.

God Stories 5

© 2010 by The Regional Church of Lancaster County
Lancaster, Pennsylvania, USA
www.regionalchurch.com
All rights reserved

ISBN: 978-0-9817765-5-2

Partnership Publications
www.h2hp.com

Printed in the United States of America

Introduction

We include a touch of history along with our contemporary accounts in *God Stories 5*. We celebrate those pioneers of faith in our region who established a legacy that continues to shape our walk with God today. Why?

Regional Church of Lancaster County

This year marks three hundred years since the first land grant to European settlers in what is now known as Lancaster County. We invited our neighboring counties to join in sharing stories that highlight the faith-shaping influence of pioneers.

On October 10, 1710, Johann Bondeli and eight others, mostly Mennonite settlers, were granted a survey for a portion of some of the richest land in Penn's Woods. Like the surveyor, the psalmist recognized that the Lord sets boundaries and designates land on which people may dwell. "The boundary lines have fallen for me in pleasant places; surely I have a delightful inheritance" (Psalm 16:6).

This first land grant to settlers in what was to become known as Lancaster County was already known as the Conestoga watershed and occupied by the Conestoga Indians. These First Nation residents saw themselves as interdependent with the land. They were stewards of the land—a legacy that is both biblical and being restored in our generation.

The purpose of *God Stories* continues to be the cultivation and celebration of oneness in the body of Christ—for which Jesus prayed. As authors and readers we may join in prayer for one another throughout South Central Pennsylvania according to the theme for each day. In response to the request of our readers, we have added an index to this edition.

As we daily participate in worship in these pages, let us continue to long for and anticipate that we may become one in the Father and Son even as they are one "that the world may believe" that the Father sent the Son (John 17:21).

—Keith Yoder, Chair, Regional Church of Lancaster County,
on behalf of the participating regional partnerships

January

Restitution

"They stood and confessed their sins and the iniquities of their fathers." *Nehemiah 9:2b (New King James Version)*

A dark moment in Lancaster's history relates to First Nations people. In his relationships with First Nations people, William Penn had met with leaders of the Susquehannock tribe, also known as Conestoga's, in order to purchase land and implement treaties. Several of these meetings took place in Lancaster city and nearby Conestoga.

But the story of Conestoga Natives ends tragically in 1763 when the remnant of this tribe was attacked in their village by a group of vigilantes from Paxtang, PA. Within a month on a Sunday afternoon in December, these same marauders broke into the jail of Lancaster city (site of the Fulton Opera House) and slaughtered the remaining Conestoga tribe members placed there for "protection." The infamous Paxton Boys were never brought to justice.

In 2003 leaders representing the church in Lancaster County met with descendents of the Iroquois Confederacy. The Iroquois had assumed legal responsibility for the well being of the Susquehannocks prior to the arrival of Europeans. Together they took ownership for this tragedy and various incidences when treaties were violated in this region. Through tears, repentance and forgiveness were exchanged between the descendents of European settlers and First Nations representatives. When they were asked what restitution for the past atrocities would "look like" to First Nation peoples, one of their leaders offered a gracious solution.

He believed that one reason God had led Europeans to come to North America was to bring the good news of Jesus Christ to First Nations peoples. Therefore, this Mohawk Nation leader affirmed that restitution would "look like" European descendents honoring the gifts of First Nations Christians and working together to lead people, particularly First Nations people, to Christ as Savior.

Redeemer, thank you for the power of forgiveness to reconcile people groups and heal the wounds of injustice. Direct us to opportunities to make restitution through partnerships in sharing the Good News.

Keith Yoder, president of Teaching The Word Ministries, is a member of The Worship Center.

Hans Herr House, Lancaster County
Photo by Mark Van Scyoc

Begin Again!

"He who was seated on the throne said, 'I am making everything new!'" *Revelation 21:5*

Last summer a pair of tiny house wrens claimed the bluebird box in our backyard. They worked diligently for days, constructing a neat little nest of sticks. But alas, just as they finished their hard work, some English sparrows displaced them. The bigger birds bullied their way into the nest box, chasing the wrens away and building their messy nest right on top of the nest that the wrens had worked so hard to make. The wrens protested noisily, but to no avail.

The next day when I looked out the window, I saw the wrens at the smaller birdhouse we had placed in a nearby tree. They were flying around and gathering sticks for a new nest, taking breaks to perch on the house and sing. Instead of sulking when they were displaced, the wrens had the courage to begin again. In fact, they raised two successful broods in that little house that summer.

Have you suffered a loss or been displaced by life's circumstances? I have, and it's not easy to start over again. In the midst of trials and losses, we have a choice to make. Will we stay where we are and mope around, causing bitterness in our own lives and in the lives of others? Or, after an appropriate time of grieving if need be, will we ask God for courage and by His grace, begin again?

Remember, He's the God of new beginnings. He sits on the throne and says, "I am making everything new!"

Lord, in this season of my life, I need a new beginning. Thank you that You know everything that has happened, and You are the God of new beginnings. Grant me the courage to start over again. Make everything new, and renew me by Your grace. In Jesus' name and for His sake, Amen.

Jane Nicholas serves as a proofreader, writer and editor. She and her husband, Bill, live in Elizabethtown and are part of the Hershey Evangelical Free Church.

Planted

"He will be like a tree firmly planted by streams of water, which yields its fruit in its season and its leaf does not wither; and in whatever he does, he prospers." *Psalm 1:3*

The verse does not say simply planted, but *firmly* planted. The resolve of the Gardener is revealed clearly. I imagine Careful Hands digging out a perfect space to place my roots and then generously watering the hole before placing my thirsty life inside it. Then I see rich, fragrant soil being poured all around the opening of the hole and Strong Hands pressing down all around the base of my life. Firmly planting all the potential of my life in an ideal place—*right* beside a stream.

There are no worries about being watered. This is a place of continual care. My thirst will be daily satisfied as I meditate day and night. My heart will be filled as I delight in the Law of the Lord, His precious Word.

I will not fear. I shall not be found in want. My leaves will not wither, but rather, my leaves will be for the healing of the nations! The Gardener's design is to bear fruit in me! And my fruit won't be premature or too late in developing; this harvest will be brought forth in its season. According to the Gardener's expectation, this planting of the Lord will be *all* that He intends it to be. Faithful is He who has done the planting; He will surely bring it to pass!

And this will be no ordinary life. No, the Gardener is an expert and He knows *exactly* what He's doing. He plans to prosper me—He gives me a future and a hope! The sky's the limit—I was *made* for this!

How glorious it is to be planted by You! I trust You, Gracious Gardener, to complete what You've begun. Be glorified through my life as I look to You alone to keep me! Amen.

Kathi Wilson and her husband Mark, coauthors of *Tired of Playing Church* and cofounders of Body Life Ministries, are members of Ephrata Community Church.

Life Language

"Every word I've spoken to you is a Spirit-word, and so it is life-making." *John 6:63 (The Message)*

I was recently asked what attracts me to Jesus. The question caught me off guard. After following Jesus for twenty-nine years, I had ceased thinking about initial attraction. So I thought about it. What attracts me to Jesus? His words. He's not exactly a "sweet-talker," but His words pull me in and capture me. They're true. Strong. Life-changing. They move me from shame to forgiveness; despair to hope; darkness to light; death to life. They are not just words. Not vain promises. His words themselves contain life. I am very attracted to this.

Where did Jesus get such words? He gives us the answer in John 8:28, "I do nothing on my own but speak just what the Father has taught Me." He took the words right out of His Father's mouth. Jesus received His words from the same place we all do...from those we live with and spend our time with. Children learn to speak the language of their parents, and later, their peers. International travelers know the best way to learn a new language is by surrounding themselves with native speakers. We begin to sound like those we live among.

Jesus spent His time with the Father and it was there He gathered these powerful, life-making words.

I want to learn a new language—His language. I want the words I speak to bring life to those who hear them. So I sit with my heavenly Father often and long. I listen to His words. Ponder them. Gather them one by one and store them in my heart. I want to take my words right out of my Father's mouth.

God, as I dwell with You, I pray Your words would fill my mind and heart so much that I begin to sound like You.

Jenny Gehman, founder of LiveWell! Ministries, gathers God-words in the predawn hours of each day in her Millersville home.

God Is Always There

"I will lift up my eyes to the hills—from whence comes my help?
My help comes from the Lord, who made heaven and earth."
Psalm 121:1–2

Monday, June 9, 2003, is a date I will never forget. I have always preached and counseled individuals about the faithfulness of God. However, on that date, God revealed His faithfulness to me in a way that was unmistakable.

My entire family had gone shopping for a wedding dress; our son was about to be married on Friday, June 13. The shopping party consisted of my wife (now deceased), mother-in-law, and future daughter-in-law. After the shopping spree, they picked up our son, the future groom, from work.

About 8:45 p.m., the police called to tell me that a terrible auto accident had occurred, and my entire family was involved. He hurriedly added that no one was killed, but seriously injured. On my way to the scene, two ambulances passed me. I arrived on the scene to the sound of the Jaws of Life dismantling what was left of our son's car in order to get him out.

As I stood rooted to the spot, I quietly prayed, "O dear Lord, what must I do?" It was then I heard the voice in my heart, *I will lift up my eyes to the hills—from whence comes my help? My help comes from the Lord, who made the heaven and the earth.* I knew beyond a shadow of a doubt that God was with me strengthening my faith and assuring me of His divine presence.

Incidentally, my son did get married on the thirteenth; God had brought us through the furnace.

Father, thank you for Your precious love and care; thank you that You are with us, and through it all, You will never forsake us.

Reverend, Dr. Peter S. Edwards is the pastor of the Goldsboro Church of God in Etters. He migrated from Jamaica, West Indies, to the United States forty-two years ago. He has been in ministry for almost fifty-four years.

Lord, My Tools Are Broken

"I can do all things through Christ who strengthens me."
Philippians 4:13

These tough economic times made us want to put in a small garden. My grandson, Kade, was excited to help with digging and planting seeds. He loves dirt! Unfortunately, my garden tools lay dormant in our garage for many years. We found them buried, in a corner, under large, heavy objects, and other useless junk. I finally saw my hoe that was my grandfather's and my heart sank—the handle was cracked and broken. After he saw it, my grandson's face darkened with disappointment. Yet, I could almost see the wheels turning in his head.

"Kade, I'm sorry, Grammy's garden tool is broken," I explained. In a moment, his face lit up, as he said, "We can fix it!" sounding a lot like "Bob the Builder." With new determination, he hunted around our yard and found a tall wooden pole. It was part of our wooden cross display for Easter.

"Look Grammy! We can use this to fix the broken handle!" My jaw dropped open, and my eyes popped out in awe.

Just a little duct tape later and we were back in business!

It was God's amazing way of providing for us, through the cross of Jesus Christ that literally restored our brokenness, enabling us to work in His garden.

We used the newly restored tool to rake off the dead leaves, which were smothering the new life underneath, freeing the tender shoots to breathe, and grow, in the warm light of God's truth. Now we could prepare the soil, as hearts soften, allowing us to plant the seeds of God's Word, then waiting for Him to bring the fruit at harvest time.

Lord, thank you for healing my brokenness. You have equipped me to do Your will. You made a way for me through Your sacrifice on the cross. I am forever grateful. Amen.

Shirley Ann Bivens serves at Christ Community Church, in the children's department. She does Christian clowning as CoCo the clown, and is a full-time grammy.

One by One

"As the sun went down that evening, people throughout the village brought sick family members to Jesus. No matter what their diseases were, the touch of his hand healed every one." *Luke 4:40 (New Living Translation)*

As I continue to battle cancer, this verse is an obvious word of hope to me. The Lord showed me these gems. It was after the sun went down, which meant it was cooler, but both Jesus and the families were probably tired. Yet, Jesus was there and the families loved enough to bring the sick. The Message translation is "When the sun went down, everyone who had anyone sick with some ailment or other brought them to him. One by one he placed his hands on them and healed them."

It was a crowd of tired, possibly dirty, anxious people. Could the sick have been anxious that Jesus would leave before He got to them? Pain, crying, moaning, desperation were quite possibly present. Perhaps the crowd was pushing and shoving their way to the front to have Jesus heal their family member. The families carried the pain, the burden of care, the desire to keep them close. The scripture doesn't tell us. It just says one by one He placed His hands on them.

Were the sick evaluated for their illness before healing? It's the result of sin; was it someone's mistake; did the sick person do something wrong; the world is full of sinfulness; was it their diet or their environment; was it passed down? Scripture doesn't say that, it only says one by one He placed his hand on them and healed them.

He placed His beautiful, capable, compassionate hand on them, what love must have radiated from His touch. Someone who is sick for an extended period of time has touch but often accompanied by pain. To have healing, caring, loving touch would have been deep ministry in itself. Along with the touch I'm certain the "one" saw great pools of love and concern and acceptance in the eyes of Jesus. It was one by one. He saw the one. You are not lost in the crowd. Wait, He sees you.

Jesus, my healer, You touched each individual person brought to You. You honored the love of family to bring those they loved. You touched them one by one. Touch us today, precious Lord.

Christina Ricker continues in the battle waiting for healing. She is a member of Petra Christian Fellowship, a wife, mother and nana.

I Cry Out in Distress

"Evening, morning and noon, I cry out in distress, and he hears my voice." *Psalm 55:17*

Everybody wants a positive outcome when it comes to cancer. But, for many of us, cancer means living with the unknown for years, maybe a lifetime.

When my elevin-year-old grandson was diagnosed with Medulloblastoma, a cancerous brain tumor, I thought I couldn't endure the pain of watching him suffer the excruciating side effects from radiation and chemotherapy, the constant vomiting that resulted in his becoming a skeleton of his former robust self, his listlessness that was so unlike his former energetic happy-go-lucky spirit. Adding to my pain was watching his parents—my son and his wife—being so brave for the sake of their son and their other three children.

I wish I could say that I had unwavering confidence that God would see us through no matter what happened, and that I was filled with joy and peace that passes understanding. But, there were some days when I felt God was much too silent for all His promises of being there.

It bothered me that fears came crashing in at the most unexpected times. Yet again and again, as I cried out to God and verbally read aloud verses of God's faithfulness, I could feel God's strength, His calmness.

It's nine months later and my grandson is in the middle of continuing chemotherapy. He is no longer nauseous and losing weight. Instead, he is gaining energy and showing amazing signs of recovery. The Lord has protected him from many of the predicted side effects of radiation and chemotherapy.

The end of his story and mine isn't known, but what is known is that God will always be there for him, for me, and for all who cry out in distress.

Lord, I cry out to You the living God. Deliver me from all my fears, real and imagined.

Lou Ann Good is a member of DOVE Christian Fellowship-Westgate and a wife, mother, grandmother of 10, and freelance writer.

Closets

"But thou, when thou prayest, enter into thy closet, and when thou hast shut thy door, pray to thy Father which is in secret; and thy Father which seeth in secret shall reward thee openly." *Matthew 6:6 (King James Version)*

My house doesn't have many closets; the ones we do have are packed pretty full of stuff. Mostly everyday junk for your everyday needs, so when I think of a closet I can tend to get a little irritated about all the junk that lies behind the door. Kind of like one of those old Flintstones cartoons where Fred opens the closet door and there is this avalanche of junk that just comes pouring out on top of him.

In the verse above, Jesus tells us to go into a closet and pray in secret to God. Now I don't know about you, but I don't think I could fit into any of my closets with all the junk I have in them. But, I don't think that's what Jesus really meant. I think what He really meant was to say, "Look, I want you to find a place, a quiet place, a secret place where you can be alone, where no one can see you or hear you and you can't see or hear anyone else. Then I want you to do something for Me; I want you to pray to your Father in heaven."

I believe Jesus just wants us to find a place where we can get away from it all, to be without distractions. That way we can better focus on God when we pray and allow Him to search us in the quietness of the moment. You know, we do need Him to search us sometimes. David said in the Psalms, "Search me, O God, and know my heart; test me and know my anxious thoughts." When was the last time you asked the Almighty God to search you?

Dear Lord, teach us to pray so we can walk in Your way. Amen.

Rob Heverling is a youth leader at Mount Aetna Bible Church, Mount Aetna.

I'll Carry the Burden

"For I will pour water on the thirsty land, and streams on the dry ground...." *Isaiah 44:3*

Through the years, I have struggled with not becoming people's saviors, but instead introducing them to Jesus, the One who can meet every need in ways that I cannot.

I was overwhelmed with all the brokenness around me. There were so many people that needed Jesus, so many that knew nothing of the kingdom of God.

God brought me a friend...a friend that was broken, a friend that needed Jesus. For eight years, I loved and prayed for her, and tried to model what a relationship with Jesus looked like. Still, my friend was broken...and the enemy continued to destroy her life.

I cried out to God, "You have given me a passion to see broken people restored and healthy. I will serve You whether I see fruit or not...but will You take my desire to see the broken healed, and keep it, because I have done all I know to do."

In a simple way, the Lord honored my prayer, and lifted the heaviness that I was feeling. I was still concerned for my friend...but the Lord was carrying the weight of the burden.

The next day, my friend called and said that she was ready to "trust Jesus with her life, to not do things her way, but His Way!" I could hardly believe the words she was saying...and I gave glory to God. Thus began the start of a new life for my friend...and the Lord restoring vision to me, that with Him *all things are possible,* that no person or situation is too broken for His Hands to heal.

Lord, continue to teach me how to be at peace in Your ability to save and restore. Keep me from striving, which is not obedience, but rather make me a vessel full of Your abundant grace and mercy.

Jennie Groff serves with The Net-Lancaster, a network of house churches in Lancaster City.

Forgiveness

"Therefore confess your sins to each other and pray for each other so that you may be healed...." *James 5:16*

In December of 2007, I started to take interest in a young woman at church. I prayed and fasted for several weeks and sought my heavenly Father's counsel. As she and I started to move forward in our relationship, we crossed physical boundaries, eventually getting pregnant. The failure is obvious, but what I want to share is how we were both amazed when we shared with friends, family, our pastors, and those we were walking closely with in ministry. We were so overwhelmed at the love and support that we received. As we continued to share with people, wondering about the response we would get, there was definitely disappointment, but always there was love and forgiveness shown.

If you are being pushed into a corner because of a failure in your life that you fear bringing to the light, because you fear rejection, God is calling you to His arms of love. Open your heart to a close friend or mentor.

Today my wife and I, and our amazing children, are chasing God's heart with full release and His love around us. Just take a step of faith today; God's desire is your full healing and freedom. "Confess your sins to each other and pray for each other so that you may be healed (James 5:16)."

Lord Jesus, I pray that You will release faith into the reader today to step into Your loving embrace and the embrace of the family You have placed around them, to walk together to freedom and victory over sin and death in Christ Jesus. Amen.

Josh Horst lives in Denver with his wife and children, and works for Caliber Hardwood Floors, Inc. They attend Petra Christian Fellowship and are involved in a ministry called Club Worship in Reading.

Show Daddy

"This is to be to my Father's glory, that you bear much fruit, showing yourselves to be my disciples." *John 15:8*

I was waiting in line at the Radiology Lab. Ahead of me sat a handsome twenty-something man confined to a wheelchair. I guessed that a catastrophic accident had put him there. He interacted affectionately with his mom. I heard the door open behind me, followed by the cheerful announcement, "Your Dad is here!"

The young man's eyes lit up at the sight of his father. Dad greeted his son warmly with a kiss. In an excited voice Mom asked her son, "Do you want to show your father what you can do?"

The group stood transfixed, silent, fully engaged in an historical moment that did not rightfully belong to us. It was impossible to keep our eyes off the young man as he handed his cane to his mother and rose from his chair. He hesitated, precarious at first. Then, with a burst of confidence, he took several lurching steps, covering the five feet between himself and his mother completely on his own.

He landed in her outstretched arms, his face awash with an exploding grin. He had walked on his own. It was obvious that this was the first time his father was seeing him walk since the accident. I thought my heart might burst! I looked up, locking eyes with the registrar nurse as we smiled through matching tears. No words were spoken, but the room was thick with the intimacy of shared joy. We had unwittingly been privy to a once-in-a-lifetime moment.

I believe that it is our heart's cry to "show our Father what we can do." I have a wonderful heavenly Father. I always have and always will want to show Him what I can do!

Father, thank you for being exactly who You are. Help me to bear much fruit that I might glorify You!

Kristin Williams Balla is a member of the Praise Team of Upper Octorara Presbyterian Church in Parkesburg.

"Where I Am Today"

"I am the vine, ye are the branches. He that abideth in me, and I in him, the same bringeth forth much fruit: for without me ye can do nothing." *John 15:5 (King James Version)*

There are so many "God Stories" in my life, ranging from life-changing, a lesson, or just turning my frown upside down, even "God Stories" in my life that went unnoticed by me...bringing me to a thought that I should write them down and keep them for later inspiration for myself and others. My God Story today is "Where I am today."

My sitting here is a result of God's hand on my life. He has sustained me through my wicked past and continues into my future. When I turned to Christ in prison, He brought me redemption! My handicaps like seven felonies, medical conditions, probation, old debt and no driver's license for a total of sixteen years, would be crushing without God. Tack on emotional damage and addictions, and it just shows how amazing God is that He can free us.

I smile because I am happy, free, and free to give what He has given. There is one way I am where I am today—God. Today I have good friends, a loving family, a girlfriend—that's another "God Story" all its own; and Christ is driving our love bus. I keep working at one job or another so He keeps my bills paid and belly full. My story is God's story, for without God, I would be in prison, an institution, or six feet under—probably the latter, the way I was going. I still have problems due to my sins and just from being here on earth but I have a God who brings security, hope, happiness, and all things good. The man who brought bad into my life is not the same man with this great story, and that is for sure.

God, thank you for changing me.

Ben Mummau lives in Elizabethtown and is part of E-town DOVE and the Bossler Road cell church.

More than Enough

"Now to him who is able to do immeasurably more than all we ask or imagine, according to his power that is at work within us."
Ephesians 3:20

While leading a ministry team deep into the Amazon jungle, we experienced God's provision in a fresh way. Each day, as we traveled by wooden canoe farther into the jungle, we stopped at riverside villages to tell the children about Jesus. Several couples on the team, who were in their early seventies, were having the experience of their lives...first time into the jungle and sensing the eagerness of children drinking in the stories of Jesus.

On one particular day, upon leaving the riverside "Jaguar Hostel" early in the morning, we had planned to visit only one village far down the river. We beached the canoes and started the walk along the jungle path leading to the village. That day's weather was unusually oppressive as it can be sometimes in the jungle. The sun rose hot and the air was steamy and humid. As we trudged along on the muddy path, our water bottles started to empty much too rapidly.

After one hour of walking, I emphatically asked our guide exactly how far this village was from the river. The guide answered in the typical jungle guide way "not far." My wife and I immediately started praying! "God, please let the village be around the next bend in the path. Please let there be clean water there for us to drink!"

It seemed as though it were twenty bends in the path later, but there the village was emerging out of the jungle. At the edge of the village, right along the path, was, to us that day, the most beautiful snack bar we had ever encountered...God not only provided for our thirst, but He provided clean liquid and more than enough.

Father, thank you for providing more than enough. You know our need and delight in providing it. Thank you for taking care of us.

Joe Nolt is the assistant to the director of DOVE Mission International, Lititz.

Secure in the Love of My Father God

"...For I know where I came from and where I am going...." *John 8:14*

Jesus was completely secure. He knew clearly where He came from, and where He was going. Most of us feel insecure in one way or another. I have felt misunderstood, left out, and rejected many times in my life. In my first year at school, I was one of those kids who was usually the last one picked to play baseball with my schoolmates. It really hurt. I felt very insecure.

I developed a lot of insecurities in my emotional makeup that I had to allow Jesus to touch. Years later, I finally realized "Jesus loves me this I know, for the Bible tells me so." It was the greatest truth I had ever learned. There was nothing I could do to make Him love me more. And there was nothing I could do to make Him love me less. I realized I could be completely secure in the fact that God loved me, period.

Jesus knew who He was. He did not react to the reactions of others because He had a fear of being discovered as unsuited to meet His responsibilities. Jesus knew who He was, where He came from, and where He was going (John 8:14). He was secure in His Father's love. That's why He could kneel down and wash His disciples' feet in the upper room, even when He knew they would betray him just hours later. He took upon himself the role of a servant because He was safe and secure that His Father would be there, on the other side of death, to raise Him up again.

When we are secure in Christ, we realize that any failure is only an event, not who we are. The Lord helps each of us to survive the ups and downs of life with its challenges. Remind yourself each day that you are loved by God. And then you will operate out of knowing your security is wrapped up in your intimate relationship with your heavenly father, not in what others say or think about you.

Lord, thank you that my true source of security comes from knowing that I am loved by my heavenly Father, period.

Larry Kreider is the international director of DOVE Christian Fellowship International

Rub-Dub-Dub Three Men in a Tub

"Cleanse me with hyssop, and I will be clean; wash me, and I will be whiter than snow." *Psalm 51:7*

Something humorous happened to me "on the way," or should I say, "at the Forum" (alias, Hempfield Recreation Center) the other day. After a routine workout, I found myself entering the Jacuzzi, better known as the common man's hot tub.

Two elderly gentlemen were already settled into the soothing waters of the tub when I diplomatically slid beneath the therapeutic jet streams of this modern-day de-stressor. Both of the gentlemen identified themselves as Lutherans. They were conferring on the good and not so good of their church experiences. One man spoke about his church splitting because of the updating of the black-covered hymnals to red covered ones. Apparently, the red color was too contemporary. The other issue, expressed by the second man, was that one of their relatives, who was Baptist, believed that Lutherans were not bound for heaven.

"Rub-Dub-Dub—Oh how we flub it!" Too often, we sow seeds of dissention instead of growing the green grass of unity. Oh, by the way, little did my hot tub friends know that I was a Presbyterian; and you know what some folks think about the "frozen chosen"!

The "bubbling waters" experience reminds me of the contemplative and insightful words that came from a young boy in Africa who said, "Christianity in America oftentimes seems to be a mile wide and an inch deep." Our propensity to be too comfortable with our critical and unkind comments may illustrate just how much our faith comes down to being a "hot tub religion."

Lord, keep me from a casual, critical, self-righteous faith; and draw me close to You so that I may be as healing waters to a hurting world.

Dr. Sandy Outlar served as headmaster of Lancaster Christian School. Prior to that, he was President of Sandy Cove in North East, Maryland. Sandy and his wife attend Wheatland Presbyterian Church.

Saltfully Thinking

"…You are the salt of the earth…." *Matthew 5:13*

I have to admit, I like a little seasoning with my food. It brings out the flavor. But don't assume that I am a good cook. The truth is that I am "kitchen challenged." Maybe it's because when I was a little girl, all of my friends were playing with their Easy Bake Ovens, while I was down in the creek catching crayfish. I like to tell people that I only have a kitchen because it came with the house. When I was first married, my husband was a guinea pig at mealtime. He could have said that my pot roast tasted more like beef jerky, my brownies were hard as subflooring and that my chicken potpie looked more like spackle. By now you're adding my name to your prayer list, right? But, he was a good sport about my lack of kitchen talent. To him, it didn't matter so much that my cooking wasn't perfect. What mattered is that I did my best to create a flavorful dish.

Isn't that how God is? God is not so interested in what's for dinner. He's more concerned with how we bring out the godly flavor in our own lives. In Matthew 5:13, Jesus said that we are the salt of the earth. Now, the way I see it, salt is salt only if it is touching something. If salt is just sitting on the table in a pretty glass shaker, it is just an ornament. It only becomes salt when it touches something. To be salt of the earth, we need to touch.

Touching people's lives can come in so many forms. It can be a simple task for someone, an encouraging word or even just a smile. Let your salt make a difference. By the way, did I mention I was in the Meal Ministry at church? Shhhhhh!

Lord, help us to see the opportunities that are around us to touch other people's lives and give us the love for the ones that are more challenging to approach. Help us to see others through Your eyes.

Lisa Garvey serves with the Hosanna Christian Fellowship, Lititz, Women's Ministry and Prayer Ministry.

What's in a Name?

"What's more, I am changing your name. It will no longer be Abram. Instead, you will be called Abraham, for you will be the father of many nations." *Genesis 17:5 (New Living Translation)*

Without question the name of Rev. Martin Luther King, Jr. draws forth images of resistance to oppression, and gives voice to the sound of justice ringing out in America's "townsquare" on the mall in Washington DC. As an ordained Baptist minister who studied the Word of God in the historic suburbs of Philadelphia and Boston, to some he is perceived as a modern day prophet, calling his nation to get in line with the great and biblical values of liberty and justice for all people.

Yet when he was born in 1929 he was originally named Michael King, Jr. That is, until his family visited Germany in 1934 and his dad changed both of their names to honor the great Christian reformer and father of the doctrine of the priesthood of all believers, Martin Luther. Ultimately King's German namesake and the doctrine associated with Luther calls all Christians who trust in the name of Jesus to unite in one administration of duties under the Lord Jesus, our eternal High Priest. Isn't it fascinating to ponder God's hand in that story, changing the name of King to match His call as a modern day voice encouraging the body of Christ to pursue an administration of godly justice in the name of Jesus?

Germany is a nation with a fascinating heritage, with God having used the vivid horrors of the Holocaust to birth the modern nation of Israel. Yet the clues to God's redemptive purposes in our day don't stop there. Before WW2, Iran was Persia until Hitler's Nazis infiltrated this ancient culture and seeded their own brand of anti-Jewish hatred. The name Iran now literally means, "Land of the Aryans," as in Hitler's uber-race that would allegedly destroy the Jews and take their place in a thousand year reign as God's chosen people.

As a byproduct of his calling, Martin Luther King, Jr. challenged Americans to sense the battles of godly justice in their nation; and on this day Christians of all nations are reminded to heed his call.

Lord, we heed Your call today toward resolving racism.

Bill Shaw is the executive director of Life Transforming Ministries in Coatesville.

The Name of Jesus

"Nor is there salvation in any other, for there is no other name under heaven given among men by which we must be saved." *Acts 4:12*

I love the name of Jesus. In that name we have salvation (Acts 4:12). In the name of Jesus, we have healing. "Then Peter said, 'Silver and gold I do not have, but what I do have I give you: In the name of Jesus Christ of Nazareth, rise up and walk.'"

"...So he, leaping up, stood and walked and entered the temple with them—walking, leaping, and praising God (Acts 3:6, 8)."

Through the name of Jesus, we access the miraculous. "...And that signs and wonders may be done through the name of Your holy servant Jesus (Acts 4:30)."

In our society today, the gospel has become diluted. New Age influences have watered down the truth of God's Word. It is acceptable to speak about "God," but it is not acceptable to speak the name of Jesus. In order to be politically correct, we are expected to accept every religion, any belief, as a way to God. Jesus very clearly spoke to this ambivalence in John 14:6 when He declared, "I am the way, the truth, and the life. No one comes to the Father except through Me."

I listen intently when chaplains offer opening prayers before NASCAR events. Will they pray in the name of Jesus? I listened intently during presidential inauguration prayers—whose name would this prayer be offered in? After sports events, to whom does the star athlete offer thanks; whose name passes his lips? When it is clearly spoken, "Jesus," I shout for joy.

Father God, thank you for sending Jesus to us, so that we can experience sweet salvation, amazing healing and stunning signs and wonders, in His name alone.

Mary Prokopchak leads a cell group for DOVE Christian Fellowship in Elizabethtown.

Humbled

"For everyone who exalts himself will be humbled...." Luke 18:14

There are many painful and terrible things, which I am fortunate enough to have never personally experienced. Unfortunately, however, many times in my happiness, wealth, health and other blessings, I have forgotten the sufferings of those around me. I would think, or even pray: "Thank You that I am not like other men."

Well, over the last couple of years, there have been a number of things in my life and in my family's lives, which have brought me to my knees in many ways. There have been health problems, financial reversals, but most of all, the lifting of a blindfold of denial that allowed God to reveal some of the truths in my life.

I am not telling this story so that anyone would feel sorry for me in any way. I am saying this because it is clear to me that God has His own ways of humbling the proud, so that we can grow closer to Him and to others.

More importantly, He has been teaching me that it is important to listen before offering advice, to keep silent instead of talking, and to move closer to Him, rather than telling Him what to do. In the life of my family, church and work, He is teaching me that I need to humble myself and recognize that if someone is hurting, it is not because they have sinned, have made mistakes or somehow deserve to suffer.

When I started hurting and got in touch with my own pain, it not only drove me closer to the Lord, but also it showed me that I can't live in a smug and isolated world choosing when, and with whom, I want to get involved. Instead, now I pray, "God, have mercy on me, a sinner."

Lord, You know exactly what I am and what I am not. Help me to treat others as I need to be treated when I am in my darkest time.

Joe Troncale is a small group leader at Petra Christian Fellowship in New Holland.

Aviate, Navigate, Communicate

"And again, 'I will put my trust in him....'" *Hebrews 2:13*

Aviate, Navigate, and Communicate. The training behind these three words saved the life of my friend navy pilot, Ron Carlson, as he flew a night mission in support of Operation Enduring Freedom soon after the events of 9/11. His S-3 Viking's cockpit filled with smoke several seconds after takeoff from the aircraft carrier, *USS Theodore Roosevelt.* With lost electronics and communication, Carlson had two choices: to eject into the water, where the possibility of being found at night was remote, or risk landing on the carrier, which was now obvious only by a nearly indiscernible deck light in the darkness.

During those few intense moments, Commander Carlson did exactly as he was trained: he aviated—by retaining control of the plane, he navigated—by keeping the one small light from the carrier in sight, and he tried to communicate with the ship—though unsuccessfully!

What is it that compels a navy pilot to trust in the training he received during the course of a career? I'm not sure what goes on in the brain of a naval aviator, but Commander Carlson's very real dilemma reminds me of a fundamental question of greater importance that each of us must answer. Can we trust in a God we can't see, especially when times are tough?

Many of our residents struggle mightily to trust others. Each remembers a time when he did extend trust to someone only to receive abuse and harm from the one deemed trustworthy. And, each carries a lingering fear that broken trust is the norm and trust in God is as futile.

How can we—resident and staff member alike—learn to trust in the God who is there especially when life makes no sense?

By the way, then Commander, now Captain, Ron Carlson, did survive the crash landing on the deck of the *Roosevelt*, and he returned to complete his tour of duty.

Lord, help me to trust You when I can't see.

Steve Brubaker is the Chief Vision Officer for Water Street Ministries, Lancaster.

Risk

"Take the thousand and give it to the one who risked the most. And get rid of this 'play-it-safe' who won't go out on a limb. Throw him out into utter darkness." *Matthew 25:28–30 (The Message)*

Two years ago, I began hearing God speak to me, one word, over and over, and over again. Reading the Parable of the Talents in the Message version, it was there. I went on a trip to London visiting churches and one of the churches had the word as a Core Value. I visited another church in Lancaster County and the word showed up again. It seemed like everywhere I went, and everything I read, this word was following me.

The word was "risk." When it kept showing up everywhere, I began realizing that this word was from God. And so, I asked God what was the risk He was calling me to undertake? His response: He wanted me to resign from my staff position at a local church and plant Veritas, as its own church; to risk in order to be a missionary to the emerging, postmodern culture. To risk by seeking to raise support, find part-time employment, and to launch out into the unknown. Sure, the questions come, what will I do for part-time employment, what if I fail, what if we plant this church and it doesn't grow? But over and over, God kept calling us to risk for the sake of the kingdom of God. And so, we are undertaking this journey of risk.

So, what is it God is calling you to risk? Maybe it's not about planting a church or maybe it is. Maybe it's walking across the yard to engage with a neighbor you don't know. Maybe it's sharing your faith with a coworker, family member or friend. Maybe it's going into ministry full-time or becoming a missionary. Whatever the call to risk is, embrace it.

Lord, may I hear Your call to risk for the kingdom and embrace it.

Ryan Braught is a church planter of Veritas, A Missional Community of Authentic Worshippers.

A Little Bottle of Hair Color

"Man looks at the outward appearance, but the Lord looks at the heart." *1 Samuel 16:7*

On a whim, I let my daughter and niece convince me to change my hair color. My hair had been white for years and many people did not know me any other way. That was especially true for my four-year-old grandson, Hudson. Hudson had gone to bed before we began the process. The next morning, he wasn't quite sure what to think. After a couple of days, he came and asked, "Grandmom, when are you going to get your white hair back?"

I've thought about his question a lot since then. Not really about my hair color, but as it relates to my spiritual journey. It was easy to apply the little bottle of color and change my appearance.

Is that what I am doing in my spiritual journey? Am I applying a little time of Bible reading, church going, and prayer? Am I doing it enough to just change my outward appearance or am I truly searching God's Word, seeking His wisdom, and listening to His heart? It only took a few minutes, and the color will last five to six weeks. Am I only spending time with Him, to last for a few weeks or a lifetime with Him? Am I showing others who I am through Christ? Is His love showing through me? Am I letting the things of this world change my appearance, my actions, and my heart? I often feel I allow the busyness of life to interfere with spending time with Him; stopping Him from changing me in a way He desires.

In the innocence of a child's question, I hear God asking, "When are you going to come fully back to Me? Let Me change your appearance."

Lord, may my appearance/life be a reflection of change that comes from knowing You.

Mona Engle serves as Practice Administrator for Drs. May Grant in Lancaster. She attends Living Word Community in York, serving as a mentor mom to young moms.

Unconditional Love

"Thank you for making me so wonderfully complex! Your workmanship is marvelous—how well I know it." *Psalm 139:14 (New Living Translation)*

As Christians, my wife and I are pro-life. I have preached full-length messages on the sanctity of human life. I also believe that God is sovereign and He never makes a mistake. What I did not know was that my faith would be put to the test with the birth of our first grandchild.

On October 6, 2006, Jaxson Dean Cover was born. It was difficult for us because our oldest son and daughter-in-law live in Mesa, Arizona. We wanted to be there to share this joyous occasion of the birth of their first child.

There were many phone calls made and received for updates. Finally, the phone call came and I answered the phone. My son said Jaxson was born, and I couldn't wait to hear all the details. But, the excitement was short lived when my son said there is a problem.

Our first grandchild has Down syndrome. I could tell that my son was disappointed that he had to tell me that our first grandchild has Downs. But, I remember reassuring him that I knew that he and his wife would love their son the same and that we would love him as well.

But I discovered that our reaction as grandparents not only reached out for our grandson but, for our son's pain as well. Yes, we are concerned about the welfare of our grandson, but our heart broke even more for our son and daughter-in-law for what they were going through as new parents. That day, we turned our grandson over to God, and God has been faithful. Jaxson is a gift.

Heavenly Father, thank you for giving us the gift of a grandson with Downs. We have learned so much from him since his birth. But, what we have learned most of all is what it means to give and receive love unconditionally, especially loving those who are different than we are.

D. Dean Cover is senior pastor of Living Waters Chapel in Lebanon.

Always with Us

"For I am persuaded that neither death nor life, nor angels nor principalities nor powers, nor things present nor things to come, nor height nor depth, nor any other created thing, shall be able to separate us from the love of God which is in Christ Jesus our Lord."
Romans 8:38–39

"Lord, Bekah doesn't deserve this!"

His presence comforted me as I lamented the dreams that were not to be realized. In the silence, the Lord spoke: "Have I remained by your side through this tragic saga? Have you continually seen My presence and involvement?"

The reels of film began to play as He reminded me of His many footprints stamped over the details of the two weeks since Bekah's accident: Beginning that first night, Bob and I had a peace that "passes all understanding" even though it was after Bekah's curfew and she didn't answer her cell phone. We had no sense of panic.

Bekah was taken care of *immediately* after hitting the tree by the homeowner and her paramedic sister until the ambulance arrived. Within three minutes of the policemen knocking at our door, I heard the assuring words, "Your daughter has no life-threatening injuries" from the emergency room doctor.

Skilled doctors, some who boldly professed their Christian faith, patiently cleaned and stitched her face and expertly set broken bones. The trauma center nurses took meticulous personal interest in caring for our daughter. Our church, school, and soccer families all rallied with an outpouring of prayers, e-mails, flowers, cards, gifts, and meals. Bob's boss drove from Baltimore to share his company's concern and support. Beginning the sixth day, Bekah improved by the minute with all medical personnel marveling at her miraculous recovery. For such a traumatic event, it was the smoothest ride possible. Jesus traveled with us on a journey we would not have chosen, for us to receive what we never would have otherwise: Himself.

Dear Lord, thank you that absolutely nothing can separate us from Your love and Your presence.

Tamalyn Jo Heim and her husband, Bob, enjoy God's presence especially when walking and bicycling together.

All I Want

"You Lord are all I want! You are my choice and you keep me safe."
Psalm 16:5 (Contemporary English Version)

The psalmist David wanted one thing more than anything else. People want a lot of things. The credit card craze is proof of that. For Christians, things need to take a backseat. The Lord must be first. In fact, Jesus said, "If anyone comes to me and does not hate his father and mother, his wife and children, his brothers and sisters—yes, even his own life—he cannot be my disciple (Luke 14:26)." We know we are not to hate anyone so what does Jesus mean? Some of the modern paraphrases take the liberty to interpret Jesus' words: "Anyone who comes to me but refuses to let go of father, mother, spouse, children, brothers, sisters—yes, even one's own self!—can't be my disciple (Luke 14:26)."

David said, "The one thing I ask of the Lord—the thing I seek most —is to live in the house of the Lord all the days of my life, delighting in the Lord's perfections and meditating in his Temple (Psalm 27:4)." Do you desire to live in His presence each moment?

Jesus promised, if we keep His Kingdom ahead of everything else the "everything else" will be given to us. Paul writes, "I want to know Christ and the power of his resurrection and the fellowship of sharing in his sufferings, becoming like him in his death (Philippians 3:10)."

Have you and I come to the place where we can say, "Lord, You are all I want?"

Lord, I surrender my all to You. I give You my time, my allegiance, my family, my job, my will. It is Yours to use as You see fit. So help me Lord.

David Eshleman is a church consultant for Lancaster Mennonite Conference and Eastern Mennonite Missions. He is author of *Now Go Forward: Reaching Out to Grow Your Congregation.*

Provision

"Look at the birds of the air; they do not sow or reap or store away in barns, and yet your heavenly Father feeds them. Are you not much more valuable than they?" *Matthew 6:26*

The real estate market had come to a standstill. Finally there was a buyer interested in one of my listings. And as God would have it, the property was scheduled to close six months to the day since my last settlement. Now, if you had told me six months ago that I would be this long without income I am certain great fear would have overcome me. OK, it's true. There *were* moments when great fear overcame me. It was so very, very good of God to give me—just one day at a time…

The day after the paperwork was signed I sat in the red Adirondack chair by the creek at the edge of our property with my Bible and journal. Contemplating where I was financially, trying to figure out how I could have avoided this and prepared for this time in my life and frankly beating myself up a bit. It had been really quiet and peaceful when all of a sudden the birds started chirping. Noisy little guys.

The Lord said to me, "*What do I say about the birds?*"

And, I opened my Bible to Matthew 6:26.

The Lord told me three things about the birds…

They don't sow.

They don't reap.

They don't store things up.

And, He assured me from His word that I was where I was because I put Him first in my life.

The Lord told me three things about me…

He loves me.

He takes care of me.

I am valuable to Him.

Father, I thank you for Your promise to never leave me or forsake me and am ever so grateful that Your provision is enough. I love You.

Marti Evans is a broker-owner for CUSTOM Real Estate and is serving on the board of directors at Lebanon Valley Youth For Christ.

Touching Jesus

"Now a woman, having a flow of blood for twelve years, who had spent all her livelihood on physicians and could not be healed by any, came from behind and touched the border of His garment. And immediately her flow of blood stopped." *Luke 8:43–44 (New King James Version)*

Traveling by bus in the cities of Russia, I am always amazed at how many people can be stuffed into just one. To exit the bus you must begin to move toward the door one or two stops prior to your desired station.

On one occasion, my wife and I, along with another young pastor, began to move toward the door, but the people were packed in so tightly that they were not willing to make a way for us. After a few mannerly comments such as "eezveeneetye" (excuse me), we changed our approach. We began to do everything possible to part the crowd and move toward the door. That door became the focal point and one way or another we were going to get to that door. I put my hands out in front of myself, and like a snowplow I started separating the people while the others followed me.

Outside the bus, we discussed how sometimes you have to use desperate measures for desperate situations. Later, in preparing a sermon on touching Jesus, I thought about how the woman with the blood illness pushed through the crowd to meet Jesus. She got desperate to get to Jesus. There are times when we must push through the obstacles in this life if we are going to touch Jesus.

Lord, as I think of my most desperate need I recognize that You are the source of all good things. I push aside every obstacle within and without of myself so that I can meet with You. I am determined in my spirit to come through the crowd and touch You today.

Darryl Henson is a member of Petra Christian Fellowship, president and founder of InSTEP Ministries International, providing support and training for pastors and church leaders in Russia and Eastern Europe.

From Fear to Faith

"…Casting all your care upon Him, for he cares for you." *1 Peter 5:7 (New King James Version)*

It was Sunday evening, and we had been ministering all day. My husband Darryl had one more meeting but I was free. I was ushered away to the home of one of the church members, to wait for the rest of the group. She spoke no English and my Russian was only a few words. We had been in this home before and I knew the meal would be tasty. I looked around at this run-down cabin and thought, back home this place would be condemned, what a firetrap. One single lightbulb hung from the ceiling.

What will I do for the next two hours? I can't help with the meal, there was no room in the kitchen and her son was helping. Her eight-year-old daughter knew a few words of English from school. So, I asked her to show me her English books. We proceeded page by page through her books. She would tell me the English words she knew and then I would ask her to say it in Russian. I wanted to take every opportunity I had to learn this difficult language.

I almost forgot where I was. When the light went off everything was dark. What is happening? Fear began to rise up in me. Is it a fire? What do I do? How do I ask? Where is Darryl? After looking around and seeing a small candle burning in the kitchen, I breathed a prayer of thanks. A half hour passed, the light shown again and the meal was *vkoosnihy* (tasty)!

Lord, thank you that You know where I am, and what is happening. Thank you that You can speak to all peoples in all languages. You care for the lilies of the field and You see the tiny sparrow fall. I resist fear and stand in faith. I know You care for me.

Joyce Henson is with Petra Christian Fellowship and serves with her husband, Darryl, traveling throughout Russia and Eastern Europe, with InSTEP Ministries International.

I Am Beautiful to Him

"The Lord your God is with you, he is mighty to save. He will take great delight in you, he will quiet you with his love, he will rejoice over you with singing." *Zephaniah 3:17*

I have always struggled with feeling and believing that I am beautiful. I remember as a teenager, telling God that since I'm not beautiful on the outside, I want Him to make me beautiful on the inside. Even though I knew in my head that God makes no mistakes and all His creation is good, I could not accept that He looked at me and actually saw me as pretty or beautiful.

One day, as I was driving home from work, God gave me a revelation. My two-year-old daughter was in the backseat, jabbering away and just being happy. I was reflecting on how thankful to God I was for the gift of my daughter. I began telling her how beautiful she is: her pretty, dark brown eyes, her soft black hair, her velvety brown skin, her tiny fingers and toes, her wonderful smile, her belly laugh, her curiosity, her love to cuddle and the joy she brings me! I told her how much I love her and can hardly believe she's my daughter. I told her how much I treasure her, and that she is so precious to me and that I love everything about her.

In that moment, God spoke so clearly, "JoAnna that is exactly how I feel about you."

I began to weep as this truth penetrated my heart, my soul, my very being! He loves me! I am beautiful to Him!

It continues to be a journey for me but now I can look in the mirror and say, "JoAnna, you are your Father's beautiful daughter!" With His help, I claim this truth each day and pass it on to all His daughters.

Father, thank you for affirming me as Your precious and beautiful daughter and choosing me as Your own. I love You!

JoAnna Hochstetler serves The Network in The Stones house church in Lancaster city.

God's Faithful Provision

"And my God will meet all your needs according to his glorious riches in Christ Jesus." *Philippians 4:19*

The year was 1995. My husband's employment was impacted by market situations. Then spring arrived and things were looking fresh and new. But, without further notice one Friday morning he was called to the Vice President's office and told he was to pack his belongings and leave—he and eleven other employees were being laid off. He was finished.

It was the beginning of a new journey for us. Our three children were still living at home and I was only working part-time. How was God going to provide for our needs? Forget about our wants!

Daily he searched the job ads, mailed resumes and waited.

That summer we decided to take a motorcycle trip, which had been planned before the layoff. While away on the trip, a phone call came offering an interview. That was a wonderful break!

Three months had gone by and finally something was happening. Soon after arriving home, he received a second call requesting an interview.

Friends were praying concerning our situation. A friend had prayed that the Holy Spirit would activate His "Ways and Means Committee" on our behalf. Another friend had prayed that doors of opportunity would be opened.

Then, would you believe, with two job offers, he had to make a decision about which position would be right for him.

God did answer all those prayers. He is faithful! Did we learn to trust Him in a deeper way? Oh, yes! It was something we had never walked through before. But, as a family we grew and our children witnessed how God provides every need.

If the Lord cares even for the sparrow, how much more does He care for you and me?

Thank you, Father, for Your provision for our family today and in the coming days. You are Jehovah Jireh (The Lord's provision shall be seen).

Nancy Wenger serves, along with her husband, as usher, zone leader and small group leader of DOVE Christian Fellowship-Westgate.

February

Two Historic Quaker Ladies

"...And help her in whatever matter she may require assistance from you, for she has been a helper of many including myself...." *Romans 16:2 (Amplified Version)*

In the history of the Lancaster County Society of Friends, two Quaker ladies were examples of faithful service.

Mercy Brown was born in 1763. When she died, her memorial read, "After a time of deep conflict and close exercise of mind, she became a qualified useful instrument in the church. In the 1800s, she felt her mind drawn in love to travel in the ministry. By 1819, her travels were commended; she felt earnest solicitude for the young generation and tenderly invited them to choose the Lord for their portion, and the God of Jacob for the loss of their inheritance. She was a truly affectionate wife, a kind sympathizing friend, and a promoter of peace and harmony among her neighbors."

The meetinghouse at Penn Hill was not large enough to seat the people who came to hear her speak. Her husband built a larger one in 1823. Mercy was ill for six months prior to her death in March 1823, so it is unlikely that she ever ministered there.

Another early Quaker lady was Elizabeth Smedley (Mrs. Eli). The Smedleys arrived in Fulton Township in 1806. Mrs. Smedley's memorial states, "In early life she delighted in the holy scriptures. Her concern for others increased, she felt constrained to invite them to partake personally of the fruits of Divine commands. Her concern was to turn their hearts 'from darkness to light, and from the power of Satan unto God.'" She last spoke at an aged neighbor's funeral. She portrayed "the awful danger of putting off the great work of the soul's salvation." Just a few days later she died, on March 24, 1858. Elizabeth and Eli are buried at Penn Hill.

Father, thank you for Your promise that those who die in the Lord are blessed. Amen.

Ross Morrison Sr. and his wife, June, are missionary associates with Village Missions. Ross writes on Lancaster County religious history. They attend Calvary Church, Lancaster.

Never Give Up!

"You need to persevere so that when you have done the will of God, you will receive what he has promised." *Hebrews 10:36*

Lyle was a young 17-year-old hearing-impaired man who was put in a state institution for the mentally retarded. His parents were a very caring kind of folk, but were overwhelmed with Lyle's behavior and communication problems. It grieved their hearts to have to send their son to an institution, but at the time, it seemed like the only choice they had. Little did they know what a disastrous choice it really was. Little did they know that they would be "chosen" to pioneer changes for individuals housed in that institution.

Lyle's parents visited regularly, at least every week, even though it was a lengthy drive and a bit of a hardship for them. Lyle's parents became involved and tried to get better funding, equipment, and services for the institution. Lyle began to get services in the Deaf Education Dept., and his speech and language skills began to develop. However, the institution still did not meet some of the most basic humane services. Soap, personal clothing, deodorant, and clean sheets were "luxury" items.

The final straw fell when all legislators and congressmen in the state of Ohio were invited to an Open House at the institution, in order for them to see for themselves the conditions at this facility. Only *two* came. The following week, there was an Open House two miles down the road from the institution, at a recently opened experimental Agricultural Center for animals. Over seventy legislators came for the ceremony. Grieved, Lyle's parents, along with three other couples, formed a special grass-root committee that began to lobby for better treatment for the approximately 1,500 mentally retarded residents of that institution. In addition to raising the awareness of government officials, they also filed a class action suit—and won!

Sadly, Lyle died in his twenties. I learned much from Lyle and his love of life. I also learned something valuable from Lyle's parents—to *never* give up!

Lord, help us to be advocates for those who cannot help themselves.

Jim Schneck is a free-lance interpreter for the Deaf, an advocate for the multi-disabled and and a doctoral student.

Angels

"For he will command his angels concerning you to guard you in all your ways...." *Psalm 91:11*

Being born and raised in Nigeria, West Africa, as a missionary kid, I was returning for a summer to work at the boarding school I had attended for grades one to nine. Although I was excited about the summer, there was one concern. I would be flying by myself from Philadelphia to Atlanta, Atlanta to London and would have to change airports in London, and then on to Nigeria. Although I had flown many times over the years, never had I made that many connecting flights on my own.

The flights did not go as expected. Storms in Atlanta delayed our arriving and departure time. I got on a later flight to London but missed my connecting flight to Nigeria. To my dismay, I was informed that I would have a twelve-hour wait in the London airport. Tired, alone and discouraged, I boarded a bus to the other airport in London.

A young woman, a little older than me, came and sat down beside me. She asked where I was going. "Please come home with me," she said. "I'm a stewardess on a Canadian airline. My parents live in London about fifteen minutes from the airport and I'm staying with them until my next flight. You can come with me and we'll bring you back to the airport." Wow! What a godsend.

I went home with her, and her mom and dad greeted me like I was one of their daughters, let me take a rest, woke me up with a cup of hot tea and had bathwater running so I could be refreshed before they took me back to the airport. To this day, I believe they were all like angels God sent to minister to me just when I needed them.

Thank you, Lord, that no matter where we are in this world, You have Your angels surrounding us. There is truly no need to be afraid!

Mary Anna Wingenroth serves the Lord as an administrative assistant at Susquehanna Valley Pregnancy Services.

God's Work to Bring Good

"And we know that in all things God works for the good of those who love him, who have been called according to his purpose."
Romans 8:28

Often the story of Joseph demonstrates God bringing good out of bad. The difficulties Joseph encountered allowed him to save a nation. However, there is another part of the story.

Joseph says to his brothers, "And now, do not be distressed and do not be angry with yourselves for selling me here, because *it was to save lives* that *God sent me ahead of you.* For two years now there has been famine in the land, and for the next five years there will not be plowing and reaping. But, *God sent me ahead of you to preserve for you a remnant on earth and to save your lives by a great deliverance.* So then, it was *not you who sent me here, but God…* (Genesis 45:5-8 emphasis mine)."

Did you catch that? He told them God *sent* him to Egypt.

It is challenging to think of God sending Joseph to Egypt, knowing what would happen to him. (Yet, think of Christ, who was sent by the Father to earth, both of them knowing fully what awaited Him).

Suffering is hard and sometimes feels hopeless. But take comfort, God not only takes the bad and uses it for good, but He sometimes (maybe always) *plans* for the bad to bring about good. In other words, God is active in the situation, instead of reactive. He doesn't sit up in heaven saying, "Oops, one of my children is going through difficulty, I guess I should find a way to bring good out of this." I think He looks at it, already knowing how it will bring Him glory and how it will accomplish His plans.

Father, thank you for having good plans for Your children.

Mandi Wissler is a financial aid and admissions counselor at Lancaster Bible College and daily sees God working for good in the lives around her.

A Still Small Voice

"Then he said, 'Go out, and stand on the mountain before the Lord.' And behold, the Lord passed by, and a great and strong wind tore into the mountains and broke the rocks in pieces before the Lord, but the Lord was not in the wind; and after the wind an earthquake, but the Lord was not in the earthquake; and after the earthquake a fire, but the Lord was not in the fire; and after the fire a still small voice."
1 Kings 19:11–12

My study Bible says that God is not just a God of the spectacular. Sometimes, perhaps many times, He speaks in a still small voice. I ask myself, "How many times have I missed that still small voice?"

Life is busy, so much to do, so many places to go. I want to carve out time to spend with the Lord so I can hear His voice but I have trouble focusing. There's that phone call I must make. I have a meeting to prepare for tomorrow evening. My husband wants me to spend time with him. Oh, I didn't read my chapters in the Bible for today. Yes, and I need to finish the grocery list before I forget.

While all these things are good and/or necessary, I'm not focusing on my Lord and Savior. I'm focusing on the "shoulds and the oughts."

Lord, help me to focus on You. I want to hear Your still small voice.

Yvonne Zeiset is a financial counselor for Consumer Credit Counseling of Central Pennsylvania a division of Tabor Community Services in Lancaster. She serves on the Evangelism Commission and the Prayer Team at her church.

Choosing Contentment

"Let your lives overflow with thanksgiving for all He has done."
Colossians 2:7 (New Living Translation)

Being a mom of two little boys, I started recognizing the "itch" to move out of the city. My husband and I have been living in Lancaster city since we got married. But, now that it's not "just us" anymore, my mind began to wonder how great it would be to pull up into a garage, get the boys out of the car and walk right into our house. No more wondering if we'd find a parking spot in front of our home, much less on our block. The list could go on with desirable changes.

We began to have our "dream home" drives around Lancaster County, window-shopping for another home. We never put our house on the market, but one day we were in touch with someone from out of state who was looking to move to Lancaster. He mentioned they'd like to look at our house if we were interested in selling it.

All of a sudden, my heart began to change. Oh no, I would really miss our city home! And, really, it isn't that bad not having a garage, and…hmmm…interesting how that all changed.

It reminded me to begin thanking God for the home we have, for all of God's blessings in our lives! Once I have a thankful heart instead of a discontented one, I have so much more peace, joy and gratitude—the ingredients of a happy wife and mom. After all, isn't that the attitude I want to pass on to my children?

Lord, thank you for all Your blessings in my life. Bring contentment and peace into the areas where I have felt discontentment. I want to be right in the center of Your will for my life. I recognize You have me in this place for a reason and I choose gratitude today. Amen.

Cindy Zeyak is the wife of Ken and the mother of Brennan and Connor, who live happily in Lancaster city! She is also a worship leader and former Pre-K teacher.

He Sustains My Rest

"…Peace be still…" *Mark 4:39*

Driving to a conference, I was a little worried about going myself, getting to my hotel, and just traveling alone. I was meeting some friends, but they had already arrived at the hotel and were getting their keys.

Upon arrival, the manager came to all of us to apologize that the hotel had overbooked, and they were sending us to a "sister" hotel, farther away from the conference. Now I had to sit through a session of the conference, with my mind wondering where the new hotel was. The conference was incredible, teaching on resting in God during the trials. I know it sounds funny, but to me, having to find this hotel at night in a new city was a trial. I was putting on a brave front, but inside I was ready to cry.

Another mix-up left me all alone, with a room for only one night. Now I was scared, alone, feeling abandoned and lying on a bed in a strange town, crying. The next morning, with a subdued spirit, I had to check out, with nowhere to go. I'll just go home I thought and forget the rest of the conference. But I heard God saying, *escape to Me, and rest in Me, and I will bring My release which brings my favor.*

Going home was my escape, not God's, and it would have brought my own results. I went to the original hotel, the manager saw me and said, "We have been expecting you, your room is ready at our expense." God had already worked on my behalf as I rested in His presence.

Jesus I thank you that You not only calm the storms in our lives, but even in the boat with the waves crashing around us, You cause us to rest in Your intimacy. Keep us from falling short of resting in You.

Kim Zimmerman is a worship leader, along with her husband Brian. They serve at The Lord's House of Prayer, Lancaster, and are the founders/directors of City Gate Lancaster.

We Need Their Prayers!

"The earnest prayer of a righteous person has great power and produces wonderful results." *James 5:16 (New Living Translation)*

In May 1992, I lay on a split-palm floor of a hut on a volcanic island in Papua New Guinea. We were in our last phase of training with Wycliffe Bible Translators. We hoped our time in the village would help us bond with nationals and learn the language. Instead, I had been lying for days staring at dark woven bamboo walls, sicker than I could ever remember.

Without electricity and running water, the chores of preparing meals, bathing children and relating to a new culture barely seemed manageable. Now Nelson had it all to do, as well as taking care of a fussy hungry baby because I didn't have enough milk for her.

My whole body ached. My head throbbed. My thoughts were muddled. "What is wrong with me? Where are You Lord? You seem so far away."

I spoke out against any evil plans of Satan, but the despairing feelings lingered.

If only I could pick up the phone to ask family and friends to pray! I felt so alone. "Please Lord," I cried, "remind our family and friends to pray. We can't fight this battle alone. We need their prayers!"

Moments passed. I have no idea how many. Slowly, a song quietly inched its way into my heart—a song that drove despair from the room. "I know that you can make it by His Spirit and by the power of His mighty hand." Over and over the words washed over me.

Suddenly I knew. Someone had prayed. The song stayed with me over the next few days as I slowly began to improve.

My faith was strengthened during those days of swirling emotion. But sometimes I wonder *what if no one had prayed?*

Father God, please remind us to pray earnestly and to delight in Your power and Your answers!

Marilyn Blank and her husband Nelson serve with Wycliffe, providing care and encouragement to missionary families. They attend Sandy Hill Community Church in Coatesville.

Lord, You Are Faithful

"Trust (lean on, rely on, and be confident) in the Lord and do good; so shall you dwell in the land and feed surely on His faithfulness, and truly you shall be fed." *Psalm 37:3 (Amplified)*

Our God is a good and merciful God, always ready to give His best to His children and to anyone who comes to Him with a sincere and humble heart that trusts Him.

I am originally from Colombia, South America. I came to this country looking for a better way of life. Because I did it in my own wisdom, I found myself in a series of problems, one of which was being illegally in the United States. As an orphan, my greatest desire was to have a family of my own and to live in this country.

I have always been friendly toward God. I knew He was God, and that He was powerful, so in the midst of my troubles I turned to Him for help. He led me to His Son, Jesus. I gave myself and everything in my life to Him—my problems and my desires. In exchange, He gave me His love. It was the greatest day of my life when I experienced His love and care for me.

As I sought the Lord with all of my heart, He revealed Himself to me, giving me two key words for my deliverance—trust and obey. He told me that if I would do this, He would legally place me in this country with a clean record and give me the home and family that I so greatly desired.

Today, thirty-two years later, I still delight myself in God's faithfulness.

I am a United States citizen; I have a good husband (Henry), and three lovable children (Sara, Kevin, and David). If we trust Him and do good, we will truly be fed.

Father, thank you for our Lord Jesus. It is because of Him that we can experience the power of Your Word and Your faithfulness in our lives. Thank you for Your mercy to us.

Marlene Bowman serves along with her husband as an elder at In the Light Ministries in Lancaster.

Buckle Up

"…From where does my help come? My help comes from the Lord, who made heaven and earth. He will not let your foot be moved… The Lord will keep you from all evil; he will keep your life. The Lord will keep your going out and your coming in from this time forth and forevermore." *Psalm 121:1–3, 7–8*

When I was a boy, seat belts were not standard equipment on cars. It took years to perfect them and make their use mandatory. While somewhat inconvenient and restricting, they can make the difference between life and death. Many years ago, a seat belt and the protective hand of a loving and merciful Father saved me from death or debilitating injury in a head-on car crash. I am a strong advocate of "Buckle Up." Seat belts are analogous to important restraints and protective devices in our lives. They protect us from being thrown about or even run over. They help us to stay in position, to remain focused and maintain our grip on whatever God has called us to.

Recently a ministry, which I was called to lead through a significant season of restoration and rebuilding, encountered an unanticipated sharp bend in the road. Instead of the clear, though challenging road we had anticipated, we encountered events and circumstances that might have thrown us about, buried us under discouragement and overwhelming obstacles, and injured those on board. Because we were "buckled up" by a clear sense of mission, well-defined core values and a compelling vision, we were able to stay on course, though with a few dents and bruises to serve as reminders.

The experience has not only strengthened our leadership team and commitment to our corporate calling, it has deepened our affection and gratitude for the awesome God we serve. He is a strong protector and stabilizing force in the face of unsettling turbulence and uncertain times.

Father, thank you not only for demonstrating Your faithfulness through care and provision, but for holding me steady and secure in the midst of tossing and turning that might have derailed or destroyed me, had You not buckled me up in Your protective arms.

Bruce Boydell and his wife, Joan, are members of Covenant Fellowship Church in Glen Mills. They encourage and build up leaders of businesses and ministries through Lifespan Coaching and Consulting Services, based in West Chester.

　　　　　　　　　　　　　　　　　　　God Stories 5

The Pink Slip

"Shouts of joy and victory resound in the tents of the righteous: 'The Lord's right hand has done mighty things!'" *Psalm 118:15*

It had been almost two years since we started our daughter's adoption, and nothing had happened in the time frames we had anticipated. We were frustrated and emotionally empty, wondering if a finalized adoption would ever come to pass. Things were stuck in both the physical and spiritual realms, and the knowledge that our daughter was growing up apart from us caused immense pain. We simply needed a pink slip, inviting us to the United States Embassy in her home country, but it was not being granted to us.

One Friday, the elders of our church invited our family to join them at the end of a scheduled day of prayer and fasting. Honestly, we didn't have much hope as we drove to the retreat center. With heavy hearts, we shared our needs, and then they began to pray for our daughter and us. Their prayers were fervent and powerful. The Holy Spirit revealed things to them that were so specific, my husband and I knew that something was happening in the spiritual realm. When their prayers ended, we both felt a peace in our hearts that we had not felt for a long time. I remember someone saying, "I can't wait to see what God does!" We left that evening with hope and anticipation.

The next business day arrived. The phone rang, my heart raced, and our adoption caseworker gave me words I had begun to doubt I would ever hear: You got your pink slip! She told me that the officials at the embassy could not explain what had happened with our paperwork, but we were cleared to bring her home. Not only that, but we could meet our daughter in two days, instead of the usual two weeks! I didn't need an explanation, because I knew: in His great mercy and might, God had moved our mountain through the prayers of His saints.

God, help us to rejoice in the eternal victory we have in Jesus! You are mighty and powerful, and You do great things.

Maria Buck is the wife of Gary Buck, worship pastor at Petra Christian Fellowship.

Fearless

"...Perfect love casts out fear." *1 John 4:18 (New King James Version)*

Have you ever been so terrified that you couldn't leave your home?

That is the way my life used to be. After fourteen years of suffering with panic attacks, I was finally set free.

In those former years, I literally could not leave my house. I could neither drive nor shop for groceries. I made my husband take me everywhere until one day he said, "No more."

I believed he was the cruelest person alive. Little did I know how his refusal would start me on a new path of freedom. I wasn't freed immediately; as a matter of fact it took almost thirteen years for that to occur. Although I gained my independence in driving, the thought of the panic attacks returning was always on my mind. I always had to have a plan for an escape route.

One day God put me right in the middle of the thing that scared me the most—a traffic jam right in the middle of bypass Route 30 with no exits nearby. I was terrified. I focused so much on my fear that I believed I was about to have a full-blown attack. I couldn't take my focus off the traffic jam. I prayed and asked God to help me and His response was "look out the window."

As I turned my head, I saw a friend of mine walking along the bypass. He was stuck as well and was walking to see what was causing the problem. Suddenly I realized that my focus on the fear had held me a prisoner. All I needed to do was take my eyes off my fear. I laughed with joy at the realization that I was free. My life has completely changed since that day, and I no longer have any fears of traffic jams or of the panic attacks returning.

Thank you, God, for healing me. I pray for those who suffer from this and hope they receive their healing from this testimony of Your faithfulness.

Eileen Christiansen is a leader of a Celebrate Recovery Group in West Sadsburyville.

Agreeing in Prayer

"...I tell you that if two of you on earth agree about anything you ask for, it will be done for you by my Father in heaven." *Matthew 18:19*

God led me to go on a missions trip in 2009 for a month with four other people I didn't know before I went.

We traveled to the Bahamas where we worked with mainly Haitian children who fled from the poor conditions in Haiti. We did twenty Vacation Bible Schools (VBS) over the course of 2 ½ weeks.

Well, to say the least, we prayed a lot together about pretty much everything we could think of. Then one day after the first VBS, we were kind of down because nobody accepted Jesus that morning. So we thought about it for a while and realized we hadn't been praying for the kids to come to know Jesus.

Right then and there we all started praying together that God would open the eyes of these kids to the truth of His love. His answer was more amazing than we (especially me) imagined. God opened the eyes of ten children, and I had the privilege of guiding them all to a personal relationship with Him.

Dear God, thank you for showing me that You answer prayer. Amen.

Alyssa Wingenroth is a senior at Cocalico High School and attends Ephrata Bible Fellowship Church.

Perfect Love

"...Perfect love casts out fear...." *1 John 4:18 (New King James Version)*

God blessed our family with Eleanor. As a young widow, she suffered from a fear of people. In 1983, someone in a local church asked if anyone could help her. My mother took her into our family. Mom led her to the Lord, and from then on Eleanor gravitated to the written Word of God. She got her peace from reading and memorizing His Word.

In 1992, my husband, Bill, and I had the opportunity to have her come to live with us. Eleanor still dealt with the fear of people. Several years later, during one of our conversations about Jesus, she mentioned she wanted to be baptized, but was afraid to do it in a church. I sensed God wanted me to baptize her in the bathtub. I know that may stir up lots of doctrinal issues, but God knew what it would do for Eleanor. Her act of faith broke the fear and healed her! She started attending church with me for several years.

During her years with our family and the church family we all were blessed by her humor and childlike faith. Eleanor went to be with Jesus at age eighty-seven without the fear of people haunting her. If I close my eyes I can almost see her dancing with Jesus and saying to Him, "Your perfect love casts out all my fear."

Dear Father, You know what we need. How great is the love that You lavished on us, that we would be called Your children. May we always represent Your love as Jesus does with us. Amen.

Debbie Davenport serves as a leader interceding and equipping others for kingdom purposes in her various roles in the body of Christ and at Cornerstone Pregnancy Care Services.

Mrs. Thoughtful

"He is not the God of the dead but of the living." *Matthew 22:32*

"Are you related to that rich guy?" I asked. I was referring to my client's last name as I drew her blood during a long shift at the hospital.

"Yeah right, that'd be nice," the lady replied sarcastically. "You don't look like a Martha, by the way."

"What do Marthas look like?"

"Not like you."

Her comment stopped my hurriedness that afternoon and I started listening. This lady was out of the ordinary; most people admitted to the hospital's oncology unit were too sick or worried to notice their caretaker's characteristics.

As I assisted "Mrs. Thoughtful" the next day, I was curious to get to know her better. Complications with cancer had left her weak in body but not in spirit. My memory of our conversation touched my heart.

Mrs. Thoughtful overheard me speaking with a coworker about praying for him and asked me to include her in my prayers, too. I said I would, and wondered aloud, "Do you know Jesus personally?"

She started to cry and said, "I couldn't fight cancer this long if I didn't. My husband died several years back, and I've been through a lot since then. When I was first diagnosed with cancer, I cried out to the Lord, 'Lord I can't do this alone. I need someone to walk through this battle with me.'" She paused. "God provided. He provided a special male friend to walk with me through this battle. God loves me so much. He is so good to me. I don't deserve this goodness."

God, the Father of Jesus Christ, thank You that You are alive; You aren't dead, and You are at work in our lives.

Martha Novak is a member of New Covenant Christian Church. She participates and leads in discipleship groups.

When You Realize You're Living Your "Worst-Case Scenario!"

"And the God of all grace, who called you to his eternal glory in Christ, after you have suffered a little while, will himself restore you and make you strong, firm and steadfast." *1 Peter 5:10*

Just when you think things couldn't get any harder, you wake up and realize that in this exact moment, it's the life that you could only imagine as being, "your worst-case scenario." You're wondering how it is that you are still able to take another breath. When you receive news that is just unbearable and it seems that giving up and crawling in a ball to die would be the best-case scenario in comparison.

There's nowhere else to go; no one can give you any valuable advice, no one has the words to say. Nothing can make it go away or comfort your wounded soul. So, you grab your Bible and you sit with tears streaming down your face in silence. It's the best noise, or lack thereof, you've heard so far. Then He whispers to you, "I got you! Trust Me. I am in this. Just stay close."

In that very moment, you realize that things really could be worse. You understand that you don't know why it had to be this way, but you know a God who knew it before it happened and has a book of promises and a plan of action. You remember that because your ways and thoughts are not anything like His, and what you hope for might look different than what He will do, you hold on to the Promise Maker as hard as you can. And, in that place, you find the strength to breathe another breath.

God, thank you that You are the answer to every problem. Thank you for never leaving us and for promising good things for those that love You and stay close to You.

Joy Ortega is an associate pastor of Living Word Fellowship, where their purpose is to "Reach people and change lives!"

Pitch Your Tent

"Now Moses used to take a tent and pitch it outside the camp some distance away, calling it the 'tent of meeting.'" *Exodus 33:7*

Moses is one of the Bible heroes we all learned about in Sunday school and Vacation Bible School. When I think of all the amazing events he experienced I'm in awe.

I wonder what his thoughts were when he looked back over his life? Today, we often hear believers say, "God is doing a new thing!"

I'm sure Moses would reply, "Let me tell you a few things!"

When I contemplate Moses' life, I am amazed at the faith and obedience he had. There are times I've made decisions knowing God asked me to step out in faith. If I'm honest, I will tell you that some of these times, in the midst of the obedience, I struggled with the question, "You did tell me to do this Lord, right?" I don't quit, I don't give up...I just question that I heard Him correctly. I'm *always* amazed when I see the end result! That's when I praise Him for being the God of my salvation, Creator of heaven and earth.

Moses pitched a tent to meet with the Lord, away from others. Ahh, here is where we all can learn. When's the last time I "pitched" a tent of meeting with the Lord?

Serving the Lord requires us to come away to our special place with Him. We can all ask ourselves, "Have I come away lately?" Perhaps it's time to pitch our tent!

Father, thank you for reminding us how important it is to set aside special time with You each day. Thank you for Your love, truth and guidance in all situations in our lives!

Karen Pennell is the CEO of CCWS Medical in Chester County and President/ CEO of Karen Pennell Consulting. She serves the Lord in full-time ministry to equip and empower others to serve in excellence.

Squeezed

"That the trial of your faith, being much more precious than of gold that perisheth, though it be tried with fire, might be found unto praise and honour and glory at the appearing of Jesus Christ:" *1 Peter 1:7 (King James Version)*

Before I went to bed last night, I prayed and saw a vision. I saw a picture of a little man. Instead of his head, he had an olive with a red pimento. The little man was tied by ropes to a tree post. I felt that the vision meant that difficulties were coming.

During the next day, my wife had a medical need that required immediate care. At first, we thought that we would have to wait a whole day before we could get it taken care of. I called up the hospital and told them the situation. The nurse was so compassionate and kind! She said that we could come right in to the Emergency Room and that the problem would be taken care of. I thanked her from the bottom of my heart and was very surprised that I choked up with tears as I spoke. This puzzled me! I didn't realize that I was as emotionally distraught as apparently I was.

As we were driving to the hospital, the Holy Spirit brought to my remembrance the vision from the night before. God revealed the meaning of the vision. The olive represents great pressure. In order to get olive oil out of olives, great pressure must be exerted. I knew that God was really squeezing us and that was why I was on the verge of tears. I knew that the only way for God to get the juice, the anointing out of us, is for Him to put the squeeze on us.

On the cross, Jesus was squeezed. Good things came out of Him because good things were in Him.

Dear Lord, let me be filled with the sweet anointing of Jesus so that when I am squeezed, goodness flows out.

Rev. John Paul Peters is with Eagle Focus International Ministries. He teaches how to hear God's voice.

A Rose on a Thorn Bush

"...Every detail in our lives of love for God is worked into something good." *Romans 8:28 (The Message)*

I will never forget the pain of the moment sixteen years ago when daddy's girl, Barbara Ann, stopped by the church office on a Sunday night before returning to college. That's when she told her mother and me that she was pregnant out of wedlock.

We were devastated. She was a senior in college and had her whole life and career ahead of her. Her dreams (or should I say mine) for her life seemed shattered.

I recovered somewhat. There was a quick wedding two months later, followed by her graduation from college on Mother's Day and the birth of our first granddaughter, Stephanie, on September 15 of the same year.

One moment that fall when I was complaining to the Lord about how much certain elements of that whole scenario still felt so painful, God seemed to bargain with me. In an almost audible voice I sensed Him saying, "I could take you back to a time before that painful Sunday night and reverse the events that broke your heart. Do you want Me to do that?"

I answered, "Sure! It still hurts."

Then I heard God say, "Oh, one more thing. You'll have to give up Stephanie!"

Ouch! "No! She's my Princess!" I shouted.

Then I added, "Oh, I think I get it, God."

You see, I realized that good and evil travel on parallel tracks and usually arrive at the same time. We can't select one without the other.

Recently I placed a wrist corsage on a beautiful woman as she was heading to her junior prom. Stephanie is the apple of my eye and I would never want to know life without her.

You see, God brings good out of every situation, no matter how painful.

Lord, some people ask why You put thorns on a rose bush. Today I marvel at the fact that You put a rose on a thorn bush. It's a matter of how I look at life.

Steve Sabol has served the River of Life Church in Lebanon for twenty years.

Godly Men Needed

"Better to dwell in a corner of a housetop, than in a house shared with a contentious woman." *Proverbs 21:9 (New King James Version)*

Some years ago I was asked to preach at a friend's wedding. When I asked him what passage of scripture he wanted me to use for the sermon, he said, "It is better to dwell on the corner of a housetop, than to dwell with a contentious woman."

He had a great sense of humor, so I thought his suggestion provided a perfect opportunity for a good laugh. But he seemed a bit offended by my laughter and said, "That is really the scripture I want."

Needless to say, I went home and prayed, "God, how can I make this into a good, compelling wedding sermon. Please help!"

God gave me a picture of a godly husband, who during Bible times, went up to his flat rooftop instead of staying downstairs and confronting an unhappy wife by trying to convince her to see things his way.

On his rooftop he could survey his kingdom and see where the attack was coming from and go to battle for his family. On the rooftop, God showed him how to go down to live at peace with his wife.

Where are the husbands and fathers today who will pay the price to pull back from strife, draw close to God to understand and determine the real enemy and do battle in prayer to find peace at home?

God, will You please raise up a generation of men who will fight to truly battle for their families, their church and their nation? In Jesus' name, Amen.

LaMarr Sensenig serves as an elder at Lancaster Evangelical Free Church in Lititz.

Learning to Trust

"Therefore, since we have such a hope, we are very bold."
2 Corinthians 3:12

I was working in construction when I injured myself, severely twisting my knee. The following morning, the knee was swollen and very painful. Even before this incident, I had problems with my knee. Now, I seemed to have no choice but to give in to surgery. I decided to stay home from work and find a doctor.

As I lay in bed, I started to feel guilty for not going to work. Second Corinthians 3:12 came to my mind. I got out my Bible and read it. I asked the Lord what He was trying to tell me. I realized He was saying *He* is my hope, and because of that, I needed to be bold and trust Him.

I went to work. We were building storm ditches in a new development and a cement truck got lost. Consequently, I sat with the foreman in a truck for five hours waiting for the truck to arrive. I ended up receiving overtime pay. A similar thing happened the next day, and again, I was paid for overtime.

That night, I had a dream in which I was running fast and freely. People were yelling at me to remember my knees, but I said, "They're healed!"

Insurance provided by the construction company would have covered my knee surgery; however, I had been asked by a friend to work in his sporting goods business, which could not offer insurance. I decided to trust God again, and I changed jobs.

For months, the pain in my knees worsened, but I remembered the scripture and the dream. Each day, I affirmed my trust in the Lord. One day I touched my knees and realized there was no more pain! I was healed and moved to a new level of trusting the Lord.

Thank You, Lord, for being trustworthy and for the opportunities to see that trust worked out in our lives.

John W. Shantz is pastor of Spring City Fellowship Church, which is part of the Hopewell Network of Churches.

Here and Now

"Give your entire attention to what God is doing right now, and don't get worked up about what may or may not happen tomorrow. God will help you deal with whatever hard things come up when the time comes." *Matthew 6:34 (The Message)*

In Joyce Meyer's *Battlefield of the Mind*, she likes to describe *worry* or *anxiety* as "spending today trying to figure out tomorrow."

We are to live life *now*. Our Father knows what we have need of before we ask. It is *now* He is interested in. If we are worrying about tomorrow's deadlines, such as what if I can't pay next week's bills, what if the car breaks down before the weekend, what if my child catches that flu, and so on, how our lists go on with what ifs.

We miss God's plan for today. We miss the signals of ministry for now. A touch of a hand, stopping and pushing aside our own agenda to hear a broken heart of a child or coworker, to lift a prayer for that friend whose name just came to mind. Even more, we miss the gentle voice of the Lover of our Soul saying come, come and sit with Me for a while.

Jesus, be Lord of my thought life. Please don't let me dwell on things that don't bring life. Please help me be in tune with Your voice and not miss the here and now with You.

Christina Ricker is a wife, mom and nana who belongs to Jesus.

Panoramic Plan

"'For I know the plans I have for you,' declares the Lord, 'plans to prosper you and not to harm you, plans to give you hope and a future.'" *Jeremiah 29:11*

When I was a boy, my family lived on top of a hill that overlooked a valley in Lancaster County. It was a beautiful sight to see a panoramic view of the farmland, trees and area towns.

I often went to the edge of our backyard to have some talks with God over my dreams and fears and all that was pressing on my mind.

As I gazed across the countryside, I wondered if the Lord would ever work through me in any significant way. The sight of the landscape in front of me had me feeling rather small. Sometimes my doubts about myself kept me from having faith in a God who is bigger than me. This caused me to have serious concerns about a productive future.

Time passed. God moved me into the area of ministry of communicating the message of God's grace and truth on radio. I thoroughly enjoy the radio ministry, and it gives me a sense of redemptive purpose.

When I returned to my parents' place a few years ago, I looked across the same panoramic view that I enjoyed as a child. It suddenly struck me that God had answered my prayer to be used by Him for His glory. He gave me that territory to minister to all the people living in the range of that view. Even more overwhelming was the realization that I could see only a fraction of the area that WJTL reaches.

I was filled with thanks and praise to God for directing my path.

Dear God, I thank You for Your faithfulness and love to move us into places where we can serve You and produce fruit for Your kingdom. May Your love so fill me that doubts and fears about tomorrow are overshadowed by faith in You, in Jesus' name.

John Shirk can be heard on the radio dial at FM 90.3 WJTL.

Storm Protection

"God is our refuge and strength, a very present help in trouble."
Psalm 46:1 (King James Version)

One Sunday afternoon, my husband and I received a telephone call from one of our grandsons. He asked if we had been watching television. I told him no. He informed us that a tornado was heading our way and would be in our area in about ten minutes.

I immediately turned on the television to hear what they had to say about the situation. The newscasters instructed people who lived in the area to go to the lower level of their homes and away from windows.

My husband is not able to go up and down steps, so he could not go to the lower level. Every room in our house has windows, so there was no getting away from the windows. I closed the blinds next to the area where he was seated. We prayed for God's protection. We both felt peace, even though it was raining very hard and we heard the winds howling outside.

After the storm had passed, we learned that homes close to where we live were destroyed by the wind and hail, but the hand of God protected us. We had no damage. I thank God for His mighty protection.

Father, I thank You for always being our refuge, not only when the storms of life attack us. I thank You for being just a prayer away.

Doris Showalter is a wife, mother, grandmother and great-grandmother and attends Mission of Love Church in Ephrata.

Good Stewards of Our Children

"Behold, children are a gift of the Lord, the fruit of the womb is a reward." *Psalm 127:3 (New American Standard Bible)*

A year ago, my daughter and I were having passionate discussions about colleges. We were weighing all the factors that one considers when selecting a college.

One of the colleges offered her a sizeable scholarship. It was a reputable school in her field of study—one of the best! It had all the positive measurable attributes that we were looking for—except one. No one could tell us about the spiritual pulse of the campus.

A second college that my daughter had not been seriously considering began to look more and more like it was the one she should attend. For various reasons they had not offered her as large a financial package. Originally the college hadn't even been among her top three choices, yet suddenly it seemed like every other factor was pointing toward this being the one.

I wrestled over and over again about how much weight the scholarship should bear in our decision-making process. We are told throughout scripture to be good stewards of our money.

As I prayed heavily over this decision, a friend reminded me that money was just one small aspect of stewardship. My daughter was also a gift from God—one of which He wanted me to be a great steward. When I considered the stewardship of my daughter—there was a completely different list of criteria!

After balancing out all the things that God wanted me to be a steward of, the second-choice college won out. We are stretched to trust God financially, but to date, we haven't regretted it. God wants us to be good stewards of all that He has blessed us with.

Precious Father, thank you for being faithful in leading us to good stewardship of all gifts that You've given to us—especially our children.

Lisa Hildebrand works for Susquehanna Valley Pregnancy Services and ministers as a teacher and speaker in local churches.

God's Overwhelming Grace

"The Lord is merciful and gracious, slow to anger and abounding in steadfast love. He does not deal with us according to our sins, nor repay us according to our iniquities." *Psalm 103:8, 10 (English Standard Version)*

Life couldn't possibly get any worse for Jeff. His life was spiraling out of control. But to everyone else, Jeff appeared as if he had life together. Jeff had the biggest smile, he taught Sunday school, led the youth group, played on the worship team, was always at church and talked to people about Jesus constantly.

Jeff realized he was trying to impress people and, ultimately, impress God. When alone, Jeff confronted the reality of who he was and when he looked in the mirror, he hated what he saw. Jeff was an addict who finally hit bottom.

Jeff realized he had a couple of choices. He could either continue in the direction he was going or choose another path that would lead to life. Jeff chose the journey he is still on to this day. Realizing this was not a journey he could take on his own, Jeff entered a twenty-eight-day treatment program. Looking back, he recalls one moment that made all the difference in his journey. He recalls reading Psalm 103, and thinking he had used up all the grace God had to offer him. Suddenly the meaning of the scripture passage became clear to him. As the sun emerged over the horizon, Jeff felt its warmth. It was like God himself wrapped His arms around Jeff and reassured him that he had not used up all His grace and that He loved him even though he had rejected Him for so long.

Today, life is a lot closer to what Jeff wanted for so long. He is experiencing the love of His heavenly Father who delights in him and, in turn, Jeff puts his hope in Him.

Father, thank you that we can never out-sin Your grace.

Dan Keefer serves as community relations director for Day Seven Ministries. Jeff's story is shared with permission.

His Timing

"Then Peter replied, 'I see very clearly that God shows no favoritism.'" *Acts 10:34 (New Living Translation)*

In 1993, my husband left me after a twenty-year marriage. How would I be able to afford my son's college tuition? How would I make house payments?

I discovered the Lord did not leave me. He proved it in so many ways. Here are two memories of God's amazing provision and timing.

My six-foot-three-inch-tall son required a suit to participate in his high school graduation ceremony. I only had the money to buy shoes. I did not know anyone from whom we could borrow a suit that fit him. Time had run out. I told my son, "Go buy the shoes and meet me at Grandma's. I am not sure what will happen, but at least you will have a new pair of shoes."

When I pulled up at my mother's house, my son walked out modeling a suit and new shoes. I found out that a local business man (who happened to be six-foot-three-inches tall) told my mother that he had a suit and wanted to get rid of it. My mother did not even know we needed a suit or why she took the suit or why he had given it to her. The suit fit my son to a tee.

A similar situation occurred when I needed $685 to pay my son's college tuition. The day before I needed to write the check for the college tuition, an unexpected check came in the mail for "overpayment" of closing costs on the house that I had purchased months before. The check was for exactly $685.

How wonderful to know that God loves my children and me and provides for our needs. God shows no favoritism and His timing is always on time.

Lord, I trust in Your timing. Thank You, Lord, for being in control of my life and my children's lives.

Barbara Luciani, Living Water Chapel, serves with her husband as house parents at Milton Hershey.

Is Your City Poised for a Revolution?

"...Can anything good come out of Nazareth?" *John 1:46*

Reading, Pennsylvania, has a bad reputation, much like Nazareth. But God enjoys bringing forth the glory of His Son out of the darkest cities of the earth. As I have prayed over this city and have studied the history of the men of God who have come through this city, I am convinced of one thing: Reading is on God's radar.

In 1949, T. L. Osborn, the great healing evangelist, came to Reading to hold a four-week crusade. I was able to obtain some of his personal handwritten journals about his time here, and they are proof that something good and something God is coming out of Reading! Look at this entry:

"The four-week Reading Crusade was an area-wide success from the beginning. Thousands of Amish and Mennonite people attended the meetings. They had been taught that the day of miracles passed, but they came to see for themselves. Thousands of them were converted and miraculously healed. That crusade's influence proved to be the beginning of a great spiritual move among them. Rev. Gerald Derstine of Florida was one of the many Mennonites whose lives were transformed during the Reading crusade."

Several of the preachers who launched healing and tent ministries in the fifties received their inspiration during the Osborn Reading tent crusade. Rev. R. W. Shambach often tells of the profound impact that was made upon him as a young Bible school student, when he stood under the tent in Reading and watched the Osborns commanding the blind to see, the deaf to hear, and the lame to walk.

Can you believe it? Right here in Reading: "Sin City USA," now transforming into the "Son City." Is your city poised for such a revolution? Let's believe it together!

Father, as darkness covers the earth, even gross darkness, let Your church arise and let Your glory be seen upon us! In Jesus' name!

Craig Nanna lives in Reading with his wife Tracie and three kids, and they together pastor Reading DOVE Christian Ministry Center. Craig also serves as the director for a group of pastors and Christian leaders called the Reading Regional Transformation Network.

Daniel Boone Homestead, Berks County
Photo by Mark Van Scyoc

March

Digging for Destiny

"This is what the Lord says, 'Stand at the crossroads and look. Ask for the ancient paths, ask where the *good way is and walk in it, and you will find rest for your souls....*'" *Jeremiah 6:16*

Today, there is a cry in my heart to know and fulfill the plan for which God created me. In previous stages of my life, I hit the snooze alarm when God was trying to wake me up. At other times I curled up too tightly in the fetal position of emotional pain to care. Even so, the DNA of God's plan stayed with me from the start, and my Savior, Jesus, redeems me to the end.

Perhaps physical land regions also have divine purposes. Perhaps these peopled landmasses can also fall asleep, be in pain, miss the blueprint and need Christ's redemption. And maybe, it's the redeemed of the land that are called to excavate God's original plan and intercede for restoration. Where to start? How about with the first native or other settlers of a region.

In my area, the earliest nonindigenous settlers of Lebanon County were Hebrews. According to historian Julius Sachse, Jewish sojourners settled the Schaefferstown area as early as 1720 to barter with the native people. He stated, "It was not long before a House of Prayer was built by them for worship of the great Jehovah; it was the first synagogue in the American Desert. It was built on the old Indian trail leading from the Conestoga to the Swatara. Here the law was elevated and the shofar blown long before it was done in the chief town of the province."[1] Clearly, this region had a blessed start by being settled by a praying people of covenant.

[1] Sachse, Julius. *German Sectarians of Pennsylvania 1708–1742.* Philadelphia, 1909.

Father God, thank you for the blood of redemption of Your Son, Jesus. Sanctify Your people and Your land. Restore us individually and corporately to the fullness of our calling in Christ. May we seek the ancient paths and walk in Your ways. Amen.

Nancy Shean serves as a Youth for Christ board member and with regional prayer teams.

The Ride

"'For I know the plans I have for you,' says the Lord. 'They are plans for good and not for disaster, to give you a future and a hope.'"
Jeremiah 29:11 (New Living Translation)

I make lists. I have been known to make a list with "make a list" at the top so I have something to cross off. When the list gets too messy, I make a new list. I color code my lists. The list to discuss with my boss, Bill, is on blue paper. You get the picture.

Two years ago, we decided to sell our home, which had been the family home for two generations and for forty of its fifty-five years of existence. We told each of our eight children and I started to make lists.

This move required downsizing, so I made lists of things to sell, to give away and of just plain question marks.

We began the roller coaster by talking to the realtor, perusing the Internet, deciding what we could afford and figuring out so many other details. Of course I made a list of the must-have's and the dream-of's that I desired for our new home.

The next few months reminded me of my growing up years in Colorado. I felt like I was floating down the Colorado River on a raft, holding on, wowed by the amazing scenery and yet confident that every bump was controlled by God.

We sold our home in two weeks, purchased a beautiful home, packed up twenty-two years of accumulation and moved in just a little more than two months.

By the way, our new house had almost everything listed on our dream list. I am so grateful that God refers to my list.

Thank You, Lord, for deepening my faith and trust in You. I still make lists, but more importantly, I enjoy the ride. You create the scenery, control the ride and provide more blessings than I can imagine. You are not limited by pen and paper. I am so grateful that I am on Your list.

Jan Pranckun-Bewley is administrative coordinator for Care Ministries at Lives Changed By Christ. She leads a ministry for single moms and for stepfamilies.

You Are His Prized Possession

"Whatever is good and perfect comes down to us from God our Father, who created all the lights in the heavens. He never changes or casts a shifting shadow. He chose to give birth to us by giving us his true word. And we, out of all creation, became his prized possession." *James 1:17–18 (New Living Translation)*

When recently asked "What is your most priceless treasure?" my initial response was to say my daughter. But she isn't my possession. Although she certainly is my treasure! It was hard raising my daughter as a single mom and the days seemed so long with earning a living, fixing meals, helping with homework, cleaning house, paying bills, grocery shopping, school activities, childcare needs, and on and on through elementary, middle school, high school. I heard someone say about parenting that the days are long, but the years go by fast. Oh, how fast they have gone!

My role as Lauren's mother has changed as I do less hands-on parenting now for my young adult daughter. She has become my very dear friend. She is a great encourager and writes me the most uplifting notes. You can't imagine how my heart swells when I read her words: that she is proud of me, that God has gifted her with a mother like me, that she has learned valuable and priceless lessons from me.

Nothing in my life has been more rewarding or given me more joy than to be a mother. And no matter the life challenge, I have always been so grateful for the precious gift of my child and for God's faithfulness to us every step of the way.

Father, I thank You for the precious gift of my child and the joy of mothering. Thank you that we are Your dearly loved children, who are Your prized possession, for we do belong to You.

Sharon Blantz is Lauren's proud, ever-loving mama and serves single-parent families, care and support ministries, as a regional pastor at Worship Center.

We Are Not Alone

"Bear one another's burdens, and so fulfill the law of Christ."
Galatians 6:2 (New King James Version)

On October 27, 2003, my wife called me. "Holly [our daughter] is in the emergency room at Abington Hospital. Her kidneys have shut down, and she may not make it." At the hospital, I shall never forget how pale and weak our daughter looked. I felt so helpless and not just a little hopeless. A woman, whom I had helped discern a pastoral call, was there to pray for us, because I could not find the words of prayer for myself.

Fear gripped me for two days. I felt so utterly helpless. Then came a voice as if it were the voice of God, "Do what you know how to do best. Build a community of prayer around her." So I went through my email address book and picked the Session of our church, colleagues from around the country, and friends in the four different communities where we have been a family together.

My request: *We covet your prayers. It is the only thing keeping us sane and in the moment right now. If we project out too far, my fear takes over, and as the writer of 1 John says, "There is no fear in love. Perfect love casts out fear." Thanks for being part of our lives and receiving this in the spirit in which it is sent; the spirit of the love which we seek to surround our family in this time of need.*

One return email in particular stands out: "So you hold your heads high while we bow ours and trust God that perfect love will take care of that fear." That day God lifted fear from my heart. I did not know if Holly would live or die, but I knew that whatever happened we were not alone. On October 28, 2004, a year to the day that Holly was placed on kidney dialysis, she received a kidney transplant from a member of that wider prayer community who had been praying for us for a year. I am a believer of today's devotional verse because I know that when we do what it says, healing comes.

Thank you, Lord, for those who pray for us when we cannot find the words to pray for ourselves. Help us never to forget that we are not alone and that we can trust the future into Your care. Amen.

Rev. Dr. Randolph T. Riggs is pastor of First Presbyterian Church in downtown Lancaster.

Reconciliation

"And all things are of God, who hath reconciled us to himself by
Jesus Christ, and hath given to us the ministry of reconciliation."
2 Corinthians 5:18 (King James Version)

Sometimes no matter how long and often you pray, things can still
seem hopeless. There were times I fasted, and times a friend would fast
with me. Surely God would see how serious we were and answer our
prayers!

Year after year I would visit my family who lived 1,600 some miles
away. Mom and my sister had been estranged for most of their adult
years. Each was tired of the hurt the other caused and hardened by
years of trying not to care. I would visit with my faith strong and expectant, only to go back home saddened and discouraged because there
did not seem to be any change.

God's intervention came in the form of a question. "Sis, I am going
to visit Mom and Dad today. Would you like to come with me?" The
answer was simple, "Yes, but I need to talk to my husband." The next
half hour seemed like an hour. I was "holding my breath" and trying
hard to keep my mouth shut. My sister and her husband then asked
their son, who had also been estranged from his grandparents, if he
wanted to come as well.

An hour later, we all piled into cars and took off to the assisted
living center. I watched in amazement as hugs and tears flowed, words
of forgiveness and laughter filled the room. And all I did was ask a
question.

That was five years ago. My Mom and sister bonded like epoxy
that day and their love and commitment to each other has not dimin-
ished. My nephew has his grandmother back, too.

If you have been praying for family members, don't give up. I
continue to pray for further reconciliation in my family. It is a little
easier now to believe and leave the outcome in God's hands.

*Father Reconciler, empower us to persevere in praying and believing
for reconciliation in our families, our neighborhoods, our country,
and the world. Thanks.*

Carol Sanchez is a follower of Jesus, loving Him and others and serving those
He loves, as He appoints.

Healing of the Nations

"On each side of the river stood the tree of life...And the leaves of the tree are for the healing of the nations." *Revelation 22:2*

Directors of pregnancy ministries from across Eastern Europe were gathering for a conference in Ukraine. Our leadership team arrived at the retreat complex a day early to set up.

By mid-afternoon our preparation was complete, and we had a few hours to relax. Several of us decided to explore the surrounding woods. As we crossed a field leading to the woods, an unusual sight caught our attention. One tree—nestled in with the others—was visibly shaking. Its leaves danced back and forth as though stirred by the wind. But it wasn't windy and none of the other trees were moving.

We didn't know what to make of it and enjoyed the rest of our walk.

The next day, conference attendees from eight nations were offering their praise and worship to God. As the music slowed, in my mind's eye I saw the shimmering tree from the day before and then thought of Revelation 22:2, "And the leaves of the tree are for the healing of the nations." It seemed God wanted to minister healing to the conference participants.

I shared what I was sensing with my friend, who was helping to discern God's leading. He'd seen the shaking tree the day before, and showed me his Bible, which he'd opened to Revelation 22. He pointed to verse two and said, "That's what God was saying to me too."

We shared this with the participants and encouraged them to open their hearts to God's healing touch. Weeping filled the room as God's Spirit ministered deeply.

Father, Your creativity in communicating with us is limitless and Your heart to bless people knows no bounds. I want to sense where You're moving and move with You.

Lisa Hosler serves at Susquehanna Valley Pregnancy Services and with teams seeking God for regional transformation.

Where Is this Abundant Life?

"But seek first his kingdom...." *Matthew 6:33*

One afternoon, I had just had it with the busyness of life. Tired of the rat race of keeping up with all my responsibilities with work and family, I stood in my living room and cried out to God, "Where is this abundant life you mention in Your Word? I don't have it!" At that moment a Bible reference came to my mind and I looked up Matthew 6:33. In Jesus' discourse on worry, He gives the antidote by commanding us to seek His kingdom first.

Instantly the Lord opened my eyes to the reason I was so exhausted and worn out. Every day I woke up with *my* agenda and everything I needed to accomplish that day. In my mind I would always tell the Lord that I would spend time with Him later when things slowed down. Of course, later never came. I just couldn't seem to find consistent time alone with Jesus. He gently told me that if I would put His command into practice of seeking to know Him first in my day, then "all these things would be given to me as well." I argued with the Lord that I just didn't know if that was possible because I was so busy.

The next morning after I started my pot of coffee, I proceeded to go out to our driveway and pick up the morning newspaper. As I headed back to the house, the Lord told me that I could find time to be with Him if I would give up the morning paper and pick up His Word instead. I could hardly argue with that! That day was the day my life changed! Prioritizing my relationship with Him and spending time alone in His Word first thing every morning brought the abundant life and joy I had been missing out on all these years.

Oh God, thank you for stating so plainly in Your Word how to find true life and joy.

Anita Keagy is founder of JoyShop Ministries and attends Manor Church of Lancaster.

Your Joy Will Come in the Spring

"Hope deferred makes the heart sick, but a longing fulfilled is a tree of life." *Proverbs 13:12*

During the winter of 1995, the greatest longing of my heart was to have a baby. When that desire wasn't fulfilled in what I deemed to be a timely manner, I began to fret and become frustrated. One evening I was reading a devotional and came upon the phrase "Your joy will come in the spring." I don't remember the rest of the context of the reading, but I felt those words leap from the page and seemingly sear my heart. I shared the experience with my husband and felt that it had been God's words, a promise, to me. I felt surely it must mean we would be expecting by springtime.

Well, spring came and went, and still no baby. However, I was thrilled the following summer to find out that, at last, we were expecting. By that time I had pretty much forgotten about that sentence from the devotional, having written it off as my own misperception. Several months later, as we held our beautiful baby girl on a chilly March day, my husband had a realization. He said to me, "Do you remember the word the Lord gave you about your joy coming in spring?" Of course, I remembered! What I had not realized though, until the moment he reminded me, was that God's personal promise to me had been fulfilled. Our precious daughter was born on the first day of spring.

Isn't it a wonderful thing to know that our heavenly Father not only knows our longings, but He desires to fill our lives with good things. However, we sometimes think that if we don't see "results" in the way or time frame that we deem best, that we have been forgotten. How good it is when we are able to grasp the truth that God works all things for our good in His own time and ways!

Father, please help me to remember that You are the giver of all good gifts, but sometimes they must come in Your timing and not mine. Grant me the grace to wait and trust in Your infinite wisdom and unfailing love toward me.

Jessi Clemmer is a church planter at Koinonia House, Pottstown.

Can't You Hear Me?

"Then Jesus said to his disciples, "If anyone would come after me, he must deny himself and take up his cross and follow me."
Matthew 16:24

"Waaaaaaaaaa!" is baby-ese for, "I don't want to take a nap." And because she thought I was not fluent in this language, my little Audrey repeated it over and over, louder and louder, in hopes that I would come rescue her from her crib. And there was crazy me, sitting in the room across the hall, listening to every wail.

I heard a very human voice inside of me saying, "Have you no heart? Can't you hear your child begging you to come to her? All she wants is a little close time with you. Go get her." That voice almost squashed the other, barely noticeable one behind it that said, "Audrey is screaming because she is tired. Of course she does not want to take a nap. Naps are boring. But can't you hear how much she needs it? Just give her a few more minutes..." And, in a few more minutes, the crying softened to a whimper, and the whimper faded into silence.

My child did not want to take a nap, although it was the best thing for her at that time. There are many things in our lives that we do not want and we may cry for our Father to take them away. But His is often that smaller, harder to hear voice, telling us to suffer through it. There is a good reason for it, even if we never know it. If we can be sure of anything, we know we will not fly through this life with the greatest of ease. It is best to buffer it with some perspective. Audrey may not have noticed that she was more cheerful after her nap. But I noticed. There is purpose in suffering.

Father, please forgive me for all my complaining. I trust You to do what is best for me. Amen.

Tracy Slonaker is a wife, mother of three, and Director of Christian Education at Harvest Fellowship of Colebrookdale.

Wintertime and Springtime Lessons

"Are not two sparrows sold for a penny? And not one of them will fall to the ground apart from your Father." *Matthew 10:29*

My wife and I are "birders." We have various kinds of bird feeders and suet logs scattered across our yard. Goldfinches, which are one of our favorite species, do not fly south for the winter. If we provide them with a fresh supply of Niger Seed, they will put on a display of their beauty all year long. In the winter months these little upside-down-eating birds are a dingy brown color. However, beginning in early March, their coloring begins to change from dingy brown back to their beautiful green and yellow splendor. As we watched this spectacular change taking place this year, I thought of how God takes us through the wintertimes of our lives, giving us hope as we draw close to Him.

Whatever we are going through in our lives, we should always remember that God will bring us through. He will take us out of that valley of fear, loneliness, inferiority or apathy and bring us into another splendid springtime. When we yield our lives completely to Him, He will "create in us a clean heart," and we will be like that tree planted by the stream, drinking from the well of living water. What a mighty God we serve!

Father, I thank You that You love us so much and continue to reveal Yourself to us in so many different ways. Whether it is watching the beauty of nature change right before our eyes, or experiencing an "Aha" moment, we "know that we know" that You have just worked a miracle in our lives. In Jesus' name, Amen.

Rich Colvin is the volunteer pastor at The Villa St. Elizabeth, an assisted living facility in West Reading.

Persevering in Prayer

"[Jesus said] Therefore I tell you, whatever you ask for in prayer, believe that you have received it and it will be yours." *Mark 11:24*

When I was a teenager, my mother started having severe depression that led to mental problems. This was a scary time for my siblings and me—wondering what to do. There was much prayer for her by friends and church.

Mom would get worse and disappear. We would call the police to find her and take her to a mental hospital where she would become stabilized and return home.

This was a nightmare to us children. We prayed constantly for her. We older ones got married and cared for our siblings while our mother would have bouts and hospital stays. I heard someone's testimony of how God had answered a thirty-five-year prayer request. That gave me hope—so we continued to pray for my mom.

Years went by and things seemed to get worse, as we continued to pray. We saw God answer other prayers which gave us faith for answers for Mom.

Mom refused help to find answers for why she struggled so much. I think she was afraid to know why. We would visit her and leave in tears, because of how crazy the visit would be. After one of these visits the Lord showed me that, when I walk out her door, after a visit, that I should thank Him that she *is* healed, no matter what it seems like. There were no more tears after that; thanking Him gave me hope!

At our last visit with Mom, we saw her happy for the first time in years. She was a totally different person—God had healed her! Open wounds that she had had on her legs for years were all healed—it was shocking to see her this way!

Thirty-two years of praying for her, we saw her happy and healed—a miracle! Praise God! She unexpectedly died the next day. If we had not visited the day before, we would have missed the miracle God had done in her.

Thank you, Lord, for answering our prayers today.

Betty Cowley is a member of Ephrata Community Church, Altar Ministry Team; member of HarvestNet Ministries; and vice president of Papa's New Generals (Outreach to Papua New Guinea).

Walking in His Will

"'For I know the plans I have for you,' says the Lord. 'They are plans for good and not for disaster, to give you a future and a hope.'"
Jeremiah 29:11 (New Living Translation)

Soon after I gave my life to God, I began to experience a nagging sense that I was supposed to do something for Him, though I didn't know what. In an effort to try to understand what God wanted me to do, I served in a number of different ministries, not one of which was "it." Each one felt like putting on a piece of clothing that didn't quite fit.

In 2003 I stumbled onto a faith-based recovery program called Celebrate Recovery and God made it very, very clear to me that this was the ministry in which He wanted me to serve. I have been involved with Celebrate Recovery ever since.

In spring 2005 God placed it on my heart to write a book about how Celebrate Recovery helped me. I worked on it for three years and recently self-published it through Partnership Publications, a division of DOVE Christian Fellowship International.

Since I have been living the call God placed on my life, fulfilling His purposes for me, I have experienced a deep feeling of certainty (I know that I know that I know) that I am exactly where I'm supposed to be, doing exactly what I was created to do. The peace that accompanies this is a peace that surpasses all human understanding. It is a peace that can only come from God. Nothing, nothing can compare to this peace.

God, please continue to use me as an instrument in Your work, pour Your light and Your power into me till it overflows and pours out of me to touch others. Please guide all who are reading this to the path of recovery so that their hurts, hang-ups, and habits may be healed and Your purpose for their lives may become clear.

Mary Detweiler leads the Celebrate Recovery ministry at Manheim Brethren in Christ Church and is the author of *When Therapy Isn't Enough*.

Laying Down Our Lives

"If his master gives him a wife and she bears him sons or daughters, the woman and her children shall belong to her master, and only the man shall go free. But if the servant declares, 'I love my master and my wife and children and do not want to go free,'...Then he will be his servant for life." *Exodus 21:4–6*

In scripture, God provided a way for man to lay down his life and freedom for his family. Even after his children were grown and his wife died, the servant had made a commitment for life.

What does it mean to lay down our lives for the sake of others? I know Jesus laid his life down for us through the cross so we could be saved, but can I lay down *my* life?

In marriage we have the opportunity to lay our lives down for our mates. In ministry we can lay our lives down for others in big and small ways.

I have a friend who volunteers at a mission for men every week. It is a program for homeless men where they are allowed to come in for showers and to have their laundry done. This man, a retired business owner, does the homeless men's laundry every week. When he shares about his time there, you can feel his love for these men. They matter to him and when he is there he lays his life down for them and does their laundry. But here is the amazing thing: he holds them in his heart and lifts them up to God daily through prayer. Daily he lays down a piece of his life.

Help me Lord to be able to lay my life down in service to You, for an hour or a day, and hopefully for a lifetime. Amen.

Anne Pierson is the executive director of Loving and Caring, a ministry dedicated to helping the fatherless of the world, located in Lancaster.

One Touch

"For my yoke is easy and my burden is light." *Matthew 11:30*

Recently I went to back-up my home computer with a remote hard drive. I am told this is wise to do. In case of a computer crash, you have a back-up of all the data on your computer to re-install. I plugged the hard drive into the computer while I was in the middle of doing e-mail and some other tasks on the computer. A window appeared and I clicked where I thought I should and nothing happened. So I worked on my other tasks for a few minutes and then went back to try and get a window to open to do the back up. After a few tries I finally got another window open. I was looking and trying all the options on the window to get the back-up to run. Nothing seemed to work.

After trying a few clicks here and there I was getting frustrated because I had other things to do. I went into the program files to try and find out how to run this. As I was looking at the program files I saw a folder titled ONETOUCH. I was about to click on it when I realized that ONETOUCH was the brand name of the remote hard drive. ONETOUCH….hmmm…I looked at the hard drive and there was a blue light on it. I picked it up and pressed where the blue light was and the hard drive started to back up data with, you guessed it, one touch!

Did you notice sometimes that we can expend a lot of energy that yields little results? Sometimes we make things very complicated when in fact God makes them very simple. The harder we try the more difficult and frustrating it seems to get.

God help us today to just keep it simple. Let us stop our striving and stop and listen to the simple action You want us to take that could unlock the mountain we feel is in front of us. Show us the "one touch" that will help us through the some of life's seemingly impossible situations.

Brian Sauder helps provide oversight and direction for DOVE Christian Fellowship International's network of churches.

Pain Free!

"…And by His stripes we are healed." *Isaiah 53:5*

I was twenty-two years old and six months pregnant when my joints started hurting. I went to the doctor and after many tests, I was told I had Rheumatoid Arthritis.

I went to see a specialist and he told me by the time I was 40 years old I would be a cripple in a wheelchair. I suffered incredible pain for ten years.

The Mennonite church that we were attending at the time was having a revival meeting. The pastor that evening was talking about allowing God to use you in any situation. He told us about a time that God used him to pray for someone's healing and the person was healed. Believe me, he had my total attention!

After the service, I went up to him, told him about my arthritis, and told him I believe God wanted to heal me. He said, "Gather a few friends and family together tomorrow evening after the service and I will pray for you." So I did. He prayed a very simple, "Lord heal her" kind of prayer.

For the next several months, my pain was almost more than I could bear. One day my husband came home and I said, "Honey, I think my pain was less today, do you think God is healing me?"

He said, "Yes." We stood on that belief that God was healing me. After six months, I was totally pain free except for at night. I would wake up in excruciating pain. I would say, "When I wake up in the morning I am going to be pain free." And I would be. That went on for quite a while. Then the pain at night stopped. I have been completely pain free for ten years now.

Lord, thank you for Your finished work on the cross, thank you for making a way for my healing, and thank you for a supportive husband who stood in prayer believing with me.

Brenda Boll is an elder along with her husband, Steve, at Newport DOVE.

No Trace!

"Now to Him who is able to do far more abundantly beyond all that we ask or think...." *Ephesians 3:20 (New American Standard Bible)*

After three extended mammography sessions and an ultrasound, I was scheduled to have a biopsy to determine the nature of a "nodule" of unknown density. While waiting in the surgeon's examining room, I glanced up and was encouraged to see a large painting depicting Jesus guiding a surgeon's hand in an operating room. What a wonderful reminder and confirmation of Whose hands I was really in! The surgeon concurred with the findings of the radiologist and showed me the X-ray that clearly showed the area of concern.

I prepared for the biopsy believing that it would prove benign, although I knew I wouldn't hear the results for several days. "Guess what was on the latest test?" the chief radiologist asked me. This question came after having the latest high-tech equipment geared to locate the area of density that was so obvious on my previous mammograms the previous week. For twenty-five minutes they searched and called him in to consult. They decided to redo the mammogram on the regular machine—the same one that detected it the previous week.

"I'd guess—nothing?" I said brightly.

"You're right—we'll see you back in six months. How do you feel about all this?"

"Thank you and all the staff for being so thorough; I am leaving with no question in my mind, and I hope there's none in yours. There have been so many people praying about this, so I'm very thankful to God for His answer!"

Lord, I had one idea of how You were going to work, yet I'm so grateful You chose the way You did! This miracle is well documented in my medical records, and I didn't even have to have a single needle! To God be the glory!

Cindy Riker is thrilled to be a wife, a mother of four children, eldercare companion and a Bible study leader for Change of Pace.

Do You Believe in Miracles?

"For God loved the world so much that he gave his one and only son so that everyone who believes in him will not perish but have eternal Life." *John 3:16 (New Living Translation)*

If you knew me and my life story, you'd see more than one miracle, but the very same is true for you. If you have accepted Jesus as Savior—you are a miracle too! The events that guided you to that place of surrender are miracles! Maybe not the sea-parting kind, but miracles, nonetheless. I believe salvation is the "greatest miracle" of all because it is one of Jesus' love for us.

Jesus takes the hurt and gives us joy unspeakable and full of glory. Jesus takes the drug addict and makes us witnesses of Good News. Jesus takes the ugly about us and makes us beautiful and new. Yes, my outside shows the scars of my sinful life, but on the inside it's all brand-new. Isn't that the most wonderful miracle of all? My dear mother never stopped praying for a miracle for me. Never quit praying for those you love.

Dear Father God, I praise You for my salvation. Please burden my heart for the lost, the lonely, the poor, the people in desperate need of Your miracle. Amen.

Alton Alexander attends Ephrata Church of the Nazarene.

Following the Gentle Nudges of the Holy Spirit

"This is what I covenanted with you when you came out of Egypt. And my Spirit remains among you. Do not fear." *Haggai 2:5*

In 2007, I had been on a trip to New York City for about three days, mainly visiting a missionary from England who was passing through the city. Having taken him to the airport for his return flight to London, I began the drive back to Pennsylvania. It was a cold, dark February evening.

Having stopped briefly along the way, I resumed the drive. As I switched on the ignition and began to drive again, I had a sudden and arresting impression that there was about to be an accident and that I should pray. I began interceding for the Lord to intervene and for Him to protect me and others. Somehow I just knew what was about to happen unless I prayed. Within a few seconds a car drove up at great speed behind me, honked the horn and swerved around me and others to avoid hitting us. I am not sure all that took place, but within a few seconds it was over, and everyone just seemed to resume their drive in peace.

Was that just me who had that thought of an upcoming collision? I don't believe so. It was sudden and strong; I don't usually have thoughts like that. I just knew that it was the spirit of God speaking urgently to me and that our loving Father wished to intervene in response to the prayers of His child. I don't know how He did it, but a collision was avoided. He had alerted me and intervened.

Thank you God that we do not need to live in fear and that You are capable of protecting us. Help me to be aware of those gentle inner nudges of Your Spirit in my life.

Peter Bunton, originally from England, has lived in the United States for over four years, based in Lititz. He serves as the director of DOVE Mission International, the mission arm of DOVE Christian Fellowship International.

Autograph Anyone?

"And when you believed in Christ, He put His seal on you...."
Ephesians 1:13 (New Living Translation)

"Do you want me to autograph that for you?" That question has been directed at me a couple of times and I remember each occasion. I answered the same way each time: "I don't believe in autographs."

There were different reactions to my statement. One got huffy, and then went back to his cell phone conversation. He was a retired professional football player passing out memorabilia. Yet he was on his cell phone the whole time and not engaging the fans in conversation. I wasn't looking for a reaction to my statement; I was just stating how I felt about collecting autographs.

Another seemed to understand what I meant, in saying such a bold statement. He was also a retired professional football player passing out memorabilia from the 1960s. He didn't have a cell phone attached to his ear, and he was engaging everyone in conversation. He really impressed me with the advice he had for the young fans. "Work hard in school and accept Jesus as your Savior."

Of course he asked the question, because I was the next in line. "Would you like me to sign that?" he asked with a big smile.

"No, thank you," I said. "I don't believe in autographs."

An even bigger smile emerged. What he understood and the others didn't was the fact that my hero is God and His Son Jesus Christ. God has signed His name across my heart and has sealed me as a child of the King.

Thank you, Lord for saving me and coming into my heart. Sealed by You, there is no other that I want.

Carol Denson is a leader of Celebrate Recovery, a twelve-step Christ-centered program in Sadsburyville.

Ginger

"Why do you look at the speck that is in your brother's eye, but do not notice the log that is in your own eye?" *Matthew 7:3 (New American Standard)*

As a young girl growing up in the country, I was blessed to have my very own horse. Ginger was a bay mare, and she was beautiful! Her black mane and tail were long and shiny. I loved brushing her and riding her. One of my favorite things to do with her was to take a nap together in the warm sunshine. She would actually let me curl up close to her and rest my head on her belly.

There was one thing about Ginger that wasn't so pretty, however, and that was her breath! In the early mornings when I would go to the barn to feed her, I would say, "Oh, Ginger, your breath!" But I loved her anyway; she was very special to me.

Well, the sad day came when, with tears in my eyes, I watched the horse trailer pull out of my driveway with Ginger in it. She was now too old to be ridden and was going to a nearby pasture to live out the rest of her days just eating and sunning herself. I wondered if she missed me snuggling with her as much as I did.

Time passed, and one early morning when I was out in the barn, I smelled Ginger's foul breath. I thought *could it still be lingering after all this time? Could I be missing her so much that I think I actually smell her?* No! It was then that I realized the bad breath I had smelled all those years, thinking it was coming from Ginger, was mine!

Lord, are there other areas of my life where I look at someone else's faults and don't even notice my own? Please help me to "take the log out of my own eye, and not look at the speck in my brother's eye."

Lisa Dorr is a part of the body of Christ, at Christ Community Church, and Christian Life Assembly, where she is richly blessed.

Picking Up Diamonds

"You were bought with a price. So then, honor God and bring glory to Him in your body." *1 Corinthians 6:20 (Amplified Bible)*

In one of my devotional times in 1999, the Lord spoke to my heart and asked me to pick up diamonds from the streets. My response was, "Lord, what diamonds?"

He answered me, "The teenager prostitutes; they are my diamonds. Pick them up because I am going to cleanse them and in due time they will shine My glory to the nations."

Since that day, I am reaching the young girls in the streets, alleyways, bars, brothels, or any other place the Lord leads me to go. I was invited to be part of the Operation Extreme Love in Thailand, where I joined a group of sixty people from the USA, Canada, Malaysia, Hong Kong, India, and other nations. Our purpose was to share the gospel with the prostitutes that work in Pattaya, a city located two hours from Bangkok. This city has twenty thousand young girls working in bars and brothels from 5 p.m. to 4 a.m.

It was an intense week. We testified, prophesied, shared the gospel, prayed for them and visited them in their working places—the bars. We made personal connections with these girls and prepared the way to invite them to a banquet sponsored by Youth With A Mission. The day of the banquet we received an envelope with money to use to pay for the time spent with the girls. We went to the bars and negotiated with the madam that controls the girls and asked how much they charged for each girl to be away for three hours. After we made the agreements, we paid the price for each individual, fifty in all.

The Holy Spirit reminded me of the prophet Hosea, when he bought back his unfaithful wife from prostitution, and two thousand years ago, the Lord Jesus Christ paid the price for each of us.

After the YWAM team testified and gave an altar call, forty-five girls accepted Jesus Christ as their personal Savior. Later, YWAM said that eight girls have left the bars and joined the program.

Lord Jesus, thank you for Your extreme love for us, for laying down Your life for mankind, for buying us back to You.

Marta Estrada, Petra Christian Fellowship, is founder and director of Restoration of the Nations and author of the book *To the Mafia With Love*.

My Lightbulb Moment

"Or do you think lightly of the riches of His kindness and forbearance and patience, not knowing that the kindness of God leads you to repentance?" *Romans 2:4 (New American Standard Bible)*

It was one of those moments. Some people call it a "lightbulb" moment, one that most deliberately birthed truth that changed a certain stronghold in my belief systems. I now can come more freely into God's presence.

I was crying out to God, "It's me again, with the same old stuff I struggled with just yesterday." I've been saved since I was a little girl and want so desperately to love Him with all my heart, mind and soul. But often I feel so inadequate to come to Him because I blow it once again. I was struggling because I had to say "I'm sorry" one more time. And then the light came on. That still, small voice reminded me…it's not about me. When I come to Jesus it's not about me or what I have or haven't done or the shame that makes me want to run. It's about Him and His love for me. My sin, my junk (as our pastor says) doesn't change God's character. It is actually that very thing by grace that enables me to run into Jesus' arms time and time again because I need Him so much. "God is Love. It's who He is. He is not limited by anything I have going on in my heart or my feeling of guilt because I deal with the same old thing or the lies I believe about myself. My focus is now on God, the one who sent His Son, Jesus for the likes of me. And I know that when I confess my sins, He is faithful to forgive me and make me clean again every single time, according to 1 John 1:9.

So as you are reading this, I pray that you too will not hesitate to run into Jesus' arms, sit on His lap with that area in your life that cries, "It's me again." Feel His arms around you, trusting it's all about who He is and His promises of Love.

Dear Jesus, once again I come to You because of who You are trusting what I know about You and Your love and faithfulness. Thank you for Your truth that sets me free. I do love You with all my heart, mind and soul. Amen.

Cyndi Garber serves on the worship and compassion teams at LCBC; she and her husband Phil serve as mentors. They have four children and two grandchildren.

Petunias

"Not that I have already obtained all this, or have already been made perfect, but I press on to take hold of that for which Christ Jesus took hold of me." *Philippians 3:12*

Eight years ago, we moved into this house without realizing what a "fixer upper" it was. Time and money have slowed our progress. We have done much so far: replaced the plumbing, totally remodeled one bathroom, installed hardwood floors in half of the house, and more. But there is still a lot of ugly, stained carpet; a bathroom with purple, chipped fixtures and tile falling off the wall; and...the list goes on and on. The house is still far from where it ought to be.

As I walked out of my front door on the way to get the mail, I scanned the green area before me. I am not sure it is accurate to call it a lawn when there is so little grass growing. I looked over the clover, chickweed, dandelions and felt discouraged. Will we ever get this house fixed? When will we get to this yard? Discouragement filled my heart. I sighed and as I inhaled, a sweet smell filled my nose; I wondered where is that coming from? I turned and saw the window boxes full of purple petunias spilling over the edges and I smiled.

When I came to God, my life was truly a "fixer upper." He has accomplished much over the years; still there is much left to do. I am so far from where I ought to be. But God has planted petunias in my heart. While I am still a sinner saved by grace, there are moments when I let the beauty of God show. There are moments when I love like God loves. And for this reason, I press on.

Dear Lord, thanks for letting me see the petunias. Thanks for not giving up on me. Continue Your deep work in me until that day when You call me home.

Karen Boyd is a contributing editor to God Stories and serves on the board of the Pennsylvania Homeschoolers Accreditation Agency.

The Planting

"And he shall be like a tree planted by the rivers...." Psalm 1:3

Sometimes plants need a bigger pot to spread their roots; this will allow the plant to grow bigger and stay healthy. If it's kept in the same size pot, it will stunt its growth or even die. At times I've started flowers indoors, only to plant them outside later. The Lord does this with us too. He may move us to a different location, according to where we will thrive the best.

If you are one of those who feels like you've missed something because you don't "fit in" your local church, have you considered the fact that God may have something for you to do outside the regular church setting? Or you may feel you are planted in the right place, yet you are unsettled. He may be getting you ready for a transplant. It could also be that you need to be placed in another function, or given more responsibility with what you are currently doing.

Be where God wants you to be, even if the people around you don't understand, obey God by following what Jesus has put in your heart. Not traditions of man, but the freedom to love God and just to be what He's created you to be. Follow the leading of the Holy Spirit in you (lining it up with God's Word); pray, praise and fellowship with the Lord and His people, wherever that may be.

I pray that you would know the perfect will that God has for your life. That you would not settle for anything less than God's best. The Lord knows where He wants to place you and where you will flourish. Not only does He want you to flourish and grow, He wants you to be in the place you will look your best and compliment others around you. Allow God to have His way with where He wants you, and give thanks in the process.

Sandra Bernhardt is the founder and president of Joy Celebration Ministries, and laid foundation with two other pastors for The Apostolic Church that meets in Lancaster.

His Word Is Near You

"But the Word is very near you, in your mouth and in your heart, that you may observe it." *Deuteronomy 30:14 (New American Standard Bible)*

Upon retiring at age sixty-five, a good friend of mine asked me, "LaMarr, what is your life going to look like now that you are retired?"

Just the way he formed the question took me off guard because I had not thought about it from that angle. But to my amazement, the instant he asked the question, there was an immediate response. The Holy Spirit gave me the answer faster than my brain could think, and I said, "In the years God gives me, I want my life to count for seeing less divorce in the church and Jesus welcomed back to America."

Keep choosing daily to be obedient to Jesus and He will continue to put His Word in Your mouth and His love will overwhelm your heart.

Lord Jesus, make us quiet and obedient before You and continue to speak Your thoughts through us, in Jesus' name, Amen.

LaMarr Sensenig serves as an elder at Lancaster Evangelical Free Church in Lititz.

The Touch of Personal Presence

"Show me your face, let me hear your voice; for your voice is sweet, and your face is lovely." *Song of Songs 2:14*

Heaven! Just the mention of that word sounds like home. It will be magnificently decorated. There will be many rooms. They will be shiny and clean. Angels will serve us. There will be endless things to do and places to explore. Heaven will be warm and cozy and intriguing.

As alluring as all that sounds, there is a more attractive draw. A house becomes a home through its occupants and their personal interactions. This fact was brought "home" to me in 1989. Four months after we lost Jonathan David at seventeen weeks' gestation, we had a record-breaking fourteen-inch snowfall the day after Easter. Our son Joshua, then five, suddenly interrupted his sledding and rushed inside. With a wonder in his voice he asked, "Mommy, will there be sledding in heaven?"

Prompted by a previous conversation about Jonathan's new home in heaven, I replied, "Yes, Josh, there will be sledding in heaven."

With more vigor, Josh bounced back outside, envisioning, I'm sure, future heavenly sledding days. Joshua fully expected to see his brother in person and play with him.

Personal encounters are memory makers. Good-byes are eclipsed by the hope of the reunion. The two lovers in the Song of Songs epitomize the excitement of each other's presence.

Seeing and being with our saved loved ones for eternity is indeed a heartwarming thought. But for now, we can only imagine that reunion. And how does one begin to envision meeting the Son of God; to see the part that Abraham was not allowed to see or he would surely die; to see *in full* our Bridegroom, the One who has prepared a place for us. Jesus is waiting to consummate our marriage with Him and will stand in the doorway welcoming us home, face-to-face.

To our Bridegroom, to see Your face—how thrilling! To hear Your voice—how exciting!

Tamalyn Jo Heim and her husband, Bob, have no greater joy than to know that their four children will meet their brother and their Savior in person.

White as Snow

"Cleanse me with hyssop, and I will be clean; wash me, and I will be whiter than snow." *Psalm 51:7*

I thumbed through placards. It was all there: drugs, alcohol, sexual addiction, thievery, suicide, death, fatherlessness, broken family relationships, hopelessness, despair and much, much more.

Within a short time, some twenty men and women would be stepping in front of the congregation, baring in a few handwritten words a piece from their past lives. They then would flip over the placard and reveal how God, through His redeeming grace, had brought them to a new place.

It was risky. How would a church congregation react? Would they lose friendships they thought they had?

I had heard some of the testimonies previously, and I had one of my own. But the overwhelming theme throughout each placard was how God never wastes a hurt when we give all of our brokenness to Him and allow Him to work in and through us. Even if the reactions were totally negative, God's goodness would be proclaimed. Friendships and understanding among those who shared would be preserved.

The testimonies were shared, one by one. Many of those watching dabbed at tears. The congregation rose in sustained applause as the "silent" testimonies ended. Some had seen parts of their own lives flash before them. Others were rejoicing in the goodness of God's love. Satan's lies, including "I am all alone," "no one cares," "there is no hope" and many others, had been destroyed, exposed to God's truth and light.

Lord, thank you for Your goodness in all things when we surrender to You. Help us to be sensitive to the needs of others who are hurting and in need of You, and to come alongside and demonstrate the same love and forgiveness that You show each of us daily. Amen.

Casey Jones, who resides in Parkesburg, is an advocate for development of comprehensive marriage and family ministries, including ministries to the hurting, in churches. He is developer of a Transformation Initiative for Building Healthy Communities Through Healthy Families.

Trusting in Him

"Now Isaiah had said, 'Let them take a cake of figs and apply it to the boil, that he may recover.'" *Isaiah 38:21*

E.P. had suffered many years of pain and experienced what would seem like tragedy after tragedy. The suffering started in early childhood from emotional and physical abuse to spiritual abuse at the hands of a cult.

E.P. self loathingly and wrongfully took responsibility for all of life's cruelties and in doing so, abused himself, self-medicating with drugs and alcohol which only led to further emotional deterioration.

One day after a complete medical examination, E.P. thought it was surely the end. The first diagnosis wasn't good. The overwhelming fear coupled with denial that often accompanies such illnesses, drove E.P. to the foot of the cross!

In desperation and with no hope in sight, a final cry to God for miraculous intervention, a cry for healing and forgiveness, was answered. The words of *Yeshua HaMashiach*, Jesus the Christ, ripping through his mind and the question on his lips: "Is it easier to heal me or forgive me? Please Lord God, forgive me and take it all away, please make it go away!"

E.P. decided to let go and let God. Within just few days, another surgical examination, a second opinion and a prescription—yes, the tiniest pill brought E.P. from the fear of death to near total healing. He went from what was thought to be death to life, sickness to health and from doubting and self-abasement to rejoicing and trusting in *Yeshua*, Jesus, "my Lord and my God."

The doctors said it was not a miracle. It was simply technology and medication. You decide.

Heavenly Father, You hold the Truth, the cure, the future and the medium for the spiritual journey of healing upon which we sojourn. The most painful moments have driven me to my knees in search of You only. Thank you, in Jesus' name, for my rescue, my salvation, my hope, Amen. —E.P.

Thomas R. Miller B.A. M.A. is pastoral counselor and minister of grace for Life Ministries (www.godswordforlife.com).

I Can Count on His Care

"The Lord is near to the brokenhearted and saves those who are crushed in spirit. Many are the afflictions of the righteous; but the Lord delivers him out of them all." *Psalms 34:18–19*

Taking these words into my heart, I see a picture of our hovering God. Much like He moved "over the surface of the waters" with the kind intention to speak life into the emptiness of the earth, He's drawn to our desolation. Our brokenness is like a magnet upon His heart. He *must* "save."

When we are hurting deeply, our God is truly moved by our pain. He doesn't simply sit back and watch how we deal with the many "afflictions" that come our way. He wishes to be with us in our despair. Although problems are permitted, we do not suffer alone.

Like a loving mother rocks her troubled little one, so our God holds and comforts us in our distress. And in spite of our many hardships, He desires to deliver us "out of them all." He will come to the rescue! How comforting to know that His endless love longs to liberate us from our misery.

I've personally experienced the precious care of my heavenly Father speaking into my sorrow. Like Psalm 119:50 so aptly expresses, "This is my comfort in my affliction, that Your Word has revived me." He breathes life into me when I feel like I'm perishing. He pours forth living water over my parched heart and revives me. I can embrace difficulties and grief because I can count on His unfailing love to carry me, comfort me and console me.

Thank you, Lord, that I really can count on Your care! You look upon my broken heart and crushed spirit and faithfully draw near. I will trust You to deliver me, no matter what may happen in my life. You are indeed my help in times of trouble. Amen.

Kathi Wilson and her husband Mark, coauthors of *Tired of Playing Church* and cofounders of Body Life Ministries, are members of Ephrata Community Church.

Lemonade

"I have calmed and quieted my soul, like a weaned child with its mother...." *Psalm131:2*

"When life gives you lemons, make lemonade!" I thought of this saying and smiled as I watched my children eagerly squeezing lemon after lemon. We were having a rough time financially. My husband Chris had been working two jobs but the money was slow in coming in. We were running out of food and diapers and had a stack of bills to pay. Yet a dear friend went shopping at a discount food auction and bought us a huge box of organic lemons for $3. When I saw them I thought, "What am I going to do with all those lemons? I need butter and milk and so many other things...not lemons!"

My children were oblivious to my concerns as they joyfully prepared for their own lemonade business. They set up a stand at the corner of our lot and waited for the hordes of customers to arrive. I watched from the kitchen window as they sat in the hot sun for an hour and no one stopped.

"Lord, send them some customers just to encourage them," I prayed. Immediately I heard God say, "As a loving parent, you want your children to succeed and be encouraged in this seemingly insignificant venture. How much more do I want to see you succeed in life? How much more do I want to encourage you by sending you provision for everything that you need?"

Soon people began stopping their cars, getting off their bikes and walking up to my children. They paid dollar bills for 25 cent cups of lemonade. My children sold the entire pitcher and were elated at their earnings! I could rest from my worries as I watched God provide for all our other needs over the next couple days. Why did I ever doubt Him?

Lord, help me to trust in Your Father's heart of love toward me.

Anne Brandenburg is a mother of six and the wife of Chris, a pastor at Life Center Ministries.

Stewards or Owners

"The land shall not be sold permanently, for the land is Mine; for you are strangers and sojourners with Me." *Leviticus 25:23 (New King James Version)*

William Penn, granted the land dubbed as "Penn's Woods," came to America to establish a society based on biblical principles. His "Holy Experiment" envisioned freedom for people of different ethnic groups and religious convictions to co-exist. One hallmark of Penn's respect for others was the trust he built with the Native Americans, or First Nation peoples. Penn honored the treaties that he formed with them. Sadly, after his death, his sons and others did not.

However, Europeans arriving to purchase land in the new world did not realize the First Nations people, who had already lived here for many years, had vastly different perceptions about religion and land ownership. Natives believed in *stewardship* of land and nature rather than the European concept of land *ownership.*

This difference created a great misunderstanding as the white man assumed he was buying land permanently and the Indian leaders thought the land was being "loaned." First Nations people lived by a principle of interdependence with the land that mirrors the biblical concept of stewardship. Even though God gave the people of Israel the blessing of "possessing" the land, He retained the ultimate ownership of the land.

We are challenged by the example of our First Nation peoples to respect and care for the land that we "possess." As we consider our life style, we may honor the biblical principle by making choices in terms of what is "green." We use renewable energy and cooperate with smart growth, farm preservation, and wildlife preservation. Conservation of soil, cleaning streams, and recycling are important, also.

"Moreover, it is required in stewards that one be found faithful (1 Corinthians 4:2)."

Lord of Creation, we embrace our responsibility as stewards. All that we have to care for ultimately belongs to You: salvation message, relationships, possessions, and our region. May those who come behind us find us faithful.

Keith Yoder, president of Teaching The Word Ministries, is a member of The Worship Center.

Harrisburg, Dauphin County
Photo by Ann Rodriguez

April

Noah, A Man of God

"[God] is able to do exceedingly abundantly above all that we ask or think...." *Ephesians 3:20 (New King James Version)*

His name was Noah. And like Noah in the Bible, he is remembered as a man of God. Noah Weber was part of Gehman Mennonite Church, Adamstown, all his life. He was handed the key in 1892, and for five years served as custodian. When the church began Sunday School on Sunday afternoons, in 1915, he became the assistant superintendent. For more than twenty-five years he served in the capacity of superintendent or the assistant.

In a meditation in *Gospel Herald*, Noah wrote of his duties as custodian. "With key in hand he is reminded of the keys of the kingdom of heaven...as shutters are opened, it reminds him of the true light."

He mentioned placing the hymnbooks in the racks, and how it reminded him of hymns "Sweet Hour of Prayer," and "Lord, I Have Shut the Door," and being alone, these thoughts may bring to mind words of Christ to enter the closet, shut the door and pray in secret. "He may sink down and heed the Spirit's call," he wrote.

His farm was just across the field from the church. Noah was among other church members that cold December night, in 1925, when fire threatened to destroy the building.

When the firefighters depleted a well across the road from the church, they went to a nearby creek, but the hoses froze. Another company was called, but as they waited they stood amazed that after all the time of waiting for additional help, the structure did not burn to the ground.

Then they learned the reason why. Noah was praying. After several weeks of repairs, the building was again ready for church and Sunday School.

Lord, help us remember whatever circumstance comes into our path, this day, You are there to see us through. Amen.

Irene Horst, Millersville, is a granddaughter of Noah Weber. She is a widow with two daughters and attends Lyndon Mennonite Church. She writes a weekly column in *Tri-County Record*, Morgantown.

It's Only Friday

"...I will turn the darkness into light before them...I will not forsake them." *Isaiah 42:16*

While preparing for a family gathering on Good Friday, I couldn't help but compare it to the year before. We had no inkling then that two family members would be diagnosed with life-threatening diseases within a few months. Looking back, life had been so carefree. But this year, the uncertain future cast a gloomy pall over dinner preparations. I pushed aside the heaviness to focus on the real purpose of Good Friday.

Life hadn't turned out the way the disciples had expected either. They believed Jesus would usher in a better life for them. Instead, Jesus was nailed to the cross and died. Darkness came over the earth as the disciples huddled together. Fear of the uncertain future gripped them. Hopeless, afraid, they thought it was the end of a life worth living.

But that isn't the end of the story. Friday passed. Easter came and with it the glorious resurrection. Eventually the whole story and purpose of that fateful day became clear.

As I read the end of the Easter story, my personal darkness disappeared and hope soared. You see, our family's story isn't finished. It's only Friday. Easter is coming.

Thank you, Lord, for the many amazing stories recorded in the Bible that show how often You turned darkness into light. You are the same—yesterday, today and forever—a faithful God who promises never to forsake us.

Lou Ann Good, her husband, four children and their spouses and ten grandchildren delight in God's faithfulness.

To the Cross

"My grace is sufficient for you, for my power is made perfect in weakness...." *2 Corinthians 12:9*

It was Good Friday morning, and I was preparing the chapel service at Water Street Mission in Lancaster City. I placed a candelabra on the table on stage. I lit the candles with a resident's cigarette lighter and handed brown paper bags to ten random men. Inside were objects that would tell the story of the Crucifixion. One by one, each of them opened their bag, read the inscription I had scribbled on parchment and brought the object to the cross at the front of the chapel. Raymond carried my mother's crown of thorns, an authentic reproduction from the Holy Land.

"I bring you this crown, my Lord, to remember where you went for me!" He laid it beneath the flickering candles. A few men coughed.

Tony had trouble reading my handwriting. But he laid three nails next to a wooden communion cup.

Allan was the ninth reader. "I don't know what to do with this," he whispered, laying the paper bag under a large stone. "They put you in the ground," he read. "But they could not contain you."

As the last reader sat down, I asked anyone who desired to write a prayer of offering. Those who had been sleeping or squirming in their seats began to file to the front of the chapel. To the Cross. They submitted their written offerings:

"My fears and past."

"I praise You Jesus my Lord my Savior and King. Thank you for rescueing me."

"God's grace is sufishnt for me."

"I lay my heart down at the Cross."

Allan, a developmentally disabled homeless man, was helped up the step by another resident. He stood at the table. "Hi, God," he whispered, rocking back and forth. "Hi, God. Hi, God. Hi, God." Slowly and quietly he turned and went back to his seat. The last of the men brought their offerings. We closed in prayer and blew out the candles.

"God's grace is sufishnt for me." Thank you, God.

Debbi Miller is the assistant to the president at Water Street Ministries. She lives with her husband, four teenagers and two dogs in Lititz.

You Can Make A Difference

"Where there is no vision, the people perish..." *Proverbs 29:18 (King James Version)*

Just a one-half hour drive from my home, I can experience Hershey, Pennsylvania. Milton Hershey, the city's founder, had a vision for a company that would expand beyond the walls of his chocolate factory. He built homes, parks, schools, public transportation, and infrastructure, enriching the lives of those around him. His wealth was also accompanied by a sense of moral responsibility and benevolence. When he and his wife realized they could not have children, they founded a school for orphaned boys. In 1918, long before his death, Milton Hershey endowed the school with his entire fortune. He was a man with a vision, and today the name *Hershey* is a household name in many places and is a confectionery enjoyed by millions.

Vision comes to us from God. The Lord is the ultimate visionary. The Bible is filled with examples of those who received a vision from God, and they changed the course of history: Abraham, a generous businessman, received a vision from the Lord to be the father of many nations. Moses was royalty in Pharaoh's household, but gave it all up for a bigger vision; deliver God's people from bondage. Esther received a vision to save her people, and Deborah fulfilled a vision to lead God's people to victory. And let's not forget Peter, who was a fisherman when he received a vision from God to catch men instead of fish. They all inspired those around them, as they communicated a vision of where they were heading and why it was important to head that way.

In the workplace or in the church, people need a God-given vision. They want to know that their work is adding up to a greater cause. Most people want to make a difference in the world.

Vision is forward thrusting, compelling, and pulling us into the future of what the Lord has for us. Why not trust God today for a vision from Him that will encourage and inspire others?

Lord, give me Your vision and then help me to make a difference in this world and the grace to inspire others.

Larry Kreider is the international director of DOVE Christian Fellowship International

May I Have This Dance?

"My soul, wait silently for God alone, for my expectation is from Him." *Psalm 62:5 (New King James Version)*

My morning devotions were sweet; the Lord expressed His love for me through His Words and gently reminded of His abiding presence through the gift of His Holy Spirit within me. He expressed His desire to be the foundation of my self-worth and the constant source of my joy and peace. He urged me to put my trust in Him above all others and to look only to Him to meet my every need. If I would focus my attention on Christ and not myself, He would shield me from the hurt of rejection. By His love He would defend me and save me from the snare of self-pity and discontent.

Yet, even with all these reminders of God's love for me, I easily stumbled into self-pity's deadly trap. This enemy most often reveals itself through personal relationships—especially when humans don't meet my "great expectations." That afternoon, as I walked into the room I overheard my daughter's surprised comment, "Dad, are you dancing?" Delighted, I figured that was my cue to walk right up and boldly invite myself into my husband's rarely displayed playfulness. He dismissed me, saying maybe later after he'd cleaned up. Later came and went, with no invitation to dance.

By the next morning, I felt miserable. In my devotions, I tried to explain to God, "Sometimes I just need a hug, I want to feel Your arms around me. I ache for a touch from You, my Lord."

The day's mail brought a message from a friend. Last year I had recommended a devotional to the young woman, which she had finished. Her note was an answer to prayer that delivered the hug for which I had longed and pleaded. I recognized the voice of my Savior whisper an invitation, "Come My child, take My hand. Dance with Me."

Thank you Father for giving me a friend who is sensitive and obedient to Your leading. Thank you for encouraging me to look to You alone for the hugs that I need. Help me to live for Christ rather than the affirmation of others. Thank you for rescuing me from the pit of self-pity so that I can dance with joy in Your presence.

Nancy Magargle is a member of Lancaster Christian Writers group.

Heart Failure

"This is what the Lord says: 'Cursed is the one who trusts in man, who depends on flesh for his strength and whose heart turns away from the Lord.'" *Jeremiah 17:5*

Some of the hardest times I have ever gone through as a Christian were the times when I took my focus off of God and placed it on someone or something else. We all struggle with wanting to fit in and needing to feel like we belong. Sometimes we go to great lengths to prove to people that we are worthy. The desire and the longing to be loved can consume us to the point where we begin to feel insignificant and weak because we are trying to fill a void in our own lives that can only be filled by God Himself.

I once was at a point in my life where I was trusting in people for my happiness and strength. The problem with living like this is that people will always let you down. And when we trust in them for our strength and happiness we run the risk of taking our focus off of God and placing it on someone else. "Cursed is the one who trusts in man," God says.

Think about it. What can anyone do for you that God cannot? What can anyone give you that God cannot? It just makes more sense to trust in God and find true strength in Him. As a result, when others let you down, your faith will not falter. Instead you will be like a wise man that built his house on the rock. The rain came down, the streams rose and the winds blew and beat against that house—yet it did not fall, because it had its foundation on the rock.

Dear Lord, as we trust in You, please give us the peace and strength we need to get through each day. Amen.

Rob Heverling is a youth leader at Mount Aetna Bible Church, Mount Aetna.

What's Your Story?

"Not to us, O Lord, not to us but to your name be the glory, because of your love and faithfulness." *Psalm 115:1 (New International Version)*

When you look back over your life, were there times when God's hand was clearly visible? During hardships, grief, illness? God shows up in each life He creates, whether that life is for a brief moment or one hundred years. Think about it right now: can you name a time and place where God showed up?

For me, His faithfulness, love, protection and even times of healing come to mind. I asked Him to "come live in my heart" when I was eight. I am so thankful that I did, because later when I had gone my own way, when my life became mired in sin, He was there for me. I called out to Him, "I can't do this anymore! You have to help me!" He heard my heart's cry and began working, drawing me back to Him while He patiently waited for me to trust Him and forgive myself.

My darkest years happened in my twenties, when I was raped. I vowed not to let anyone know the real me, hardened my heart, and began living a promiscuous life, thinking I was looking for love, but really I was never so alone. At that point, I couldn't give or receive love. All I could do was fall deeper into sin. One night, after three years of this, I called out to God and He heard me. My life did not change instantaneously, though He could do that. The God who created me and knew me took me on a slow journey and let me become the person I was before it all happened, and then led me to recommit my life to Him, study His character in Bible studies and find healing. Eventually, I became a new person, a better person than I was before, and I began to feel alive for the first time in my life.

What has He done for you? Thank Him today.

Father God, Your love and faithfulness overwhelm me! Thank You! Not to us, but to You be the glory and honor and praise.

Sharon Neal serves on the shepherding team at Lancaster Evangelical Free Church.

APRIL 8

New Start

"But you are God, ready to pardon, gracious and merciful, slow to anger, abundant in kindness...." *Nehemiah 9:17 (New King James Version)*

Despite lily white legs, I decided to don a pair of shorts the other day. I reached into my drawer for my favorite pair of jean ones. Pulling them out, I was appalled. Ragged strings hung down like the bangs of a toddler-turned-hairdresser and paint drips streaked the front in a random pattern. I couldn't believe it. When did these shorts get so bad?

Waxing poetic, I thought of the bazillion parallels to life. When did those weeds get so high? When did the cabinet under the girls' sink become such a mosh pit of miscellaneous girl stuff requiring a shovel to extract a single hair barrette?

Later that day, I opened my Bible at random. Falling on Nehemiah 9, I came across the story of God's people, his covenant with them, their betrayal, their repentance, his forgiveness, their betrayal again, their repentance *again*, and his forgiveness *again*.

How often we get so busy with our lives. The important things get pushed aside out of view, under the cabinet or in the drawer with the summer clothes: our relationship with God, our God-given need for Christian fellowship and our Bible studies. We turn around one day and our Christian walk that used to fit in God's plan is now in rags, paint spattered and misshapen. We look on with horror and wonder just where we went wrong.

When did the licks and bites add up to extra weight in our heart and in our jean shorts? But praise the Lord for His forgiveness. Because of His love for us, His creation, He keeps letting us come back, clothing us in fresh robes and giving us a new start!

Lord, help me not let life catch me unaware. You know my heart and are waiting to help me organize and clean out.

Sarah Peppel is a communications professor at Valley Forge Christian College and president of women's ministries in the Philadelphia Metro-West Presbytery.

Walk with the King

"For we walk by faith, not by sight." *2 Corinthians 5:7 (New King James Version)*

My husband and I had airline tickets booked a month in advance to fly to Mexico, where he was scheduled to undergo a medical procedure to stop aggressive cancer.

When we were ready to board the plane, we were told the flight was overbooked, and we would not be allowed on the plane. The airline promised to pay for our meals, overnight lodging and to book us for a flight at 7 a.m. the following day. We were not concerned because our doctor's appointment was not scheduled until the following day.

The next morning, we boarded the plane and were almost ready for takeoff when the flight attendant told us that she was sorry, but they'd made a mistake. They had forgotten to enter our names in the computer and someone else was assigned our seats. We would need to get off the plane and take a later flight.

The people sitting around us protested. They pointed out that my husband's appointment for the cancer procedure was scheduled for that afternoon. The attendant was apologetic but adamant. We would need to get off the plane.

"We walk with the King. He has a plan for all this," I said.

While we waited for the next flight, numerous airline personnel apologized. Soon all the passengers surrounding us had heard about our predicament and expressed outrage. Again and again, we assured them that we were not angry.

"We walk with the King. He has everything under control," I said. My husband and I freely shared how faith in God enabled us to live confident in His care.

We don't know exactly what all God had in mind by that delay, but we do know that we arrived in time for our scheduled appointment. We ended up with four free tickets to fly anywhere in the United States. Best of all, countless people heard how it is possible to live without worry by walking with the King.

God, You are so good. It's exciting to walk with the King who reigns over all circumstances.

Arlene Weaver is a wife and grandmother of fifteen.

Giving Voice to the Voiceless

"Speak up for those who cannot speak for themselves, for the rights of all who are destitute." *Proverbs 31:8*

Isn't it fascinating how often God calls us to a work that we think is about one thing and it turns out that He ultimately wanted us to do something entirely different! After a number of years of serving with a ministry that does home repair for low-income homeowners, my role has evolved in many ways. I know God has given me a heart of compassion and mercy which I have felt was best manifested by caring for people's physical, emotional and spiritual needs and encouraging others to do so as well.

Recently though, being an "advocate" has welled up in me. Defending the rights of the weak and vulnerable, speaking up for the disenfranchised and seeking justice for the powerless…quite frankly, I thought was someone else's calling. I have felt that I will do my part and others will do their part. However, God has redirected my thinking to not only have gratitude for the very blessed life that He has given me, and to continue to show that gratitude by caring for the practical needs of the underprivileged (doing my part!), but that I must also do what I can "to speak up for those who cannot speak for themselves" (someone else's part!).

One of the definitions of *advocacy* is "one who pleads another's cause." More than ever many of the homeowners who apply to the nonprofit I serve are truly destitute. And our staff does whatever we are able to do to meet their needs. There will always be a place for that kind of hands-on ministry, and I feel privileged to be a part of serving others in this way. But a passion for "giving voice to the voiceless" has taken on new meaning to me. What that entails, only God knows. I just know He now has my attention and by His grace may I prove to be faithful.

Lord Jesus, thank you for being our advocate on high. Help us to boldly speak up for those who cannot speak for themselves. Amen.

Patti Wilcox is assistant director of Good Works, Inc.

What Are You Bringing Home?

"It is good neither to eat meat nor drink wine nor do anything by
which your brother stumbles or is offended or is made weak."
Romans 14:21 (New King James Version)

Our home is under attack by armies of annoying little ants and an
assortment of other indescribable insects. It is so unnerving to wake up
at night with something creepy crawling over me in the dark!

It's upsetting, but we try to laugh about it. Sometimes, we pretend
we are on a missions trip in a third-world country and are without a
mosquito net.

My diligent husband has been waging war against these pests. We
think he is winning since he has discovered a new baitlike substance,
which attracts ants. They devour it and take it back to their nests. This
poison kills the whole colony as the insects gobble it up like a sweet
treat.

This situation reminds me to question what I am bringing into our
home that may be a similar sugar-coated poisonlike substance that could
infect or kill my family. Am I voicing a root of bitterness, of
unforgiveness or gossip within earshot of my impressionable young
ones? Maybe it's my ungrateful heart, dangerously comparing my "stuff"
to their "stuff" in envy or coveting. Am I ushering into my home the
worldly cancers of pornography or other addictions such as performance drugs and alcohol?

Sometimes these poisons are so alluring and attractive to my flesh,
just like the poisonous bait is for the ants. Eventually, the poisonous
things I carry into my home will infect and kill me and my family. The
poisons will destroy healthy relationships, interactions and true spiritual growth, which is life from God.

*Lord, help me have discernment. Give me true wisdom. Keep the
door to my home and my heart closed to that which is disguised as
good but is truly evil.*

Shirley Ann Bivens serves in the children's department at Christ Community
Church. She does Christian clowning as "CoCo the Clown" and is a full-time
grammy.

Transforming the Mind

"Therefore if anyone is in Christ, he is a new creation; the old has gone, the new has come." *2 Corinthians 5:17*

The old has gone, and the new has come! We saw this in action last month at the pregnancy center where I work. Our clients come from every walk of life and their stories are as different as can be. So often they make the choice to follow Christ but must return to homes that do not encourage them to walk with Christ.

For each of us, the life of a Christian is truly a journey of transformation. Sometimes it is a difficult journey. Yet, we are never abandoned by God to wander all alone. He is always with us to guide our steps. He begins to renew our way of thinking as soon as we yield to Him. And when life is beyond our control, God redirects our thinking so that we will respond in ways which glorify Him.

One of the young dads was a perfect picture of this concept. Shortly after the young dad accepted Jesus as his Savior, he lost his job. In tears he told our counselor that he wanted so badly to walk away from his life and leave his family. Before he came to Christ, he would have left in a heartbeat, he said. But now, something inside of him told him he could not walk away, but that he must stay and deal with the issues.

We praise God that He renews our minds and brings about in us a work we could never do on our own.

Precious Father, thank you for being there, for transforming us and giving us what we need for this journey.

Lisa Hildebrand works for Susquehanna Valley Pregnancy Services and ministers as a teacher and speaker in local churches.

Seeds Planted

"Now faith is the substance of things hoped for, the evidence of things not seen." *Hebrews 11:1 (New King James Version)*

As a novice gardener, my "faith" in the God-created-process of new life, was admittedly challenged this spring as I planted my vegetables and herbs. Each time I pushed a tiny seed into the soil, I couldn't help but think of all the things that could go wrong; a sense of doubt that these seeds would ever "work" overcame me almost as a matter of fact.

Each day I would go out to the garden and look for a sign that something was happening. Eventually, tiny green sprouts began popping up all over the place—were those weeds or my plants? A few days later, I could see their individually shaped leaves, and I knew that I had made it.

How often do I go around checking the soil of my life, only to become discouraged and despair that "it will never happen"? I have not yet harvested any of my vegetables, but those tiny green sprouts give me reason to believe I will. As I wait on the Lord to fulfill His word in my life, I must look at the "sprouts" He has placed all around me. The things God has done in me and throughout time speak to the fact that He will fulfill His promises. We have every reason to believe that the "seeds" He has planted in our hearts will "work."

Father, help me to trust You with the unseen, faith-building process that You have planned for me. Give me eyes to see beyond the physical realities and limitations of this world. I know that You have begun a good work in me, and You will be faithful to bring it to the day of completion. In Jesus' name, Amen.

Emily Yoder lives in Lancaster City with her husband Travis and their daughters Hollyn and Lyrie; she serves at In the Light Ministries as the early childhood coordinator.

Like an Arrow

"I will instruct you and teach you in the way which you should go; I will counsel you with My eye upon you." *Psalm 32:8*

You've heard the phrase "I need to watch you like a hawk," right? A determined gaze comes to mind. It reminds me of how carefully I watched my children at the beach when they were just toddlers. My eye was *surely* upon them. And I was quick to advise them when needed!

That's the kind of heart God has toward us! He keeps a close watch over each one of us with a sincere desire to instruct our hearts. "Oh, that My people would listen to Me, and walk in My ways" is His cry!

The Lord really wants to give us direction that we might walk wisely. He clearly cares about the path we take. As the verse says, there is a "way" which we "should go." The Lord has specific intentions for our lives!

I'm fascinated by the definition given by the Hebrew Lexicon for the word *teach* in the verse we're chewing on. We can more accurately understand the heart of what's being said if we imagine an archer pointing his arrow toward the chosen target. He carefully aims, shooting the arrow with precision and care. Likewise, the Lord will direct and release us.

Keep in mind that the flight of an arrow depends completely on the competence of the one pulling the bow. Once the arrow is shot, it flies freely to its mark, not by any effort of its own. It hits the mark due to the aim of the one holding the bow. It's all in the aim of the archer.

Pull back Your bow, Lord, and send me where You wish for me to go! I have confidence that Your eye will ever be upon me and trust that Your presence will go with me, to make known to me the pathway of life!

Kathi Wilson and her husband Mark, coauthors of *Tired of Playing Church* and cofounders of Body Life Ministries, are members of Ephrata Community Church.

God Means It for Good

"…But God meant it for good, to bring it about that many people should be kept alive, as they are today." *Genesis 50:20*

I love to read an engaging story, one that provides mental stimulation and inspiration. One day I got caught up in re-reading the whole story of Joseph in the book of Genesis. It is a familiar but stirring account, rich with drama and discovery. It tells of jealousy, greed, and deceit. Hopes are dashed and hope is renewed. There is great grief and refreshing joy. Themes of guilt, shame, remorse and forgiveness are explored.

Through it all, the major story line develops as the history of Jacob's sons unfolds. We can shudder at the treachery of Joseph's brothers, empathize with Jacob's grief and pity the lustful wife of Potiphar, but God's protective design is displayed in every chapter. The plot resolves with this amazing statement from Joseph to his brothers. "Do not fear, for am I in the place of God? As for you, you meant evil against me, but God meant it for good, to bring it about that many people should be kept alive, as they are today. So do not fear, I will provide for you and your little ones."

With that strong word freshly burned into my soul, I turned to answer the phone and received news that I did not want to hear. I learned that I would be facing a long separation from dear ones as they relocated in a distant land. Though there was none of the drama of treachery or sin in this situation, the application was clear and immediate. God was saying to me, "I mean this for good, and it will bring life to others. Do not fear, I will provide for you and your little ones."

Thank you, God, for stories from Your Word that teach and nourish in such a timely way.

Joan Boydell and her husband, Bruce, provide counsel and coaching through Lifespan.

Donkey Grass

"I know what it is to be in need, and I know what it is to have plenty. I have learned the secret of being content in any and every situation, whether well fed or hungry, whether living in plenty or in want." *Philippians 4:12*

"The boundary lines have fallen for me in pleasant places; surely I have a delightful inheritance." *Psalm 16:6*

Bloom where you are planted. Count your blessings. Our culture is full of little adages. "The grass is always greener..." came to mind one day while driving past a field. It was spring and the field was lush with bright green grass, a common sight in Lancaster, Pennsylvania. It stood out this particular day because a donkey stood by the fence with his head askew, squeezed through the fence straining to get the grass outside his pasture on the roadside. What was he thinking?

Have you ever strained and stretched and fussed, thinking you should be doing something different? A ministry position, or to be accepted, to be one of *them*, or squeezed passed boundaries hoping for fulfillment only to find out God hadn't given you permission or anointing to be there. Turn around; the field is ready in your pasture. It is lush and green and God has given it to you. Ask for God's eyes to see what He has placed before you. Speak a word in season to the checkout clerk. Pray for, or better yet, pray with your waitress. Encourage a child. Seek God's heart and best for the person who really annoys you. Are you there next to this person to be God's hands? Are you salt and light to your coworkers? Turn that wait at the red light or grocery line to a holy place by praying for the people around you.

"I'm giving you every square inch of the land you set your foot on—just as I promised Moses (Joshua 1:3)."

You can be content with the full lush abundance of ministry opportunities within your pasture. Ask God to show you.

Father, forgive me. Open my eyes and heart to Your placement. Amen.

Christina Ricker is a seeker of God, wife, mom and nana serving with Petra Christian Fellowship.

Your Own Place in the Dirt

"…The kingdom of heaven is like a man who sowed good seed in his field." *Matthew 13:24*

It is April, and it's planting season. I love the fresh, cool dirt between my fingers. Getting close to God's creation while placing each seed in its "place in the dirt" I anxiously wait for the first signs of plant life. After several days, I see small evidence of mounds of dirt being lifted by the strength of the leaves reaching upward to the sun.

I love walking about the seedlings watching, *impatiently* for the plants to reveal themselves. I was very careful to accurately label each seed pot so I would know one seedling from another. All the different seedlings start off looking amazingly alike; I would not know what these seeds will be until they bear fruit!

Wow…how God spoke to me at that time…Jesus *knows* who we are and has planted His Spirit in us for His purpose. God's hands are all over His creation. We may look somewhat alike…but it is the fruit which we bear which distinguishes Who we belong to. We are created for His purpose to fellowship with Him. What we do matters to Him. I am thankful I serve a God who does not *anxiously* or *impatiently* walk about us; Jesus is steadfast, faithful, patient and a loving Savior who desires to have a relationship with us. "So they will be called oaks of righteousness, The planting of the Lord, that He may be glorified (Isaiah 61:3)."

Lord Jesus, thank you for Your steadfast love, and Your faithfulness. Thank you that what we do matters to You. Lord Jesus, search our hearts and cleanse Your people so we may be the oaks of righteousness, the planting of You, Lord, that You may be glorified in all we say and do.

Julie Carroll Alexander is missions director at Ephrata Church of the Nazarene.

Lasting Change

"Let us not be weary in well doing...." *Galatians 6:9*

I was headed through Harrisburg on my way to help with the food distribution of Harrisburg Food Ministry. Twice a week bags of groceries are given to the needy of the city. I often wondered if there was any lasting change being made in people's lives through this ministry, or were we just a source of free food? I stopped at the 13th Street light and a lady crossed the street in front of my car and turned to look at me. I noticed that she was very well dressed for that neighborhood in a flower-printed dress and heeled shoes.

Much to my surprise, she appeared later in the food line at the host church. We have teams that offer prayer along with the food and I got to hear her story. She had just been released from prison that morning! She had no money, food, clothes or even a place to stay. She asked for prayer for her children to be released to her from foster care and for help to overcome a drinking problem. I was able to pray with her and offer some counsel. I strongly advised her of the need for an accountability partner. She connected with a lady from the church who knew of a women's shelter.

Months later I was with my wife at a yard sale in our rural community about fifteen miles south of Harrisburg. Suddenly a lady stuck a finger in my face and said, "I remember you. You're the guy who prayed with me at Allison Hill." She excitedly told me how God answered her prayers. She had a job and an apartment and best of all, the foster care system would be returning her children shortly. God provided this divine appointment to let me know the true value of doing His work.

Lord, cause me to see the value in each of Your children and how You work in their lives.

Phil Mayeski is a board member of Harrisburg Food Ministry and member of Christ Community Church, Camp Hill.

The Name of God

"He who dwells in the shelter of the Most High will rest in the shadow of the Almighty. I will say of the Lord 'He is my refuge and my fortress, my God, in whom I trust.'" *Psalm 91:1–2*

After many years in an emotionally abusive relationship, I felt like my world was crashing down around me when the abuse became physical and my life was threatened. During those terrifying days, my relationship with the Lord grew stronger and deeper. When absolutely nothing in my world felt safe or secure, God taught me to trust Him completely and run to His shelter. Psalm 91:1–2 became my life scripture as I realized that my life is held in the hands of the Most High. That knowledge removed the fear and brought rest to my soul.

An in-depth look at the original Hebrew reveals four different and unique names of God that communicate important truths about the nature of God and how He relates to us. Most High is *El Elyon*, emphasizing God's strength and sovereignty. Almighty is *El Shaddai*; the word *shaddai* is derived from a word meaning "mountain," picturing God as the overpowering majestic mighty one. Lord is YHWH, the most significant name for God in the Old Testament. YHWH occurs 6,823 times in the Old Testament and is especially associated with God's holiness. It has a two-fold meaning: the active, self-existent one (I AM), and Israel's redeemer. God is *Elohim*, meaning strong one, mighty leader, supreme Deity. This is the same name of God used in Genesis 1:1 ("In the beginning God…"). The form of the word *Elohim* is plural, indicating the revelation of the triunity of the Godhead.

What a divine revelation of the power and sovereignty of our Lord and His desire to be the shelter and protection for His own.

Holy Father, we desire to fully experience You as our redeemer, the sovereign, majestic, and mighty I AM.

Sharon McCamant serves as director of the Lebanon Pregnancy Clinic with Susquehanna Valley Pregnancy Services and as a ministry leader at the Ephrata Nazarene Celebrate Recovery.

Sharing Your Day

"Be joyful always; pray continually; give thanks in all circumstances, for this is God's will for you in Christ Jesus."
1 Thessalonians 5:16–18

"Turn your radio on and listen to the Master's radio. Get in touch with God, turn your radio on...." This popular song by Ray Stevens in 1972 was a favorite of mine—upbeat with a great message I could relate to. And as my father would say, "I can whistle it," meaning it had a recognizable melody.

But today I find that I intentionally do just the opposite of Ray's suggestion...I turn the radio off. Of course, the song's message was to turn on your "inner radio" and listen to God's still voice. But taking that concept a bit further, I started thinking of all the time that could be better spent in not just "listening," but being in "conversation" with God.

In today's fast-paced world, our need-to-know antenna has us hooked not only to radio and television but to i-pods and a host of other stay-connected devices. We're overwhelmed with distractions. Often we hear preachers suggest we take occasional "media breaks" by turning off all electronic distractions. *Finding time* to do this is the problem.

Something that works for me is this: I have turned the car radio off, permanently. Time alone in the car is time alone with God. Ray's song tells us, "Everybody has a radio receiver." Well, we also have a microphone. We have a voice. I believe that God wants to *hear* what I'm thinking. Just as I cherish conversation with my kids, God delights in hearing my voice. Whether serious or lighthearted, communication is important to both parties.

Try turning your inner-radio on, but formatting it into a talk show. You just may be amazed, and amused, by His input!

Dear God, thank you for the insight and joy You put into my heart new each day. May my focus and commitment to You be continually renewed and refreshed daily through our talk-show conversations.

Janet Medrow serves as a deacon at Great Valley Presbyterian Church in Malvern.

Standing with the Suffering

"Sometimes you were publicly exposed to insult and persecution; at other times you stood side by side with those who were so treated."
Hebrews 10:33

It was a worship service like many others that I had visited in the developing world. There were men, women, youth and children in the little chapel enthusiastically praising God, clapping or raising their hands and dancing before the Lord. Their joy was contagious and their love of our Savior was overflowing. The presence of the Spirit was nearly palpable and though I did not understand the languages, they were clearly my brothers and sisters.

There was a shared experience between these worshipers. They were from Orissa, India, and the homes and all of the possessions of these thirty families had been destroyed by Hindu extremists. They had all fled for their lives into the jungle. Some of them watched family members being killed, others their husbands being abducted and jailed and a few lost loved ones to disease in the jungle, far from medical care.

Despite having lost so much, they still had the joy of the Lord, and amazingly, they were planning how to return to their home regions so they could resume ministering in the name of Christ! We had come to minister through medicine, but greater was their spiritual ministry to us!

Few of us can relate to the first half of the verse from Hebrews, but all of us can be challenged by the second. Stay informed through Open Doors or Voice of the Martyrs, pray for the persecuted church, or support ministries who toil for these suffering members of our family; stand side by side with those who are so treated!

Lord, give strength to our brothers and sisters who are suffering for Your name all around the world. Raise up an army of Your people to intercede on their behalf. Amen.

Chip Mershon, MD, is a family physician at Cornerstone Family Health Associates in Lititz and serves on the elder board at Lancaster Evangelical Free Church.

Forgiveness God's Way

"Bless those who curse you. Pray for those who hurt you." *Luke 6:28*

Forgiveness is a choice, not a feeling. I've heard it many times. And from experience, I know just how long it can be until my emotions catch up with my will. Which means the time span between the two is crammed full of battles: reiterating that forgiveness has been given, wrestling with anger, refusing thoughts of retaliation. It's an exhausting week, or more, before my feelings match my decision.

And then I discovered God's shortcut—a more excellent, not to mention expedient way. The time between forgiveness and emotional peace need only be as long as it takes to speak a blessing over the one who offended me. It works when I speak the blessing through gritted teeth. It works whatever my emotions. The change in my emotions (and blood pressure) is close to instantaneous.

Because I never know when the opportunity (rude drivers, family members) to bless will arise, I keep an index card handy. On it I have typed an extravagant blessing.

God sends rain (a huge blessing in the semiarid Palestine) on both the just and the unjust. When I bless those who offend me, I am walking in my Father's footprints.

Heavenly Father, I forgive _____. Bless their life with riches and honor, healing and wholeness. Bless the good work of their hands. Cause Your face to shine upon them and grant them peace.

Ruth Morris is a member of Worship Center. She is a special projects writer for several parachurch ministries.

Taking Time to Listen

"…Speak, Lord, for your servant is listening…." *1 Samuel 3:9*

For many years, my prayers were mostly one-way conversations with God. I thanked, confessed, blessed and petitioned. But I forgot to listen!

However, after I was introduced to an ancient way of praying with scripture (*Lectio Divina*), my prayer life changed. In this approach, I read a short passage of scripture, reflect on its link to my life and respond to it in prayer. Sometimes I ask God questions about something I've read. Many times, my response is expressing gratitude for God's work in my life and the world. Concerns and requests to Him are filtered through the knowledge I've gained from reading my "guidebook," the Bible.

Something is missing from my prayer time until I stop speaking and sit quietly, often with closed eyes. Just as I clean the house for a special friend's visit, I sweep away distracting thoughts from my mind in preparation to welcome God. This is the Lord's time. Like Samuel, I wait in expectation. Sometimes I become aware of a sin in my life; sometimes loving words of affirmation fill my mind. I may be nudged to bless someone with an act of kindness or reminded of a task I've neglected. Peace and stillness prevail as I bask in God's presence.

God, indeed, does speak to us when we take time to listen. Each of us can have a two-way conversation that will strengthen our relationship with God forever.

Oh, Lord, forgive us for being too busy to allow You to speak! Teach us to listen for Your voice. Amen.

Leona Myer, with her husband, Everett, serves on the pastoral elder team at Hosanna! A Fellowship of Christians, in Lititz.

Responsive Living

"Trust God from the bottom of your heart; don't try to figure out everything on your own. Listen for God's voice in everything you do, everywhere you go; he's the one who will keep you on track."
Proverbs 3:5–6 (*The Message*)

The Deacons at our church are out there listening to God and serving in a dozen ways. Our Stephen Ministers offer continual support and encouragement to many in crisis and transitions.

One such caring person is Emily. Emily is responsible to update our prayer list and follow up with people who are discharged from the hospital. Last week she called a man in our congregation, James, to see if he wanted us to keep his dad on our prayer list. Her timing was perfect. James had just discovered that his ninety-year-old father would need eye surgery. He was upset and worried.

Emily's call helped him settle down and reminded him that he was not alone. Thank you, Emily, for your faithful work of caring for others. You listened to the Holy Spirit as to when to call James. That is what I call responsive living. You hear the Spirit whispering and then you go and do it!

O God, our worlds are spinning out of control. We find ourselves in confusing and hard times. Jesus, Creator of the World, come and create order in our chaos. You are in charge. We trust You. Help us to listen and respond to You. Employ us in Your healing, transforming and missional work. In Christ, Amen.

Don Hackett is a pastor at First Presbyterian Church in Lancaster.

Something about Him Is Different

"I have never been a good speaker. I wasn't one before you spoke to me, and I'm not one now. I am slow at speaking, and I can never think of what to say." [Moses]

"I will be with you and give you the words to say." [The Lord]
Exodus 4:10–12 (Contemporary English Version)

Several years ago I was conducting a weeklong series of renewal messages in a church east of Lancaster. One evening I noticed a woman seated in the audience. She and I attended the same one-room school many years ago. I had not seen her since our school days. She told me later that evening that she heard I was preaching in this church near her home. She could not believe that the preacher was the same person she knew in school or that he could be standing before an audience and preaching. She just had to come out to see and hear him.

You see, when I was in grade school I was very timid and shy. You know, when the Lord whispered to me, at twelve years of age, that I would one day be a preacher, I had some reservation about it too. Several years after I was ordained as the pastor of my church, we had a visiting speaker who gave a teaching on the Holy Spirit. He invited his audience to make a complete surrender of all of life to the control of the Spirit. I responded to that invitation. I committed my mind, my voice, my facial expression, my hand gestures and all of me to the control of the Spirit. Shortly after this, one of our members asked my son, "What happened to your dad? Something about him is different."

Thank you, Lord, for giving me Your Holy Spirit.

H. Howard Witmer is now retired. He and his wife Miriam are living at the Landis Homes Retirement Community.

Laugh Out Loud, You Just Might Feel Better

"A merry heart does good like medicine…." *Proverbs 17:22*

When I was a little girl, I wanted to host the show *Candid Camera*. I watched it faithfully. I wanted to be the one to carry out pranks and make the other person laugh. Then I look at some of the crazy things that happened to me and the things I did, such as making room in the trunk of my car for the groceries, only to turn around and to see the cart going out of the parking lot, as if it was going on a road trip. Or the time I walked into the men's bathroom at the store. I was so embarrassed as three men just stood there and looked at me. Can't you just see God getting a chuckle at some of the things we do and some of the things our little children say? Laughter is so important to have. It is good to laugh and to be able to laugh at ourselves and some of the circumstances that happen to us.

I remember one day I had just gotten done washing the kitchen floor and my husband came home from work. As he walked through the kitchen, he left a trail of dry mud particles that looked like Tender Vittles cat food. I really wanted to get mad, but I ended up laughing. I had two choices. I could either get angry or I could choose to laugh. At that moment, I chose to laugh because I would rather be laughing than be angry. I know it doesn't always work that way, but it is a choice.

God wants us to enjoy our lives. He is always encouraging us through His Word. Try to see God's humor in the little things. Maybe if we do more of that, we will actually see more of God's character in our own lives. Hmmmmm. I wonder if there's mud in heaven.

Lord, help us to be able to laugh at ourselves more and be less uptight over things that might not even matter much. Help us to increase our attitude of thanksgiving and open our eyes to more of You. Amen.

Lisa Garvey serves at Hosanna Christian Fellowship, Lititz, with their Women's Ministry and Prayer Ministry.

Still Believing

"Now faith is the substance of things hoped for, the evidence of things not seen." *Hebrews 11:1*

"Lord, can you change his heart? Lord, please remove the scales from his eyes. Lord, can you change him?" I pleaded with God for my wayward child.

"Daughter, I have your children in the palm of My hand. I am trying to change you," God responded.

I realized I had some lessons to learn: What did faith in God truly mean? Did I really believe that the God of the universe had a plan for my children? Be it good or bad, did I trust God fully?

I was reminded that it is not about my pain, my disappointment, my desires, or what I think is best—it is about God's plan, God's desire and God's will. It is *all* about God.

To watch your child struggle and wrestle with the world and all it has to offer is disheartening. "God, I raised my children in your Word. Why? God, I homeschooled my children and taught them your Word. Why? God, I sent them to a Christian school and gave them biblical principles to live by. Why?"

All the while I could hear God whisper, "Anita, do you trust Me? Anita, do you really trust Me? Anita, trust Me."

Lord, I know more about You, the pain I cause You with my sin, and trusting You as a loving Father, than I could have learned had I not had seven years with my prodigal children. I am still believing, Lord, in You; my faith is in You, Lord, that You will bring all the evil to good, in Your time.

Anita Casteel has been in Christian ministry for ten years, serving God at Dayspring Christian Academy. She is the mother of three young adult men. Currently, she is working on her Master's in Education, and serving God as the Director of Admissions and Development.

Your Heart's Desire

"Delight yourself in the Lord and he will give you the desires of your heart." *Psalm 37:4*

I was raised in a Christian home and was always taught to believe that God answers my prayers. Knowledge like that is easy to tell others, but often difficult to draw strength from in difficult times. I found that prayer in my life tended to be habitual and ritualistic. I don't think that was a bad thing, because it kept me focused on giving my life to Christ; however it often made my prayers impersonal and disingenuous.

That was before my wife and I experienced our greatest struggle to date. We had been married for three and a half years and having a child had become our number one priority. We both sensed, especially my wife Emilie, that God would provide a child for us, and that we would make great parents. After a year and a miscarriage we were discouraged and frustrated.

Being a slow learner, it finally started to occur to me that this might not happen without some serious prayer. I started to make it a priority to bring this to God every day. My wife was praying for this all along, but I am ashamed to say it took me some time to realize that we needed God's provision.

Two weeks ago we heard our baby's heartbeat for the first time, praise God. Depending on Him for this miracle has changed my prayer life and has made it more sincere and personal. I have experienced that God wants to forgive me of my sins and give me the desires of my heart.

Father, thank you for hearing my prayers and always faithfully answering them.

Grant Gehman serves as the director of TNT Youth Ministry in Ephrata.

On Display

"...This happened so that the work of God might be displayed in his life." *John 9:3*

My teenager came home from school and informed me he needed a new pair of dress pants for a mock job interview the very next day. So, off we went to the local mall. Walking the halls, I couldn't help but notice the storefront windows. Meant to stop us in our tracks, capture our attention, and whet our appetites for more, the display items in these windows also represented what's found inside the doors. They were actually quite helpful. Without them, I'd have only a store name to rely on and may end up entering a shop where I'd rather not be found! After all, without previous experience, how else would I know "Apple" was full of computers, "Payless" with shoes, and that "American Eagle" would hold the very pants my son and I were searching for?

It struck me that, as followers of Jesus, *we* are the display items in which God reveals who *He* is and what is found in Him. Our Creator God puts Himself on display in us so others will see and desire more of Him. Different characteristics are on display in each of His children, but all are meant to attract others to Him: stopping them in their tracks, capturing their attention and inviting them to come inside for greater discoveries.

We're told God displayed His unlimited patience in Paul (1 Timothy 1:16); His power in Pharaoh (Romans 9:17); and His mighty works in the blind man (John 9:3). What's on display in your life and mine? What, of God, do passers-by see in us?...and does it leave them longing for more?

Creator God, put Yourself on display in me in such a way that captures the attention of passers-by and draws them deeper into Your heart.

Jenny Gehman, founder of LiveWell! Ministries, is on display in Millersville.

Faith and Peace

"Trust in the Lord with all of your heart and lean not on your own understanding; in all your ways acknowledge Him, and He will make your paths straight." *Proverbs 3:5–6*

Recently, like a lot of other people, I have had the misfortune of losing my job. Normally I would panic or worry about the loss of finances.

I was reminded of the scripture above from Proverbs, by the Holy Spirit I believe, and thought, okay, this is "where the rubber meets the road" as the old saying goes. I felt like I was being challenged. Do I, or, do I not, believe in the scripture I so often quote, or, even, memorized?

Well I don't have a job yet, but I do have something much more valuable: faith and peace. I can honestly say I am not worried. It is a blessing to be able to say I trust that the Lord will take care of us.

So, if you're going through any trials like those that scripture says, "Consider it pure joy…" putting your faith to the test can be a blessing if you let it.

Thank you Lord, for allowing me to put my trust in You because You are faithful.

Jean Henry, along with her husband, attends "Stones" which is part of the Micro Church Network.

The Great Meeting

"And continuing daily with one accord...with gladness and single-ness of heart." *Acts 2:46 (21st Century King James Version)*

In 1715, Jacob Boehm III arrived from his Swiss Reformed community in Europe to a new colony planted by the Mennonites in Lancaster, Pennsylvania. Ten years later Martin Boehm was born. The Byerland Church community chose thirty-one-year-old Martin by lot to serve as one of the early pastors. After failing to preach for an agonizing two years, Martin sensed the Holy Spirit impressing the word *lost*. That day while plowing in the field he knelt repentantly before the Father and received salvation. Leaving the plow and the horses, he ran to the house to inform his wife of his newfound relationship with the Lord. Martin was filled with a new enthusiasm for preaching the gospel in the power of the Holy Spirit.

Word began to spread about the impact this country preacher was having. House meetings other than Sunday morning were held in the Boehm home where fifty to one hundred people heard the Word of God. This fresh move of God was evident in all the churches of the colonial era in the formation of regional gatherings attended by Mennonites, Amish, Dunkers, German Reformed and Lutheran.

The greatest meeting on record was held at Isaac Long's barn near Landis Valley Museum on Pentecost Sunday, May 10, 1767. Regional church leaders from as far away as Virginia preached. Martin stood before 1,000 people who had gathered and spoke of his own conversion experience. The scene that followed will never be forgotten. Philip William Otterbein, a university-trained minister of the York Reformed Church, unable to repress his emotions, rose from his seat and went directly to the short, bearded plain-dressed Mennonite pastor. He embraced Martin and declared, "We are brethern." The people were deeply touched, wept for joy and loudly gave praise to God. Could this have been the seed of the regional church coming together in one accord?

Father God, reveal to Your church in this generation the biblical principle of coming together in one accord (culturally, denominationally, ethnically).

Joe Garber is a bi-vocational pastor/dairy farmer who serves at Byerland Mennonite Church and Spring Lawn Farm.

Long's Barn, Lancaster County
Photo by Mark Van Scyoc

Find Refuge

"So to the descendants of Aaron the priest they gave Hebron (a city of refuge for one accused of murder)...." *Joshua 21:13*

On the northwest side of the city of Lebanon, nestled among a Puerto Rican restaurant, a gas station, and a beer distributor, stands Light's Fort. A centuries-old building constructed by the family of John Light, an early settler of the Lebanon area, it is strongly built of gray and white stone, fitted with a high-side roof and a small entryway.

As European settlement of the area strengthened through the first half of the eighteenth century, Native Americans began to respond to the intrusions upon their land. Add to that tension the drama of the French and Indian War in the 1750s and 1760s. The German settlers of the area living on farms dotting the countryside were forced to seek refuge together. They found that refuge at Light's Fort in the city of Lebanon (known at the time as Steitztown). Consequently, the Moravian settlers in this land first called the city Hebron before formally naming it Lebanon in 1778.[1]

To this day, Lebanon continues to be a city of refuge. People running from all sorts of things find safe haven in this city. Be it past mistakes, blown ambitions, the law, family strife, inner turmoil, dark memories or painful circumstances, the land of Lebanon is one that declares safety, security and beauty. While sin and defilement on the land often twists this design to deception and manipulation, Lebanon has stood as a city of refuge for hundreds of years, and it is in the redemptive design of the land of Lebanon to declare that "God is our refuge and strength, a very present help in trouble (Psalm 46:1)."

May the grace of God make it so.

[1] Carmean, Edna J. *Lebanon County, Pennsylvania: A History.* Lebanon County Historical Society: 1976.

Father God, may we find refuge in You alone, for You alone are a truly safe haven. Amen.

Jay McCumber serves as lead pastor of Cornerstone Christian Fellowship and president of the Lebanon222 Team in Lebanon.

We Are All Precious

"For God so loved the world that he gave his one and only Son."
John 3:16

Over a twenty-eight-year career I spent way too much time at the Metro airport in Detroit, Michigan. But one such occasion was memorable. As I sat waiting for my flight, I was inwardly praying:

Lord, You are invited
Come to dinner at our house
Walk on our pond
Climb into our boat
Drive Your breakfast wagon onto our worksite
Show us as much of Your beauty as we can stand.
Charm Your children, Lord
Let us laugh loudly
And live lovingly
As Your kingdom comes!

A most amazing thing started to happen. I became aware of a group of young men jokingly ribbing one another behind me. Ten feet off to my right was a group of three men and a woman similarly enjoying each other's company. One young lady sat on the floor to my left, her back resting against a big, round concrete pillar, contentedly typing on her laptop. Three seats to my right was an absolutely gorgeous young woman. She wore very little makeup, was clearly fit and had the face of an angel. Suddenly it seemed like Jesus was showing me how he saw all of these dear folks—with heartfelt delight in them, His very own precious children. It was as though His presence packed that grungy, old, rancid-smelling gate area with warm good humor and beauty. I have no idea whether my prayer in any way contributed to that scene, or whether it simply made me aware of God's love and presence. Either way, I boarded the plane that day with a new appreciation of God's love for *all* His human children. It seemed like he had given me just a hint of what He had intended when He created us.

Oh Lord, give us the grace to see all of Your children as precious, just as You do.

Everett Myer serves as a pastoral elder at Hosanna! A Fellowship of Christians in Lititz.

One Week Without God

"Do not cast me from your presence or take your Holy Spirit from me." *Psalm 51:11*

It seemed like the beginning of any other school day until two vivacious high school students came bounding into my office. One young lady began to reveal a thought that sparked in her heart while she was riding on the school bus. For some time she had been concerned about the spiritual lethargy in her life and in the life of some of her peers within the Christian school setting. Her concern emanated out of what can occur in any of our lives and ministries when the routine and regiment of religion overtakes the richness and relevance of a personal, daily relationship with our Lord.

Julie began with a question. "Dr. Outlar, What if we deleted everything referring to God and Christianity from school life for one week?" Her reason? To see first if anyone would notice the difference and second, that both students and staff might consider whether such a shocking action would jump-start a deeper appreciation for what we have in Christ.

The words, "And a little child [young person] shall lead them (Isaiah 11:6)," came to my mind, as Julie's concerns were probing my own soul. For in fact what appears to be happening in our Christian society today is the pushing of the "delete key" when it comes to God's involvement in our everyday lives.

The words of Annie S. Hawks and Robert Lowry, in the hymn, "I Need Thee Every Hour," speak to the antidote for our arrogance, at times, toward our loving Savior.

I need thee every hour, Most gracious Lord
No tender voice like Thine can peace afford.
I need thee every hour, Stay Thou nearby
Temptations lose their power, When Thou art nigh.

Forgive me, Lord, for seeing You only as a resource and a rescuer in times of crisis, to be like a valet, responding to my beck and call; rather than realizing You are my daily Source and the reason for my very existence.

Dr. Sandy Outlar is headmaster of Lancaster Christian School.

Today!

"Therefore God...set a certain day, calling it Today...." *Hebrews 4:7*

The battle was rough...we prayed and stood in faith, knowing that we were doing all God called us to do, yet it appeared to be getting worse. We had made some big decisions out of obedience to God in the way He was directing us. Now as the change was taking place, the finances for Cornerstone Pregnancy Care Services were going down. Unbelief started to enter...did we really hear correctly?

One evening, as I closed my eyes to sleep, I said, "Lord, I am finished, I have done all I know to do and have walked in what we felt you say. CPCS is Yours."

In the morning as I was waking, I heard the Lord speak to me one word, "Today."

I repeated back, "Today?" In the silence, *hope* stirred in the depths of my soul.

Activities at CPCS were normal that day...actually a few more negative (in appearance) changes took place...but rest and hope was growing. I was at rest with whatever God chose to do. That weekend I sensed the Lord directing me to turn to Hebrews 4. That is when I understood the "Today." I asked the Lord to forgive me for not resting in Him and allowing unbelief to enter.

The following week God released the finances. Little by little within a few weeks debt was paid off and a miracle happened...a debt was erased! Only God could have done such a work. I stand in awe at the completeness of His work in my heart and His ministry.

Dear God, You are always on time. Thank you for Today and for the rest You give to those who believe.

Debbie Davenport serves as a leader interceding and equipping others for kingdom purposes in her varied roles in the body of Christ and at Cornerstone Pregnancy Care Services.

The Extra Mile

"...He gives power to the tired and worn out, and strength to the weak." *Isaiah 28 (The Living Bible)*

I felt sympathetic and exhausted while watching my son run the quarter-mile track behind our house. His slender, trim, legs paced evenly to keep going far beyond what a normal nine-year-old could endure. He seemed determined to reach the goal he had set for himself; however, the heat of the day, the aches in his legs and the distractions all around him were definitely slowing him down.

Halfway around his sixth lap, he broke open with a sudden burst of energy. The look on his face started to change as his pace almost doubled in speed. He was more determined than ever to accomplish his goal.

"What's come over him?" I questioned my husband. "He's run a mile and a half, and now he's doubled his pace!"

Greg explained that there is a peak where a runner feels no pain. The body is revived with new energy to finish the race. "It must be very satisfying to get to there," he remarked.

It wasn't until a few days later that God used that parable in my life. Satan tried to drag me down, taking away all my spiritual energy so I would eventually lose sight of God's plan for my life. It took all I had just to keep my spiritual pace. While down on my knees asking for supernatural strength, a burst of God's power revived me. As with my son's physical revival, my spirit received fresh, new energy from the Holy Spirit so I could accomplish the goal set before me.

Through this timely lesson, God has etched in my heart that He will never leave us nor forsake us as we turn to Him for renewed strength. He will carry us through any trial and we "shall mount up with wings like eagles (Isaiah 40:31)." How satisfying, indeed, it is to know that over and over again, the Lord will renew our strength.

Dear Heavenly Father, thank you that we can depend on You for renewed physical and spiritual power even on days when we feel all our strength is gone.

Jan Dorward is a Messianic Jew who resides in Ephrata where she attends DOVE Christian Fellowship, Westgate. Jan loves to write and she presents Messianic Passovers.

The Dove of Peace Sends a Message

"May the God of hope fill you with all joy and peace as you trust in Him, so that you may overflow with hope by the power of the Holy Spirit." *Romans 15:13*

It was the week of National Day of Prayer. We must always brace ourselves for the enemy's attacks. He swings his blows any way he can to distract our attention from the real thing—the real work of God, His Son and the Holy Spirit.

Taking a defense class for our community in the form of putting on the whole armor of God keeps us with our dukes up and ready for battle. Quoting scripture verses in the name of Jesus helps the enemy flee.

But May 7, 2009, was especially tough! The economy hit us hard! The costs for National Day of Prayer were very high. Then the phone rang! Our very close friend had emergency open heart surgery. "Not on this very week of National Day of Prayer, Lord!"

As I was prayerfully approaching another new day, I was standing at my kitchen window observing the gray skies and rain drops which were predicted for the entire week, including National Day of Prayer day. Then I experienced the presence of God in the dreariness. On the branch outside the window sat a turtle dove cooing back at me as if to say, "All is well, our Master is in control. Relax, believe and trust God."

By God's grace, the skies cleared and the police reported eighteen thousand attended our evening celebration of prayer! Our close friend's recovery from open heart surgery has been remarkable. The finances? Well, God has never failed us, so we know the dove of peace was God's way of sending us His message of promise.

Oh God, as we trust, believe and obey, we praise You for all the great and marvelous things You accomplish when God's people humble themselves and pray. Amen.

Dona Fisher is chairman of the local National Day of Prayer, president of Change of Pace Bible Studies and is a freelance writer for Lancaster Sunday Newspaper.

A Different Kind of Mother's Day

"Delight thyself also in the Lord: and he shall give thee the desires of thine heart." *Psalm 37:4 (King James Version)*

My husband Dick and I have been traveling to Russia/Latvia/Siberia for ministry over the last fifteen years. In all our trips, I recall this one as especially difficult as we would be in Siberia away from all four children on Mother's Day.

This day was always so special as I would receive breakfast in bed, followed by cards, flowers and gifts. On this particular morning in Siberia I awoke and Dick told me we would be going into a prison that morning. I promptly answered that I would not go and wanted to stay. I was near tears because of the distance between me and our children. He firmly told me that I was going along. In my heart I knew he was right, so off we went.

It turned out I was the first woman ever to go inside this prison. We were greeted by some guards and a few prisoners who hugged and kissed my husband as he'd been there the previous year and taught them the Bible. They were overjoyed to have him back and meet me.

As we walked upstairs, they were excited to show us their first ever chapel in a Siberian prison. Escorting us as honored guests, we went to the front of the chapel and there on the altar was our family photo. They said, "We pray for your family every day!" I was so touched and humbled.

Then I had the honor of singing for these hardened men (I thought) until they looked me in the eyes and I saw Jesus and His light shining from them. It was the best gift God could give me to be in a room with His beloved children in a prison.

Oh God make me willing to be used of You anytime and anywhere You lead and on any occasion for You will surely give me the desire of my heart. In Jesus' name, Amen.

Jeannette Taylor and husband Dick are full-time staff with the Navigators. Jeannette is also a volunteer with REST Ministries in Coatesville.

My Mother's Legacy

"The wise woman builds her house..." *Proverbs 14:1*

"Mom, Grandma died!" those desperate words echoed over the phone from our youngest son. I stood paralyzed, unable to move or breathe, as thoughts of denial flooded my mind. A pulmonary embolism, a blood clot, stole the life of my seventy-year-old mother on Sunday, September 22, 2002. What remains and not stolen is her legacy to our family.

If you were to ask her children and grandchildren about her, they would tell you the things she taught them—faith is the most important thing, family comes before business and hard work matters. She was not perfect. Mom was a farmer's wife, who worked at home and who willingly poured herself into her family's lives. Nothing glamorous about her, she was practical; the only jewelry she wore was a wedding band. That gold band carried a commitment that helped her weather the joys and sorrows during fifty years of marriage. She faithfully taught a first grade Sunday School class. Her reputation as the "candy lady" preceded her at church with the children and teens because of what she carried in her pocketbook.

She loved each of us and made us feel important. Managing to include a favorite dish or dessert for every family member, her holiday meals became feasts. Feeding the people she loved was her hands-on way of loving them. She believed when you nourished someone, essentially, that you are saying that you want him or her to thrive, to be happy and healthy.

Her listening ear, her confidence in us and the freedom she gave to make our own decisions about life, along with her moral support and her prayers, has served us well over the years. She was a mother chosen from God to mold our lives, and we dearly miss her.

Every life tells a story, through our words, deeds and choices, through our homes and even through our clothes and jewelry. Let us tell God's story through our stories to the next generation.

Father, help me through my life, my story, to leave Your legacy to my family.

Coleen Gehman enjoys being a wife and mother serving with her husband, Bryan, at Lancaster Evangelical Free Church.

It's All about Him

"You do not have because you do not ask." *James 4:2*

Bob and I could identify with Mary and Martha. We both experienced a traumatic event: their brother's death and our daughter's serious auto accident. All of us were confused, but we ran boldly to the Lord with honest and breaking hearts. Jesus grieved with us, His presence visibly surrounding us.

"And do you deserve all that I give you?" He asked.

"No," I quietly thought. Prayer, being in the presence of the Lord, humbles us into the truthful and "real" perspective of God's point of view. I perceived that Bekah, a "good teenager" didn't deserve to suffer; however, because of our sin nature no one truly deserves the goodness of God's blessings.

In the midst of allowing this truth to sink in, I heard that still, small voice: "You do not have because you do not ask."

"Excuse me, Lord, am I hearing you right? What are you getting at?" Hope and joy stirred within me as I realized God extending His kindness, His grace.

"You keep praying your wildest prayers! You have already seen Me working in Bekah's situation. She's home after only eight days in the hospital." (Bekah only missed three weeks of school and was almost back to "normal.")

"But I'm not done with her yet. Remember Lazarus? I magnificently displayed My glory through Lazarus so that no one, even the Pharisees, could deny My handiwork. (They tried to murder it, but couldn't deny it.)

"Bekah also has a bold testimony on her lips. The people who hear her accident account will not be able to deny My involvement, and My glory will continue to work in other individual hearts. And one day in the future you'll hear, 'Now for the rest of the stories...'"

Dear Lord, thank you for extending Your grace and answering our prayers beyond our wildest dreams. Give us the words to say as we tell others how You have worked in our lives to give You the honor and glory.

Tamalyn Jo Heim and her husband, Bob, are empty-nesters and pray their wildest prayers to attend Bekah's freshman collegiate soccer games.

Your Greatest Moment

"Teach us to realize the brevity of life, so that we may grow in wisdom." *Psalm 90:12 (New Living Translation)*

Many of us understand the principles of tithing our finances or being generous with our possessions. But the concept of asking the Lord to make the most of our time may be a different kind of giving to Him.

If someone were to ask you about the greatest moment in your life, how would you respond? Many of us would think about when we first accepted Jesus or when we married or when we graduated from college. We think in terms of history. But, could the greatest moment actually be the one you are having right now? Yesterday is gone and the future is somewhere out there, but God is present with you now and offering to partner with you through this day.

You have today to embrace or to endure–it's your choice. Tomorrow can be a somewhat dangerous and, perhaps, even more nebulous word. We can put a lot of things off until tomorrow, even our salvation (Hebrews 3:7, 8, 13). Over three hundred years ago, Brother Lawrence, a lay minister who lived and served at the Carmelite Monastery in the 1600s, said we are to commune with God continually through His Spirit in our spirit and that we are not to try to go faster than grace each and every moment of each and every day.

Believe it or not, everything does not depend upon you or me today. Allow Jesus to teach you to make the most of His time through you. You may experience a divine appointment or an opportunity to actually enjoy many great moments this very day.

Father, I ask You to order my day because You are with me and I recognize that I have the privilege of hanging out with the Creator of the universe this very moment. What fun!

Steve Prokopchak helps provide oversight and direction for DOVE Christian Fellowship International's network of churches.

God Calls a Farm Boy to Be a City Boy

"Do not be overcome by evil, but overcome evil with good."
Romans 12:21

"Wow, I am not in Kansas (or Oxford, PA) anymore," I said to myself. This realization came to me in 2006, soon after coming to work at Water Street Ministries in urban Lancaster. Just like Dorothy, the country girl, in *The Wizard of Oz* recognized that the life she once knew was not to be any longer, I found myself seeing and experiencing the newness of city life.

Evil has surrounded the lives of many men, women and children who have run out of options and come to the mission. Lies, broken promises and commitments, sickness, poor decisions—all have been part of the life that led folks to the door asking for "help." On the flip side, I have seen God provide for the daily, material needs of over two hundred people. Some are not looking for redemption in Jesus Christ; yet He has allowed the hands and feet of His people to minister to their hearts through meals and beds. Amazingly, I am privileged to be part of this work, as are the unsung community members who have given money, food, clothing, prayers and encouragement. The list goes on. Good is winning out over evil.

"Wow, I am glad I am not in Kansas anymore!" I frequently say to myself as I walk over the mission's campus. Dodging cow pies on a dairy farm was my first thirty-one years of life. Now I greet, hug and counsel real people like Mike, John or Steve, who can be impacted by the goodness of the glory of God. *The Message* translation of the Bible declares: "Don't let evil get the best of you; get the best of evil by doing good."

Father, allow me to be used effectively as a small piece of Your Kingdom in sharing good in an evil environment. Let me be Jesus' salt and light in every situation.

Jim Stanton is a chaplain at Water Street Mission and now lives with his wife, Laurie, in Lancaster City.

God's Works Are Great!

"Great are the works of the Lord; they are pondered by all who delight in them...He has caused His works to be remembered."
Psalm 111:2, 4

As newlyweds, my wife and I began a journal which we titled, *Book of Miracles*. It was a way of keeping a record of God's works in our lives and I believe it was initiated by God.

Recently I read the above verses and it reminded me of our miracles journal. I dug it out from my night stand and read through it again. I had been experiencing discouragement in my life and remembering God's works brought revival and refreshment. His works in our lives include the birth of our children, lost keys found, healings, transformed relationships, significant dreams, miraculous provision and much more. A journal entry from my wife reads:

Several months ago I had a dream about Tom (name changed). He kept trying to end a relationship with his girlfriend but couldn't. I saw that Satan was keeping him involved. Later I told Tom the dream. One month ago Tom called and told me that he ended the relationship. Today I spoke with him again. A week after ending his relationship with the girlfriend, he made a decision to enter the ministry! He said he has never felt as good or right about a decision before. Tom told me that his family had been praying for him to make such a decision. I told him that I've prayed for him also, to turn back to God. God does answer prayer. I feel encouraged today. Thank you Lord!

God's works really are great and a worthy delight to ponder. We can observe His wonderful works in nature, in the stories of the Bible, in Christian literature, in the testimonies of friends and family and in the daily experience of our lives. May you be encouraged and strengthened this day as you ponder the works of God in and around you.

Father, thank you that You will cause Your wonders to be remembered today. We affirm that Your works are truly great.

Barry Stoner, The Door Christian Fellowship, serves at Black Rock Retreat and with marketplace leaders.

Lavish Love

"How great is the love the Father has lavished on us…" *1 John 3:1*

When my husband and I took our son back to school in Nashville after spring break, he was excited about showing us "his town." But no more than we were. We wanted to see everything that was a part of his new life—where he ate, slept, studied and worshiped. When he asked if we wanted to go to a concert where one of his buddies was playing, we jumped at the chance—even when he warned us that we might not "exactly" like the music. As we walked down the street to the concert, we passed a parking lot attendant who asked if we were going to see *Brad* (country music star Brad Paisley was also playing in Nashville that night). When we said, "No, we're headed to Rocketown," he burst out laughing.

"It's not your mother's rock and roll anymore," was his veiled warning. It wasn't long before we understood what he meant. In a crowd of over a thousand, Chip and I must have been the only ones over forty-five. When we finally entered the hall, we found our "spot" on an over-looking balcony. This proved to be a wise decision because as the band started playing, the crowd below emerged into two sections—the *shove pit* and the *thrash pit*. I was surprised to learn that the lead vocalist didn't have to know how to sing. Not even one melody line. It turned out to be our initiation into the genre of *screamo*.

I would do it all over again. Why? Because I love our son. I wanted to be with him. I think that's a glimpse of God's love. He wants to be with us…to walk where we walk, see what we see, hear what we hear. He left heaven to do it. Such love says a lot about who we are. It speaks even louder than *screamo*.

Father, help us see Your love for us.

Becky Toews leads the women's ministry at New Covenant Christian Church and is an adjunct professor at Lancaster Bible College.

Explosion!

"We love because he first loved us." *1 John:19*

I was in Junior High and had been attending a new church with a friend of mine. I had no interest in God. I was trying to sing the loud and crazy worship songs I didn't know. A guest speaker was there, and I can't even remember what he talked about. He invited us to come up to receive prayer. I didn't consider getting prayer, yet I found myself up front. When the speaker prayed for the guy beside me, he started crying like something was touching his very soul.

"I wonder if this preacher will know that I don't believe in this stuff," I thought to myself as he approached me.

"You are having doubts about all this stuff," he said as though he was reading my mind. Suddenly the youth pastor was right next to me and asking, "Do you want to receive Jesus into your heart?"

I had never thought about asking Jesus into my heart. I didn't even know what that meant. Before my mind could tell me "yes" or "no," I heard myself saying, "Yes!"

I repeated the prayer that the pastor prayed for me. Immediately I felt something explode in my heart, and my eyes were opened to a wondrous reality I never knew. I spent the next week in a glorious daze! Everything was lovely and new. I never realized how beautiful a tree was! How amazing a doorknob could be! Or how much I loved my parents! The world was different because now I knew that God loved me. That was nineteen years ago. Since then I have learned that long before I ever thought about God, He was pursuing me. Even when I wasn't seeking Him, He was seeking me. I am so glad He found me. Isn't it time that you let God find you?

Lord, please forgive my sins and come into my heart and show me that You are real and that You love me.

Anne Brandenburg is a mother of six and the wife of Chris, a pastor at Life Center Ministries.

The Faithfulness of Abraham

"I beseech you therefore, brethren, by the mercies of God, that you present your bodies a living sacrifice, holy, acceptable unto God, which is your reasonable service." *Romans 12:1*

My grandson "Buddy" who was about eighteen months old at the time, had a stomach virus. My daughter was repeatedly assured that it would pass within a few days; but instead of passing it got worse.

I was there when my daughter changed his diaper and saw blood in his stool. We immediately took him to Lancaster General Hospital, where they sent him to Hershey Medical Center via helicopter. Buddy's bowel had turned inside out, a condition called *intussusception*. We spent the night watching Buddy being prodded and sent off for all sorts of tests. Buddy was in excruciating pain and held his frail body in a fetal position on the bosom of his father or mother, as we waited. The doctors told us they would have to do surgery, as he wasn't responding to the treatments.

I remembered how the Lord had given me a word of wisdom for my brother many years earlier, when his daughter, age five, had been diagnosed with leukemia. I ran down to the chapel at Hershey and began to read the Psalms. The Holy Spirit began to speak to me and I began to do spiritual warfare, and thanked God for his faithfulness. Then the Lord said, "Remember Abraham, who gave me a living sacrifice. I required Abraham to give up Isaac in his heart. When he did I provided a way out."

I gave this word to my daughter and son-in-law. We prayed and gave Buddy to God as a living sacrifice. The doctors came in shortly afterward, as they had taken one more X-ray before surgery. Buddy was healed! Just like my brother's daughter, years earlier, who went into remission a few days after he and I prayed and released her to God. She is twenty-nine and has never had another bout with cancer.

Lord, we sacrifice ourselves to You!

Donna Brown is a "Street Evangelist/Muralist" who attends Wayside Presbyterian Church and ministers with Breakout Ministries at Water Street Ministries.

How Do I Present Jesus to Others?

"Be wise in the way you act toward outsiders; make the most of every opportunity. Let your conversation be always full of grace, seasoned with salt, so that you may know how to answer everyone."
Colossians 4:5–6

I recently heard a statistic that alarmed me. It confirms a burden many of us feel for people we come in contact with every day. Forty-five thousand people die every day without hearing the Good News. This kind of staggering number makes me think about my life's priorities and direction. What am I doing every day that leads people closer to Christ? To me, this is evangelism—the process of leading others to the event of coming to faith.

When I was a new Christian, I was zealous and insensitive in the way I shared. I had a friend whom I desperately wanted to come to know Jesus. I spoke with him, and he told me in many ways, "I'm not interested." I kept pushing and pushing. He became so turned off to me and Jesus that it hurt our relationship for years.

It wasn't until I began thinking more about him and his needs that we have made progress. Today, he and I have loving discussions about Jesus. He hasn't decided to cross the line of faith yet, but his heart is open and God is doing a work.

If forty-five thousand people die every day without hearing the Good News, how many die every day because Jesus isn't presented in a way they can receive? Could people end up in hell because of the way I present Jesus?

Oh God, help us to live and share in a way that people see You and not us or a method. Help our churches be places that welcome others and present You in an uncompromised and authentic way.

Joe Castronova serves as an assistant pastor of evangelism and discipleship at Worship Center. He leads their Alpha course and helps other churches start and run Alpha in the region.

Still Learning to Rest in God

"Return to your rest, O my soul, For the Lord has dealt bountifully with you." *Psalm 116:7 (New American Standard Bible)*

I watched in amazement as the young child flung herself into the seven-foot depth of water in the pool. She was wearing a floatation device, so she knew that she was safe and secure. Observing her I thought, "I wish I could fling myself with such abandon into the lovingkindness of my God." Unfortunately, I am a kindred spirit with the patriarch Jacob, the one who wrestled with God. Some days I become weary of the battle, tired of being a weak human. Thankfully, the Lord's lovingkindness is more than abundant for me. He has to continually prod me to reject the shackles that seek to paralyze me with fear and misgivings.

The seeds of my insecurity were planted five decades ago, when I was unsafe physically and emotionally. The resultant fear has been a formidable enemy. Had it not been for the Lord's love, grace and mercy, I would have been destroyed long ago. He has dealt bountifully with me, yet like a dumb sheep I become restless so easily.

My soul has been restless because of the nature of my employment. After working so hard to complete my bachelor's degree between the ages of fifty-two and fifty-four, I find myself working in a retail environment—the same work of my high school days. My thoughts swirl: Doesn't it matter to the Lord that I studied so hard at Lancaster Bible College? Is He mocking me? Pulling all-nighters was worthless! Then the Lord gently reminds me that receiving a biblical education is a priceless privilege. Feeling ashamed, I apologize to Him. A timely song with the words of Proverbs 3:5–6 penetrates my heart as my Lord lovingly invites me to trust His shepherding care, enabling my soul to rest in Him.

Oh my Lord and my God, thank you for loving me, even when I disappoint You with my foolish thoughts.

Susan Marie Davis is employed by Goodwill and is a member with her husband Karl at Calvary Church in Lancaster.

Calling Fear's Bluff

"I sought the Lord and he answered me; he delivered me from all my fears." *Psalm 34:4*

"Your wife has endometrial cancer." The doctor's words fell like lead weights. Diane had had some problems and they had called in an oncologist, just in case, but we were not prepared for what he said. Perhaps the most fear-producing word in the medical profession—cancer! Instantly my heart went back to the time many years ago when my first wife died of leukemia. *How can this be happening to me again! And now we have two children. What will they do?* Then a CAT scan revealed spots in her liver. The solemn attitudes of the physician's staff indicated this was serious. Our class at church, family and friends rallied around us. I'll admit I was scared!

One sleepless night I turned to the scripture cited above. As I read, calm spread over me. At church through our worship, I was reminded of Job who in the midst of all his tragedy declared, "Blessed be the name of the Lord." So we resolved to consciously "praise the Lord anyhow."

Soon a biopsy revealed no cancer in the liver, so the doctors set Diane on a course of radiation. She got pretty tired, but only missed a few days of work. All in all, it was not as difficult for her as recovering from previous surgeries. A few days after her last treatment, the doctor met with us. He examined her and without any further tests declared, "It's gone." We were dumbfounded. Such good news, so quickly. A year later, there is still no sign of it.

I had been full of fear for what? Nothing. Just a word—"cancer." It had us fooled for a while, until by God's strength we were able to call fear's bluff.

Lord, we bless Your name, no matter what comes.

Craig Hickey is a program counselor for the Men's Residential Recovery Program of Water Street Ministries. He lives in Lititz with his wife Diane and two daughters, Carissa and Joelle.

Walking in Favor

"I entreated Your favor with my whole heart; Be merciful to me according to Your word…I made haste, and did not delay to keep Your commandments." *Psalm 119:58, 60*

"And all these blessings shall come upon you and overtake you, because you obey the voice of the LORD your God."
Deuteronomy 28:2

Everything seemed to be adding delays as I drove my rental car back to the airport. "I have only carry-on luggage," I reasoned, as I rushed to make my noon flight. I was entreating the Lord as I drove, asking for favor as another traffic light turned yellow. Having returned the car, I ran full speed to the ticketing counter and pushed my credit card into the kiosk to print my boarding passes for the two-leg trip home.

No passes were produced, only a screen image declaring the flight closed. I gained the attention of a ticketing agent who confirmed that they had just closed the flight. He said he would try to help me then busied his fingers on the keyboard only to look up and say, "I can get you into Harrisburg at 7:30 p.m." This was not what I wanted to hear. I imagine that my face communicated just that. He said it was the best he could do and then God moved. The agent called the gate and pled my case for me without me even asking. He then printed boarding passes for me and sent me through saying, "You will have to run." I made it to the gate with my shoes under my arm as the last few passengers were boarding—just in time!

I settled into my seat filled with praise as He confirmed in my spirit that it was His doing that changed my circumstances. It was not critical that I get home by 4:30. Seven-thirty would have been no hardship. He just blessed me because He loves me and wanted me to know that I walk in His favor.

Thank you Father, for blessing me.

John M. Hughes, together with Suellen, leads the Centerville House Church.

Gardening

"The thorny ground represents those who hear and accept the Good News, but all too quickly the message is crowded out by the cares of this life and the lure of wealth, so no crop is produced."
Matthew 13:22

"And all of us have had that veil removed so that we can be mirrors that brightly reflect the glory of the Lord. And as the Spirit of the Lord works within us, we become more and more like him and reflect his glory even more." *2 Corinthians 3:18*

I was sitting in the yard when I noticed six or seven big weeds in an area that had recently been mulched. As I pulled the weeds, I noticed that most broke off at the surface or just below. I had been seeking the Lord about some personal issues and I felt Him saying these weeds were symbolic of what was happening in my life. I was recognizing some of the weeds and starting to allow Him to deal with them, but I would need to continue allowing Him to dig deep and pull out the entire root in order to be free.

Now, a year later, I'm still keeping after those weeds, but I've noticed that the big ones are gone. Some little weeds pop up from time to time, but the roots don't go so deep and usually come all the way out on the first try. I had been feeling rather discouraged about things in my life, but the Lord so graciously reminded me of the progress in my little gardens—both the backyard and the garden of my life. My prayer is that I will be continually open to His gentle hand as He prunes me.

Father, thank you for Your tender mercy. Give me the courage to allow you to dig deep down into the soil of my life today. Root up all that is not pleasing to You. I give You my cares and concerns today. I invite You to tend this garden for Your glory and trust You to fulfill Your purposes and plans for me in the mighty name of Jesus. Amen.

Liz Ingold is a wife, mother, grandmother and co-laborer.

A Mother's Prayer

"Train a child in the way he should go, and when he is old he will not depart from it." *Proverbs 22:6*

Every night when I put my son to bed, I pray for him. I pray for the normal things, like that Caleb would be intelligent and do well in school. I pray that he would grow strong and healthy. More importantly, I pray that he would come to know the Lord at an early age, and that God would give us wisdom on how to raise Caleb right. I also pray that he would be filled with compassion and know right from wrong and choose to do right.

I also ask God to put godly people and friends into his life that would help Caleb to follow and serve Him. And I pray that the Lord would use him in a great and might way. Lastly I pray that God would give Caleb a godly spouse.

But there is one more thing that I prayed for, and that was that God would spare Caleb from the many problems and trials that kids face today. And that got me thinking once again. As a mother, it's natural to want the best for our children and to protect them. We don't want anything horrible to happen to them. However, if nothing bad happened, then they wouldn't grow. And their faith wouldn't increase in the Lord. They wouldn't become dependent on the Lord like they need to.

So if you're a mother, remember to pray for your children. But more importantly remember to let them go and let God have His way with them. Our children will be in much better hands in the Lord's than they ever would be in ours.

Dear Lord, thank you so much for children. Help us to remember that children come with much responsibility. May You give us the strength to raise them up right and release them into Your hands. Amen.

Jenn Paules is a part-time DJ for WJTL, FM 90.3, an ESL instructor, but more importantly a full-time wife and mother.

Miscarriage

"...To comfort those who mourn, and provide for those who grieve ...to bestow on them a crown of beauty instead of ashes, the oil of gladness instead of mourning, and a garment of praise instead of despair." *Isaiah 61:1–3*

Last Tuesday my baby lost a baby. My youngest daughter Katie was four month's pregnant. She and Jason were happily anticipating the birth of their first child, but the doctors told her Tuesday that a miscarriage had occurred.

Miscarriage is an interesting and disturbing word. It is intended to soften the reality that a life has ended prematurely. A life that a mother and father have partnered with God to create. A life that already has reality in the womb. A life to which the parents, especially the mother, are already connected.

It doesn't really soften the pain. The immediate impact is some-times devastating, in fact. Time will tell how it will affect Katie and Jason. My prayer is that it will draw them closer to one another and to God. My oldest daughter Christi also suffered a miscarriage in her first pregnancy. My son-in-law Tim consoled her with a blessed response, "God knew something was wrong and decided to take care of it now." Whether his answer eased her pain, I don't know; but his words were true. After Christi's recovery they started over and my grandson Jake is now over a year old. His presence has now become a light of God's love for their lives.

A miscarriage is one of those terrible valleys of shadow of death David described to us. He never said such places were not painful, heart-wrenching—but he reminded us that we are never alone when we must walk that path. God walks even more closely with us when we must take uncertain steps in those shadowy valleys. And any grief we experience, He will comfort and remove—replacing it with His joy.

Thank you for walking with us through the valleys, Lord.

Dr. Steve Dunn is the lead pastor of the Church of God of Landisville and the director of the School of Evangelism for the Churches of God, Eastern Region.

In The Garden

"He will teach us his ways, so that we may walk in his paths."
Isaiah 2:3

My brother and his wife gave me a basket full of "flip-flop" things for my summer birthday—plaques and magnets, a pair of pink and yellow flowered flip-flops and lots more. One day my four-year-old grandson, Clay, found the basket in the closet. We headed out to the backyard with the ceramic flip-flops resembling garden stones. As Clay and I were deciding where to place them, I lined them up as if they were taking a step. I told Clay it looks like someone is walking in the garden. Then he said, "Maybe it's God!"

It reminded me of the chorus of the old hymn that is precious to our family, so I taught Clay the words: "And He walks with me; And He talks with me; And He tells me I am His own. And the joy we share as we tarry there; none other has ever known."

The story goes like this…when Clay's Grandpa, Curt, was a little boy, about three years old, his family was in church and this hymn had just been sung. Curt looked up at his mother and asked, "Who's Andy?" Precious.

God is walking in my garden and I experienced inexpressible joy as Clay and I met Him there.

Father, I thank You for the privilege of sharing You with the next generation, for meeting us in the everyday events of our lives and showing Yourself real and alive to us. Thank you for teaching us Your ways.

Marti Evans is broker-owner of CUSTOM Real Estate, Inc, otherwise known as Grandma MJ to six adorable little boys and a long-awaited princess.

God Hears Our Prayers

"You may ask me for anything in my name, and I will do it."
John 14:14

My wife and I started a business several years ago. As part of the business, Carolyn set up a retail website. She picked an ideal name, but we found that someone owned a similar domain name, which could divert traffic away from us. In order to buy it, we repeatedly attempted to contact the owner, including sending him a certified letter. We received no response.

Over the course of the next couple of years, we prayed about it often, without resolution. Recently, we felt it was time to try again. We got current contact information for the owner and amazingly, he called back. Unfortunately, he wanted five to ten times what we were willing to pay for the name. We had to turn him down, but prayed he would have a change of heart. I don't know why, but I was surprised when he emailed me the next day saying he wanted to sell it to us and would cut the price in half. We explained this was still two and a half times what we could afford. Again we prayed that God would change the man's heart and he would reduce his price. The next day, he informed us that he would sell at the price we could afford.

It is easy for me to forget that God hears my prayers, especially when I have not received the answer I wanted. I find that just when I start feeling this way, God answers a prayer at an unexpected time, like he did with this purchase. God is faithful to remind me He loves me and wants me to have good things. Our timing is not always the right timing. His timing is always perfect.

Father, we thank you that we can trust You to provide our needs and many of our wants. Help us today to remember that Your timing is perfect. Help us to rest in You today.

Darryl Schlicher and his wife reside in Elizabethtown with their five children. They attend DOVE Elizabethtown and run www.liquidwholefood.com.

Gather, Don't Scatter!

"He who is not with me is against me, and he who does not gather with me scatters." *Matthew 12:30*

I love playing games, but there is one game I never want to play again. It's called "52 pick up." I'm sure most of us are familiar with this game. You probably learned it from an older brother or sister who one day approached you all nice and friendly. For a moment it seems like your sibling is your best friend as he asks if you want to play a game. "Sure," you say, "what shall we play?

"How does '52 pick up' sound?" he asks. You are just so happy that your brother even asks to play a game with you, so you let down your guard and you agree to play. That's when you find out just how rotten older siblings can be. He takes the whole deck of cards, all fifty-two, and throws them into the air scattering them over the floor in a huge mess. As he walks away, he says with a wide grin, "Okay pick them up!"

As Christians, we have to be careful of making messes with our lives. Today's verse says that if we are not with Jesus, we are against Him. If we do not gather with Him, we will scatter, just like those cards.

There are lots of times in our lives when we think we've finally got it together. We say, "This time it's going to be different." We are going to live for God no matter what. But what happens? In a couple of days or weeks we find that we are right back in a rut. Why? I think we often fail to act on what we claim is true. In other words, we say we believe in God but it's not evident in the way we live our lives. When Christians live this way they are not gathering—instead they are scattering.

Your sin nature is at war with the Spirit inside you trying to get you to do what you know is wrong, but your faith is what gives you the strength to live above your emotions. It's what should drive you to do what is right because you know it's right and it is what God wants you to do.

Lord, help me to live by faith and not by sight.

Rob Heverling is youth leader at Mount Aetna Bible Church, Mount Aetna.

Celebrate God's Goodness

"You gave [human beings] charge of everything you made, putting all things under their authority—the flocks and herds and all the wild animals, the birds in the sky, the fish in the sea and everything that swims the ocean currents." *Psalm 8:6–8 (New Living Translation)*

It was a beautiful, sunny day with perfect temperatures for the beach. Our family unloaded surfboards and sand toys and made our trek through the hot sand toward the breaking waves. The smells of salt and sunscreen filled the air, and the kids could hardly wait to jump in the water!

Our anticipation built…but quickly faded as we neared the water's edge. There before us were swarms of jellyfish invading the waters. As we gazed down the shoreline, we noticed that most families were staying clear of the waves, apart from a few risk-takers hoping to avoid getting stung.

What a disappointment! It wasn't the beach trip we had envisioned. As I tried to reassure my daughter, Brianna, I was suddenly flooded with some truths the Father was teaching me earlier that morning. In Psalm 8, I had read that God actually gives us charge over everything He has made, even the "fish of the sea and everything that swims the ocean currents."

Wow! Was it really true that God was waiting for us to walk in the authority He had given us to see those jellyfish leave? I grabbed Brianna's hand and we headed off toward the water to pray. We simply agreed together, commanding those jellyfish to leave in the mighty name of Jesus!

We were amazed as we watched the waters clear up over the next hour. Our family celebrated God's goodness in teaching us His ways as we splashed in the waves the rest of the day!

Father, You are good and Your Word is true! How we praise You! Thank you for allowing us to partner with You to see Your Kingdom come in our lives!

Bonita Keener helps to unite prayer in the region and serves as an elder with her husband, Brent at New Life Fellowship, Ephrata. They have four precious children.

A Matter of Attitude

"Everyone who exalts himself will be humbled, and he who humbles himself will be exalted." *Luke 18:14*

Today's scripture text follows Jesus' account of the two men who went up to the temple to pray—one a pompous, self-righteous Pharisee and the other a humble, self-debasing tax collector. The Pharisee haughtily reminded God how good he was. The tax collector smote his breast and pleaded for God's mercy. *What a difference in attitudes!*

A number of years ago I was in a church setting where the sister in charge of the meeting began by saying, *"If there's any resistance to my suggestions or what I have to say this evening, it's not of the Lord!"* and immediately my defenses went up as I thought about her bold arrogance. While I didn't say it aloud, I was secretly reminded of that little light on your dashboard that comes on and flashes things like *Coolant Low! Check Oil! Service Soon! That little light is an indication of a deeper problem.*

Contrast this account with the long-ago farmer in a local Brethren congregation who struggled with an ongoing drinking problem. It got to the point where two deacons were sent to deal with the situation. When the two church officials arrived, they went directly to the barn. But when they got under the fore bay, the stable door was open. And there in the feeding entry, they saw the man on his knees, humbly pleading aloud with God to deliver him from his addiction. *The deacons left quietly without saying a word!*

Lord, help me to be conscious of the times I've been proud and haughty and arrogant, and in humility and penitence, make me willing to confess and turn from my sinful ways. In the name of Him who gives victory, even Jesus, the Christ. Amen.

Paul Brubaker serves on the ministry team at the Middle Creek Church of the Brethren in Lititz.

God's Heart

"…As far as the east is from the west, so far has he removed our transgressions from us." *Psalm 103:12*

In our morning snuggles conversation with my five-year-old daughter we were talking about God. She asked, "Mommy, if God has a heart, how big is it?"

I had to laugh…what a cute, innocent, yet mind-probing question! Right away I called my parents so they could get a good laugh, too. My Dad's answer to her was "immeasurable." I agree, and the more I thought about it the more I am amazed.

His heart is big enough to forgive and forget our sin and to cast it as far as the east is from the west. His heart is compassionate. His heart longs to connect with His children. His heart longs to redeem us. His heart feels our pain. His heart longs to heal and help us. His heart desires the best for us. His heart desires to encourage us. His heart desires relationship.

Rachael then asked, "Mommy is his heart bigger than the cross?"

"Yes, His heart is bigger than the cross, that's why he sent Jesus to die for our sins."

"Wow," she said, "that's big!"

Think about this, God's heart was big enough to overcome the pain of seeing His Son die the most hideous death possible, the death upon a cross, to reconcile us. His heart was big enough to see His Son take upon himself the sins of the world and the sin of each individual person, past, present and future. I don't believe it was the cross that killed Jesus; I believe it was our sin and the separation our sin caused between the Father and the Son that ultimately killed Jesus.

From the perspective of children, amazing truths can be revealed as we open up our hearts to listen to the lessons God reveals through them.

Father God, thank you for redeeming us through Jesus and revealing Your heart of compassion to us.

Diana Sheehan is a mom of three and attends DOVE Christian Fellowship Westgate in Ephrata.

TP and Sin

"If you do not do well, sin is crouching at the door, its desire is for you, but you must rule over it." *Genesis 4:7 (English Standard Version)*

Toilet paper on a desk. I get it...I just don't do it. I understand why several of my associates plus the perky girl behind the newspaper desk in town have TP on their desk, but it just seems out-of-place. It's like having eating utensils in a rest room, a tennis racket in a church sanctuary or fishing tackle at a hunting lodge. There may be an explanation for all of the above, but to the outside observer something is askew.

My desk may be a mess, but you will not find a roll or separate sheets of TP on it. I do have a box of tissues on the credenza. But I refuse to have TP on the desk, in a desk drawer, under the desk or hanging over the desk. It will remain in its designated location—the rest room.

Here's something that is even more out-of-place—sin in the life of a Christian. Oh, it's ever-present in the lives of many of us, but it's a oxymoron when you get right down to it. The scriptures call us *new creatures* when we become a part of the family of God—"old things are passed away, behold all things are new." Yet, we keep holding onto those "old things."

The battle is great. "Sin is crouching at the door," God told Cain, "desiring to have you, but you *must* master it" (my emphasis and the point of this devotional). The *must* puts the responsibility on us to not allow that sin to enter in and, if it does, to show it the door! 1 Corinthians 10:13 and Philippians 4:13 confirm that we can do it, with God's help. But we must be vigilant, always cleaning house.

As out-of-place is TP on a desk, despite have legitimacy in its use, so is the sin, even the *besetting* ones in the life of a believer attempting to be holy.

So at the very least, if you use TP for a facial orifice that is "running," put it in the desk drawer until you need it. If it's sin in your life ...expel that completely!

Lord, we all struggle with sin. Give us victory.

Dr. Dan Allen is a pastor, writer, conference speaker, radio commentator and Director of Pinebrook Bible Conference, East Stroudsburg.

Legacy at Rawlinsville Camp Meeting

"God also said to Moses, 'Say to the Israelites, "The Lord, the God of your fathers—the God of Abraham, the God of Isaac and the God of Jacob—has sent me to you." This is my name forever, the name by which I am to be remembered from generation to generation.'"
Exodus 3:15

Wayne Winters came to Rawlinsville Camp Meeting last year—for the 92nd time. And Charlie Eshleman, for the 88th time. Days after the 124th session closed on August 9, 2009, Charlie went home to Jesus.

As Wayne and Charlie worshiped in the Tabernacle in the Providence Township woods, some 50 preschoolers were overflowing their boardinghouse classroom at the top of the hill. Not to mention 75 grades K-4 kids, about 25 fifth and sixth graders and 135 teenagers in their own tabernacles.

RCM celebrates its 125th anniversary in 2010. The camp was established by the southern-end Methodist "circuits"—Mount Nebo, Boehms, Quarryville and Fulton—and held its first full session in 1886.

Yet a camp's spiritual heritage isn't measured in years, but in lives changed by Christ. Lives like Wayne's. And Charlie's.

At one service last summer, our spiritual director, the Rev. Mike Sigman, asked everyone who had accepted Jesus at RCM to stand. Everyone who had rededicated themselves to Christ at RCM. All who first heard the call to mission or ministry at camp.

People stood all over the tabernacle. I was one of them. I heard the Lord call me to ministry at RCM in 2003. My daughter came to Christ at RCM at age 8.

That's the spiritual heritage of Rawlinsville Camp Meeting. From generation to generation, we remember the name of the Lord. And He remembers us.

Dear Lord, thank you for generations who praise You and remember You at Rawlinsville Camp Meeting. May this be a place for future generations to find You. May Your name be glorified among us!

Helen Colwell Adams is a Sunday News reporter and pastor of Stehman Memorial United Methodist Church, Manor Township. She and husband Marv have a daughter, Abby.

June

Pray in Faith; Act in Certainty

"Call to Me, and I will answer you, and show you great and mighty things, which you do not know." *Jeremiah 33:3 (New King James Version)*

Back around 1930, a Jewish businessman was driving north on old Route 222, near Green Dragon market. Suddenly he got a feeling he was going to have an accident. He pulled to the side of the road, stopped and prayed: "Lord, I feel I'm going to have an accident. What do You want me to do?"

The Lord spoke to him: "Go into Ephrata, go to the Buick garage and ask for Sam."

Sam Erb, the mechanic at Eberly's knew just what to do. He went to his quiet place at the back of the garage and knelt down to pray. And the Lord told him, "Look at the front left spindle (axle)." Sam put the car up on the lift and saw that the axle was almost off the coupling—a simple thing to fix, back in those days.

The rest of the story is about what didn't happen. The axle didn't snap or fly loose along the road. There was no accident. No one got killed or hurt. But, on the other hand, there were no headlines in the *Ephrata Review* or the *New York Times* saying, "Man arrives safely home!"

The point of the story is that two men of different faiths called upon the same God, with full faith that He would answer. It happens every day, all over the world. Maybe if it did make the newspaper headlines or the TV evening news, a lot more people would try it.

Father, we know You are faithful to answer when we call on You in prayer. Make us Your "newspaper" and "TV news." Let us never forget to testify when You answer our prayers...so we can encourage a lot more people to try it.

Norman Saville, along with his wife, Joyce, worship at Hope of the Nations Christian Center in Reading, and work with Ken and Betty Eberly at Behold Your God Ministries.

Divine Destiny

"From one man he made every nation of men that they should inhabit the whole earth; and he determined the times he set for them and the exact places where they should live." Acts 17:26

According to this scripture my city, Lebanon; my state, Pennsylvania; and my country, America were divinely set here within its appointed time and place. I have to ask. For what reason? What spiritual streams entered this area from its inception? What are the foundations upon which my county and state were built? And do the answers to these questions shed light on God's plans and purposes for this region?

The First Nations tribe known as the Lenni Lenape or the Delaware anchored the land when the covenant-keeping Hebrews settled. Soon after the establishment of this Jewish community, reforming Lutherans, mission-minded Moravians and Presbyterian Scotch Irish arrived. Many other streams of spiritual influence flowed into the area.

William Penn, our state's founder, embraced this diversity and called for unity in purpose. Penn prophesied that this state would seed a nation through the power of God. Inscribed on the ceiling in the rotunda of our state capitol building, William Penn's foundational words reverberate into the present century:

> There may be room there for such a Holy Experiment
> For the nations want a precedent
> And my God will make it the Seed of a Nation.
> That an example may be set up to the Nations
> That we may do the thing that is truly wise and just.

Today there continue to be many spiritual streams flowing into the region. I see sectarian walls breaking down and ministries partnering together. Perhaps God is redirecting our little regional stream back to His source and into the larger concourse of God's plan for Pennsylvania—a river broadening into the sea of God's will for the nations. Penn's Holy Experiment is still alive.

I pray for a unity of purpose brought under Christ's headship through an outpouring of the Holy Spirit over this entire region.

Nancy Shean serves as a Youth for Christ board member and with regional prayer teams.

Surpassing Peace

"And the peace of God, which surpasses all comprehension shall guard your hearts and your minds in Christ Jesus." *Philippians 4:7*

In May 2008 I was diagnosed with keratoconus: cone-shaped corneas. I was legally blind. My left eye was the worst, at 20/150. The only medical cure was a cornea transplant. The surgery on my left eye was scheduled for June 24, 2008. I, and others, were praying and believing God for a miracle. As the surgery neared, I knew God was going to use it to deal with other issues in my life. Before surgery I put it all in God's hands. It did not matter what happened. God was in control.

When they took me to prepare me the day of the surgery, I had a peace I had never felt before. After the surgery, I heard the surgeon say, "Isn't this the best cornea transplant you've ever seen?" I knew it was because God had His hand in it. When I went for my postoperative visit the doctor had me read the eye chart. He was amazed at how far down the chart I could read, and told me that people can't read that far the day after surgery. At every checkup, the doctor was amazed at my progress. He called it luck or providence. I knew it was God and told him so.

After eight months my vision was 20/25. On March 10, 2009, I had surgery on my right eye. The doctor told me not to expect the same results, as he had done over five hundred surgeries and only a handful had turned out like mine. Six weeks after surgery my right eye was better than the left eye had been at six weeks. God didn't do the same with the right eye. God did better! I'm anxious to see what God is going to do next.

Thank you, Lord, for Your peace that surpasses all understanding. Thank you that You have control of everything, even when things seem impossible to us. And thank you for Your healing power. It's so wonderful to know that You care about the littlest things in our lives.

Julie Gehman attends Ephrata Community Church.

Baking Day

"Taste and see that the Lord is good...." *Psalm 34:8*

It was baking day. I usually try to conceal the food before the end of school when my ravenous teenager reappears. But much to my son's delight, the usual plan had failed. On this day muffins lined the counter, calling his name as he entered the kitchen. My name was the next being called. "Mom, can I have two muffins?" I agreed and made a mental note to get the food put away more quickly! Before he had time to swallow I was hearing, "Mom, could I have one more...please?" His compliments and pleading blue eyes wore me down and I consented.

"You're wonderful," he crooned, taking another bite. "I know," I replied, "and I would be wonderful even if I *didn't* give you that last muffin."

"Yes, you would," he agreed, "but I just wouldn't be thinking so at the moment!"

After a good laugh, and a mad dash to hide the rest of the food, the truth of my son's comment hit bottom. How often do I think that very way concerning God? When He gives me what I want, I'm singing His praises. But what if He delivers a "no" where I wanted a "yes"? Then what? He's still wonderful, but "I'm not thinking so at the moment." Reminds me of the saying, "God is good, *all* the time." It's true. He is. We just may not be thinking so at the moment.

God, You're wonderful. All the time! And I love You.

Jenny Gehman is a writer, retreat speaker, and mentor—that is, when she's not baking!

Trusting God Always

"Trust in the Lord with all thine heart..." *Proverbs 3:5*
(King James Version)

As a child, I was taught to trust in the Lord, to put my faith and hope in Him. Over the years, I continued to put my trust in Him; yet when life's circumstances brought challenges, I often found myself full of worry, anxiety, and sometimes even fear. I thought how could I experience all these emotions if I truly trusted God? The solution did not come easily, nor in a way I expected.

One day as I was listening to a preacher on TV, I heard a different way to exercise our faith. The preacher went on to say that we should envision the hand of God holding onto our hand, leading us through the tough times, the sad times and even through life's disappointments. Little did I know that this knowledge would soon be put to the test.

An annual physical necessitated the need for further testing. The results showed that I needed a follow-up test. During this lapse of time, anxiety and worry overshadowed me. How could I go through yet another test, fearing the results? It was then that the preacher's words came to mind. I began to envision Jesus reaching out His hand to me. I, in turn, offered up my hand. As He took my hand, in my mind's eye, I immediately began to feel at peace. It was as though I could hear Him say, "Do not be afraid, all will be well with you." Throughout the weeks that followed, I continued to envision His hand holding mine, assuring me that all was well.

When the day for the test arrived, I was so at peace that I found myself praying for another lady who was having the same test, and obviously experiencing anxiety. What did I learn? Trust in Him, He will never leave you.

Lord, thank you for teaching me how to put my trust in You. Amen.

Janet Young is the owner of Over The Teacup, Camp Hill.

A Mighty Work of God in a Small Town

"...Being confident of this, that he who began a good work in you will carry it on to completion until the day of Christ Jesus."
Philippians 1:6

In 1859 a group of Old Order Mennonites were meeting in homes in the area of Fairville (now Terre Hill), Lancaster County, Pennsylvania, for weekly prayer meetings. Since that practice was frowned upon at the time, the group separated themselves from the church and took the name Evangelical Mennonites. They met in a stable in the west end of town and said just as their Lord started His ministry in a stable so did they. This small group joined a group of other like minded Mennonites from the Lehigh Valley headed by William Gehman. They became Evangelical United Mennonites in 1881. After much prayer, they purchased a property across the street and constructed a new church for worship. Early in the church's history, they were part of a preaching circuit where they shared a pastor with churches in Fleetwood and Blanton of Berks County.

In 1947, they had grown enough to support their own pastor and they built a house for him and his family to live in. The church was very active in their community. Often children would come to the Berean Mennonite Brethren in Christ Sunday school and then go down the street to the other two churches in town. A group of believers in the church felt called to start a "daughter church," near Ephrata, in the mid-60s. That church grew into a strong voice for God in that community. Meanwhile, the church changed its name one more time and became the Bible Fellowship Church. The church still desires to reach the lost, in that small town, through many outreaches including a day camp that reaches over one hundred children per year. The church God started in a stable one hundred and fifty years ago continues to give Him glory for all that He has done.

Lord, thank you for the ministry of Berean BFC in Terre Hill. Please continue to use it to reach the lost in eastern Lancaster County.

Kevin Kirkpatrick is the current pastor of *that* small church in *that* small town.

Strengthened through Challenges

"Even though the fig trees have no blossoms, and there are no grapes on the vines; even though the olive crop fails, and the fields lie empty and barren; even though the flocks die in the fields, and the cattle barns are empty, yet I will rejoice in the Lord! I will be joyful in the God of my salvation!" *Habakkuk 3:17–18 (New Living Translation)*

A number of years ago, this was a verse I clung to for strength. It was a very difficult time financially for our family. We had two children and our third was due in six weeks. Then I had a physical condition that prevented me from driving for a year. Since I was in sales, I was unable to work. It was one of those times when you find out if you really believe God is your provider or you just say you do!

One story of how God provided happened when my wife, Lois, and I attended a previously scheduled Marriage Encounter Weekend. It was just a short time before Christmas and we were concerned how we were going to buy gifts for the children. We stopped by my in-laws on the way to the Marriage Encounter and they gave us cash for Christmas.

If you have been to a Marriage Encounter Weekend, you know there is no cost to go. All expenses are paid by someone else who attended previously. So, when Sunday came, they asked everyone to pray about how much to give to enable someone else to attend at a later date. We both prayed and believed God said, "Give the money you just received from your parents." This made no logical sense, but we gave all the money!

When we pulled into our driveway at home we noticed an envelope attached to the garage door. In the envelope was money—two and a half times the amount we had just given. This happened many years ago, but the lesson learned still impacts our attitude for giving.

Thank you, Lord, for Your faithfulness. Increase our obedience in all we do that we may do it as unto You.

Larry Hess and his wife, Lois, attend Lancaster County Bible Church where they serve as life group leaders.

Abide

"He that dwelleth in the secret place of the most High shall abide under the shadow of the Almighty." *Psalm 91:1 (King James Version)*

It was the strangest thing that I have ever encountered; I would talk and the word *abide* would come out of my mouth. It didn't make sense to what I was saying, I hadn't read any verses with it, and of course, it's not your everyday word; what was going on?

I was talking with one of my friends on the phone prior to getting ready for work and the same thing happened. She said that it must be God trying to tell me something. After getting off the phone, I felt led by the Spirit to read a devotion. I picked it up and couldn't believe my eyes—there it was, Psalm 91. Of all versions, it was King James, where the word *abide* is used.

Psalm 91 has played a big part in my life since I accepted Christ back in 2002. It has brought me through some very difficult times. I am currently experiencing some rough waters and have been overwhelmed with chaos in my life. I believe the Lord was bringing that word to my mind for a reason. A friend of mine explained that when we are trying to make decisions in our life and it's all about rational thinking—we are being led by self and not the Lord. I realized that this is what was causing my chaos. I had so much on my mind that I couldn't find peace with anything. So I decided to do what Psalms and the Lord was leading me to—abiding.

I haven't made any decisions concerning the things that have been overwhelming me, yet I am at complete rest. I know that I am protected as long as I dwell with Him at all times. He will tell me when I need to move forward with all the matters that need attention in my life.

Thank you Lord, for putting words in my mouth! Your Spirit leads me day and night, and I am so thankful that You love me that much. Help all of us to abide with You every day.

Eileen Christiansen is a leader with Celebrate Recovery, a Twelve-Step Christ-centered recovery group in West Sadsburyville.

Enough, Enough

"For he himself is our peace...." *Ephesians 2:14*

The word *enough* is funny. To me, *enough* can be used in two opposite ways. To *have enough* and want no more, and to *be enough* as if nothing else matters.

With the first *enough* we might say, "No thank you, I have enough..." or "Stop! That's enough." With the second *enough* we might say, "Jesus, You are enough for me—I need nothing else—nothing besides You matters."

In the book of Job we hear Job saying, "Naked I came from my Mother's womb, and naked I will depart. The Lord gave and the Lord has taken away; may the name of the Lord be praised."

Do you think Job said, "Enough Lord!" when the messenger came with the news that he had just lost everything: his oxen and donkeys, his servants, his sheep and more servants, his camels and the rest of his servants, then his sons and daughters. Or do you think Job was saying, "You are enough for me—You alone—without anything else."

If you're like me, when I sing songs of worship like, "You're all I need" and "All of You is more than enough for all of me. You satisfy me with Your love because all I have in You is more than enough," I want this to be true, but I've never had everything taken away from me like Job to really know God would be enough. If He started taking things away, I might be saying, "Stop! Enough."

For now, I'll sing the song and trust that He knows which "enough" is enough.

Father, I want You to be enough because I love You and if I had nothing else—You would be enough, but I also want to be honest. I love You and need You.

Lisa Dorr is a wife, mother, writer, editor and public speaker.

Obedience and Responsibility in Spite of Faith

"And he said, Take now thy son, thine only son Isaac, whom thou lovest...and offer him...for a burnt offering upon one of the mountains which I will tell thee of."

"And Isaac spake unto Abraham his father, and said, My father: and he said, Here am I, my son. And he said, Behold the fire and the wood: but where is the lamb for a burnt offering? And Abraham said, My son, God will provide himself a lamb for a burnt offering: so they went both of them together." *Genesis 22:2, 7–8 (King James Version)*

As Christians do we sometimes choose to "trust God in faith" so we can avoid facing a tough situation? How often do we hide behind faith, to avoid making and executing difficult decisions, instead of following Abraham's example of basing his faith on clear promises of God? Abraham could have easily rationalized his way out of this tough assignment. After all, didn't God promise through Isaac his offspring would be greater than the number of stars in the sky? Surely God didn't actually want him to sacrifice his son Isaac. But Abraham never wavered in obedience or faith. He didn't rationalize his way out of carrying out a difficult decision. He trusted God to fulfill His promise and provide a sacrifice. He acted in obedience to God's command trusting Him fully for the outcome.

In today's tough economic environment when realities of many situations are difficult to confront, it's easy to rationalize away the brutal facts. We may be tempted to compromise financial standards for borrowing or lending; we may be tempted to believe God has to fund a particular project or initiative to get His work done. So we plow ahead "in faith" without properly considering difficult alternatives. We anesthetize ourselves in "faith speak" not truly listening for God's voice with a commitment to obedience. When we are willing to surrender fully to God in obedience in spite of our faith, God will honor His promises just as He did for Abraham.

Lord, grant me the gift of discernment to see both the need for faith in You, and obedience to You and the wisdom and grace to do both.

Kent Martin is President/CEO of Signature Custom Cabinetry, Inc.

A Cookie Lesson

"...His pride led to his downfall." *2 Chronicles 26:16*

I am a firm believer that offering a smile or a kind word affirms the value of someone who is homeless. Even if it's short, a healthy interaction can make someone feel alive.

As I was walking down the sidewalk in front of the Water Street Mission the other day, I saw a homeless woman eating a huge chocolate chip cookie. She held a second cookie in her other hand. I smiled and commented on how delicious they looked. What happened next jolted me. With her belongings in bags at her feet and slung over her shoulder, the woman asked if I wanted her other cookie.

I tried to hide my surprise, but I'm afraid my gaping mouth may have given me away. Amidst my stammering, I was finally able to politely (I hope) decline. As I walked away, I was embarrassed at my degree of shock. I realized I had begun to fall into the trap of "us" and "them." I had begun to think that "us" were the kind folks who give, and "them" were the folks who take.

So yes, it's true; kind words can affirm someone's value and make them feel alive. I know because one sunny day, a homeless woman respected me enough as a human being to offer kind words. She helped crack open my pride and remind me that, no matter our circumstances, we all have something to give.

God, forgive me for my pride. Forgive me for my assumptions and judgments. Please help me to see the value You have placed in each human being, no matter his/her circumstances.

Maria Schaszberger is the Director of Communications at Water Street Ministries. She attends Mount Calvary Church in Elizabethtown.

Distractions

"For Demas has forsaken me, having loved this present world and has departed...." *2 Timothy 4:10 (New King James Version)*

We all deal with distractions. Distractions can take our attention away from our purpose. But not all distractions are bad or to be ignored. Jesus while on His way to places of ministry often met people in need and spent the time necessary to heal and deliver. Although temporarily distracted from getting to his intended destination, Jesus continued operating in the realm of His purpose for being here.

There are three types of distractions, which I classify as the good, the bad and the awful. The good fall within our realm of service to God. The awful are the deaths and sudden losses we experience, which demand our immediate attention. The bad are fleeting momentary digressions of thoughts leading us away from our purpose. We should remind ourselves that thoughts, continually dwelt on, influence lifestyle choices. The biblical personification of this is the man called Demas.

Demas, although mentioned only three times in scripture, characterizes an extremely clear picture of a man distracted. In Colossians 4:14 and Philemon 2:4 he is listed as a fellow laborer in ministry with the apostle Paul, Luke and Mark. To me, one of the saddest New Testament scriptures is 2 Timothy 4:10. "For Demas has forsaken me, having loved this present world and has departed...."

Demas became disloyal to Paul by being distracted. Demas' distractions pulled him away from the mission and the people with whom he had traveled.

The Demas example of the progression away from effectiveness began by his growing love for the things of this world, which, no doubt caused him to question, "what am I getting?" Then loyalty to Paul no longer mattered and he walked away!

Jesus, my desire is to continue living an effective Christian life. Equip me to pay proper attention to the good and awful distractions. Save me from falling prey to distractions which would direct my heart from serving others. Keep me from "walking away"!

Richard Armstrong serves as assistant director of The Worship Center Global Ministries in Lancaster.

Perfect Fit

"Give your entire attention to what God is doing right now, and don't get worked up about what may or may not happen tomorrow. God will help you deal with whatever hard things come up when the time comes." *Matthew 6:34 (The Message)*

We had graciously received a scholarship this year to go to *Joni and Friends* camp as a family. Excitedly we prepared; we had heard such good reports about it and marveled that we would be assigned a "buddy" for our son, someone who paid their own way and would spend five days as a short-term missionary to serve families with a member with a special need or disability.

My concern, however, was that it is a challenge for someone with autism to transition to new situations and relate to new people. We would be there from Monday through Friday, but how long would it take for Jordon to adjust to his "buddy"?

As we arrived, we were informed the leaders pray specifically over each match; then they told us about his buddy. He had flown in from Colorado, and though there are several camps throughout the United States, he had requested to come to the one in Pennsylvania. As we met Mark, we immediately recognized several features and mannerisms that reminded us of my nephew. Since the likeness was remarkable, our son quickly related to Mark as though he'd known him for years.

How like God, to prepare our son in such a loving way by bringing someone in from halfway across the country who reminded us of a beloved relative so that he could be "at peace" and bypass the initial adjustment time! In all my speculations, I had not imagined such a perfect fit!

Thank you, Lord, that while You hold all the stars in place, You also are intimately acquainted with the details of our lives. Thank You for Your love shown in such creative ways, and shown through Your body.

Cindy Riker is thrilled to be a wife, a mother of four children, eldercare companion, and a Bible study leader for Change of Pace.

Workplace Battles

"If you keep biting and devouring each other, watch out or you will be destroyed by each other." *Galatians 5:15*

When a coeditor told me that she had overheard a coworker talking with my supervisor, twisting some facts and taking credit for a project I had done, all the real and imagined wrongs about the offensive coworker came rushing to my mind. He was scheming and always trying to get ahead at the expense of the rest of the staff.

Fellow employees urged me to go to management with additional facts that would shed a negative light on the coworker if it were revealed. I hesitated. Part of me wanted to set the record straight, but another part knew that as Christians, we are often called to lay down our rights and let God be our defense.

A bit grudgingly, I prayed for strength to forgive my offending coworker. Although I mouthed the right words, I certainly didn't feel any better.

Later, a few of my coworkers presented more ammunition for me to take to the boss. As they talked, I realized how my failure to forgive my coworker was like a cancer and quickly spreading to other employees. I realized that our department could become a continuous battleground of biting and devouring each other with words.

I knew what I needed to do. So, I said, "I don't need to defend myself. If I do, it will pit us as opponents and not coworkers. I don't want that. I'm not going to make an issue of it."

Amazingly, when I said those words, all the anger and negative emotions I had felt drained away. I no longer cared who received credit for the project.

Ironically, that afternoon, a person from another department was talking with my supervisor and expressed appreciation for the work I had done on the project. In the process the details about the situation were revealed from an unexpected source, and I hadn't even needed to open my mouth.

Lord, let my workplace be a place where we are a team and not opponents destroying each other with words.

Lou Ann Good is retired, but this is an excerpt from her personal devotional journal written while she was employed as a newspaper editor.

Amazed by God's Love

"...He cares for you." *1 Peter 5:7*

I was having a sweet time of worship at church that Sunday. The weeping of the young lady nearby felt intrusive until her pain caused compassion to bloom in me. Suddenly, I clearly heard a voice speaking. "Tell her I said she didn't lose it."

I actually looked around for the speaker but quickly realized it was God speaking to my heart. I wondered what she might have lost but made no move to obey until I heard "The Voice" again. This time the tone was a stern reprimand, "I said for you to tell her that I said she didn't lose it."

His tone left *no* room for disobedience. I quickly tapped her and said, "This probably sounds crazy but God just told me to tell you that He said, 'You didn't lose it.' I don't know what that means but I had to tell you." She looked confused and without a word got up and left. Embarrassed, I thought, *maybe she didn't lose it, but I think I have!*

On Wednesday, she shared her testimony. That weekend was the first time her parents trusted her to stay home alone. On Friday, she went out with friends and forgot her purse at a restaurant. They quickly returned but it was *gone*—along with her wallet, money, driver's license and keys! The manager promised to call if it was found. A spare key got her into her home but who might have keys to her house and car?

The next day's return to the restaurant proved fruitless. The thought of disappointing her parents had her in tears. God's message sent her rushing to the restaurant one last time. The manager said it had not been found but appeased her and looked in the safe. There was the missing purse! She hadn't lost it! Her hurting heart was amazed by God's love for her.

Father, give me Your compassion for the hurts of those You place in my path today and the courage to speak Your words.

Esther Mayeski is a member of Christ Community Church, Camp Hill.

My Feet Had Almost Slipped

"Surely God is good to Israel, to those who are pure in heart. But as for me, my feet had almost slipped...." *Psalm 73:1–2*

It was my wife's birthday. The plans were that, later that day, the children and I would make a cake "for Mom." But that was not to be the case. For around 9 a.m., while trimming a grand old maple tree, I was knocked off my ladder by a falling branch. The branch, chain saw and I all fell nearly twenty feet. My son, who was helping, watched helplessly as I landed on the back of my head. My motionless body led him to believe I was dead. I remember nothing of what took place. He made certain that an ambulance was immediately on its way. Soon we learned that I had broken my back.

That summer, as I lay in a hospital bed, which was moved into our living room, I had plenty of time to think about that fall. I was alive and I wasn't paralyzed. My pain had been minimized by means of medications. Now, I had plenty of time to think, pray, read and memorize scripture. For years, Psalm 73 had been my favorite Psalm and for years I had thought, "I should memorize that Psalm." Finally, I did.

Psalm 73, a Psalm of Asaph, is a good reminder that while sometimes things seem unfair—the righteous struggling (or laid up in bed) while the ungodly apparently flourish—God is aware of everything. Asaph's "feet had almost slipped" in that, he had almost been beguiled into believing that it doesn't actually pay to live righteously. But in the end, he realizes God does honor those who live as He pleases. To question His hand over my life would have been a *real* fall.

Lord, save us from falling—truly falling—into that trap of deceit that questions the merits of an obedient life. In Jesus' name, Amen.

Doug Winne is senior pastor of the Lancaster Evangelical Free Church in Lititz.

Fly Away into Jesus' Arms

"If the Son therefore shall make you free, ye shall be free indeed."
John 8:36 (King James Version)

Richelle went to heaven leaving two young children, a loving dad and mom, and brother and his family and many who love her including this writer. With the love of the Lord I served Richelle for years as she resided in a nursing home seriously ill, partially paralyzed, having a brain tumor and other major health problems. But now in heaven, she is in perfect health serving the Lord she loved so much.

Richelle knew and lived the Word of God. Her dad and mom, and others routinely read her the Word and explained how it applied to life, especially hers. Richelle ministered to the nurses, those that cleaned her room, those that brought her clean clothes to her room and so many more. She was a Spirit-filled lady.

Her pastor ministered to her life and to all of us in the message celebrating her going to heaven. I served with honor by helping to minister at the gravesite. This is where the continuing story begins. As we walked down the hillside to the grave, a hawk had rested in the tree atop the hillside. This hawk has become friendly to the graveside of Richelle. It has been seen always close by, and some have said the hawk is considered a sign from God. It is now months later and the hawk still "protects." It often gets close to the humans at the gravesite.

Her dad wrote, "I stood outside and looked up into the blue cloud-filled sky, and my heart cried out, 'Fly away Richelle; the Son of God has set you free from the body wracked with sickness, pain and paralysis. Fly away my little girl; Jesus our risen Savior has set you free from the confines of your wheelchair that had you bound. Fly away my precious one; fly high into the heavens into the arms of our Lord who has set you free this earth filled with sin and death. Fly away, fly away, I love you. Dad will always love you, fly away.'"

Thank you, Lord, that there is no more pain or tears in heaven. We pray for those today who are seriously ill, that they may find comfort in Your care today.

Bob Burns serves as pastor, GT Pastoral Care Team in West Lawn and continues to serve as pastor and shepherd of Spiritual Growth Ministries, a guiding ministry to church leaders in areas of spiritual growth.

Gone Fishing

"Come, follow me," Jesus said, "and I will make you fishers of men." *Mark 1:17*

I was in the middle of a crowded fish market with three of my Arab friends looking for the perfect fish for our dinner. I soaked in the noise of the crowds and the overwhelming smell of fish. After going back and forth between the different sellers to barter for the best price, we picked out two nice-sized uncooked fish. We carried our selections to a nearby restaurant which was a BYOF (bring your own food!) kind of establishment. You bring the food, and they cook it for you. As the four of us sat around our little table, the waiters placed a piece of newspaper on our table and our cooked fish on top of the paper. We all began to grab pieces of meat with our hands and ate—no utensils or plates needed.

I was immensely enjoying the fish and the great Arabic speaking practice I was getting. Just then, one of my friends leaned over and asked me about my religion and what I believe. I took the opportunity to share about how much Jesus means to me and how He changed my life. As I was sharing my testimony they all began to lean in closer, wide-eyed and so eager to hear my story. This was the first time I was able to share at length in Arabic about my relationship with Jesus to my friends.

The best part of this story is that one of my friends is showing interest in hearing more, and we are regularly meeting to talk. He is showing interest to begin reading the Bible. I have a long way to go in my ability to speak the language and there is so much more that I wanted to be able to say, but words can hardly express the excitement of being able to share in a new language!

Lord, thank you for the opportunities You give us daily to be fishers of men. Help us to take advantage of these opportunities today.

Rob G, from DOVE Christian Fellowship Elizabethtown, is currently a social development worker in the Middle East.

Daddy

"…You received the Spirit of adoption by whom we cry out, 'Abba, Father.'" *Romans 8:15*

I will never forget the day I finally embraced God as *Abba*, Father. I was raised in a tradition where I only saw God as a Father who would "get" me if I did anything wrong. I didn't see Him as a "Daddy" who loved me as His child—His princess.

In my twenties I started hearing of this side of God's love. I was unfamiliar with this love but so longed for it. I would hear people calling God "Daddy" and thought it was dishonoring God. I kept telling myself, "If I call God Daddy, I will bring God down to my level." Then one day I had a revelation. I don't bring God down to my level by calling Him Daddy but Jesus raises me up to have this type of relationship with God. He is my Daddy. I remember journaling to my Daddy that day. As I kept writing "Daddy, Daddy, Daddy," freedom came to me and His love flowed into me in a new and fresh way.

God desires to be Daddy to all His children. As His children, He desires for each of us to embrace Him as Father (the one who corrects and disciplines) and Daddy (the one we can cuddle with, and just be loved by).

Precious Father God, thank you for adopting us into Your family— an adoption that gives us the awesome privilege of calling You Abba Father—Daddy. Your love is so complete, so pure. And You desire to pour Your love into each of Your children. May we be open vessels for Your love.

Kathy Nolt lives in Lititz with her husband Gary and is an administrative assistant for the Regional Church of Lancaster County.

I Have the Best Dad

"Because those who are led by the Spirit of God are sons of God. For you did not receive a spirit that makes you a slave again to fear, but you received the Spirit of sonship. And by him we cry, 'Abba, Father.' The Spirit himself testifies with our spirit that we are God's children." *Romans 8:14–16*

I love being a daddy, to have two beautiful children, to pick up and hold, squeeze them tightly and hear them laugh when I tickle them. There is nothing like hearing the joyful words "Daddy!" when I come home. I cherish my one-on-one times with them, talking about God, and His love for us or answering questions about the sky, trees or basic questions about life. I also love coming to the rescue when they are hurt, bandaging their boo boos, wiping tears and kissing it all better. Yes, being a daddy is a great life to live.

Once I became a dad, I only then started to realize God's love for me. In fact only the last couple of years have I really found God's "Daddy" love for me, and I thank my children for being vessels for God to teach me that love. He, too, loves to hear us call Him *Daddy,* to hear us laugh, and ask questions about life, and to call out to Him for rescue, when we are wounded.

So often I viewed God as a taskmaster demanding good performance in order to gain His favor and love. How silly that theory is because if I, a worldly father, never respond that way to my children, why on earth would the God who created me be that way? He is the perfect Father, desiring a deep, loving relationship with us His children. Think about that statement, "His children." That has an awesome ring to it. No matter what happens in this life, nothing can ever take away the fact that you are His child.

This Father's Day, don't just say, "I love you" to your earthly fathers, give love, thanks, and praise to your heavenly Father. Know that love, breathe it in and live in that love. Happy Father's Day, God, You are the ultimate example of what a daddy truly is.

Thank you for accepting me as Your child. I love You and I will put my trust, hurts, fears, joys and doubts in Your loving arms today.

Mike Wenger is executive director of TNT Youth Ministry.

Showers

"Rejoicing...and having my delight in the sons of men." *Proverbs 8:31 (New American Standard Bible)*

Ugh! It's raining. What a shame—our one day to go to Dutch Won-derland, I thought. My daughter had another thought, *Yay! Today's the day we get to go!*

After mentally debating "practicality vs. adventure," I decided we'd chance it that the weather would clear. She had a free ticket, but I'd still have to pay for mine.

We talked about it on the way. "I really didn't want to go today. However, my desire to have fun with you there is greater than my desire to stay home. In a family, what's important to you is important to me."

We stood in line to get my ticket. It had cleared some, but impending rain was still threatening. *At least we won't have to wait in line for the rides today. Not many people here.* A man caught my eye, came up to me, thrust a ticket into my hand and quickly left. Stunned, I looked at the ticket. Yes, it was valid, and it was free! I looked up to thank him but he had disappeared and was absolutely nowhere in sight.

Suddenly my spirit rose to the occasion and matched the words I had spoken in the car. Though it rained most of the afternoon, we enjoyed all the "water rides" and actually had a blast! I pictured God's smile on us. It is now a fond memory of ours—the day we splashed our way through the amusement park together. I am thankful for our benefactor—whether he was man or angel—for his act of kindness and generosity sparked my day from a "duty" to a "delight"!

Thank you, Lord, for the surprises You shower on us and that what is important to us is important to You! We also declare that what is important to You is important to us and we join in the adventure You have called us to.

Cindy Riker is thrilled to be a wife, a mother, elderly companion, and a Bible study leader.

Hard Reign

"Then I heard again what sounded like the shout of a vast crowd or the roar of mighty ocean waves or the crash of loud thunder: 'Praise the Lord! For the Lord our God, the Almighty, reigns.'"
Revelation 19:6

It was summer in the mountains of Mexico, and our ministry group anticipated a night of artistic worship and prayer within a huge cement building. The Holy Spirit began to lead the night and souls experienced Jesus. But then, a priest from a local church, seeped in idolatry, started opposing us over the town's loudspeakers. Another problem was swarms of mosquitoes. Despite these distractions, locals continued to gather. By mid-service however, our electric was turned off by the opposition, leaving it pitch black.

I thought the night was over, but I was wrong. More people joined us through the cover of darkness, overcoming their fear of social rejection. And without the light, there were fewer mosquitoes! Fear took a backseat and abandoned worship took center stage. I started to pray. "Rain down Lord! You Reign! Rain Up!"

Rain Up? Yes.

I continued, "I feel Your rain because Your Kingdom reigns! Your Kingdom is now, Your Kingdom is in me. Let Your sons and daughters 'rain up' Your Kingdom in worship as You reign down Your Kingdom!"

This revelation saturated my whole being. Within seconds, an eruption in worship escalated to everyone applauding God. With eyes closed, I heard the sound of heavy rain. Hands clapping within the building sounded like hard rain pounding on a metal roof. I opened my eyes because I thought it was raining! I heard God's hard reign through the worship and warfare. At times, God's Kingdom can seem so distant from my life. What Abba taught me was to remember that His Kingdom involves people. The work of His Kingdom involves you and me. In ways, it's a mystery. I experienced Abba's hard reign via the Holy Spirit and human beings.

Thank you, Abba Father!

Rachael Leah Kahler serves at Susquehanna Valley Pregnancy Services and attends Cornerstone Christian Fellowship.

Questions and Choices

"Lord, remind me how brief my time on earth will be. Remind me that my days are numbered—how fleeting my life is. You have made my life no longer than the width of my hand. My entire lifetime is just a moment to you; at best, each of us is but a breath." *Psalm 39:4–5 (New Living Translation)*

In this Psalm, David recognizes that his earthly days are numbered. Not one of us knows how long our lives, or the lives of those precious to us will be. Physical death is an unfortunate reality that we all eventually face. Admittedly I think about this more than the average person does, simply because in my profession (Critical Care Nursing) it's a subject that must be dealt with often: A young mother tries to cope with the sudden loss of her husband as her children hold tightly to her side. A husband of fifty years sobs unashamedly outside the room of his deceased wife as his contagious grief affects everyone within earshot. An unconscious grandfather found at home rushed to the hospital by ambulance who sadly never regains consciousness. Each individual in these sad situations had to face the death of a loved one and choose how to deal with the loss.

Ten years ago this reality hit home for me as my mother died suddenly, the victim of a violent crime. The fact that we live in a fallen world makes these sorts of situations a possibility, but I chose not to blame God. The words of my pastor helped me make sense of this tragedy: "God was in that room when Sheila died…BUT…God did not point that gun, and God did not pull that trigger, and God's heart broke when that bullet left the barrel." Many unbelievers were present for that funeral message. They were faced with the choice of blaming God or believing God's Word. Today you may be questioning God because of a very difficult situation, maybe the death of a person very close to you…will you ask God to reveal His Truth to you today?

Oh Lord our God, we call on You as King David did when his heart was overwhelmed with grief. You are our Rock. Will you lead us today by the light of Your Truth…the light that casts out darkness and brings revelation to our hearts and minds? In the midst of desperation and trouble we call on You alone for healing.

Ken Zeyak is a critical care RN in Lancaster. He and his wife Cindy have two sons.

The Special Bike Ride

"[God] is a rewarder of them that diligently seek him."
Hebrews 11:6 (King James Version)

The problem was so heavy on my mind that I could barely get through the day. I sat and stared at the wall for over an hour and still came up with no solution.

"Well, this isn't doing me any good," I shouted to my family. I'm going for a bike ride...a long one!" I had often gone on bike rides for enjoyment, but this time it was for prayer and meditation.

Secured to the back of my bike was a fruit drink with a straw taped to its side. The sweet beverage was to be a little pleasure that I could look forward to in case of another standstill with my problem.

After about three miles of riding with no peaceful answer, I decided to stop and have my drink. Unfortunately, it was gone! It had obviously fallen off my bike. I had become thirsty, but not so thirsty that I couldn't have gone straight home. Besides, the escapade with my bike had taken me in four different directions. How would I ever find it? None of that really mattered. I wanted that drink and was determined to find it.

Agitated, I backtracked well over a mile looking for that dumb box of juice until I finally found it. "Well," I admitted to myself, "at least I found it, but the straw is gone." Continuing a few more yards, I found the straw. As soon as I bent down to pick it up, a verse came to mind: God rewards His faithful who diligently seek Him. As I gulped down the juice, I voiced praise that all things do work together for good to those who love and seek the Lord.

Eventually, the problem was worked out as I continued to seek God's answer. I thanked Him for His answer to my prayer that day and also for the added exercise!

Dear Father, sometimes I'm so persistent in going around in circles with a problem that I can't see the answer which is right in front of me. Thank you for Your guidance no matter how You choose to show me.

Jan Dorward is a Messianic Jew who resides in Ephrata where she attends DOVE Christian Fellowship, Westgate. Jan loves to write and she presents Messianic Passovers.

McDonalds—6:00 am

"The King will reply, 'I tell you the truth, whatever you did for one of the least of these brothers of mine, you did for me.'" *Matthew 25:40*

My wife Dianne and I took a three-day vacation to Baltimore and the Inner Harbor. We got a great hotel deal, so we stayed downtown—handy to Camden Yards, where my beloved Detroit Tigers were playing the Orioles and handy to Inner Harbor, a great gathering of shops, museums and other interesting sights.

Typically Dianne and I are on two different sleep schedules. I am generally asleep by 10 p.m. and up around 4 a.m. She is asleep by midnight or later and up four to five hours after I have risen. I try to stay in hotels that have complimentary breakfasts so I can eat around 5:30 or 6:00 a.m. and then have a "second" breakfast around 9:00 or 9:30 a.m. when she is ready.

This hotel did not accommodate me. Fortunately, McDonalds is open at 6:00 a.m. But as in many major American cities, a tourist will share the streets with the homeless and other street people. When I arrived at McDonalds, a beggar persisted until he got my attention (I couldn't get in the door without talking to him.) "Sir, can I get a hot meal?" I said, "I'll bring something out."

Inside, one of the men in line said to me, "He does this every morning. He really can go to work but he prefers to beg for a meal." I have enough savvy to know that's always a possibility, but since I had given my word, I took him breakfast as I left to return to the hotel.

Was he taking advantage of me? Maybe. A friend once said that the only way not to be taken advantage of is to never help. As I gave him the meal, he said, "Sir you have done a good deed for the day."

Jesus, I know that a good deed—a cup of cold water in Your name— is always a good thing. So even if the street guy was taking advantage of me, You were pleased because I was simply following Your command and values.

Dr. Steve Dunn has been the lead pastor for the Church of God of Landisville since September 2001. He and Dianne have been married 37 years.

Throwing Up on Paper

"Trust in the Lord with all thine heart, and lean not unto thine own understanding. In all ways acknowledge Him, and He shall direct thy paths." *Proverbs 3:5–6 (King James Version)*

What am I going to write? I pondered this question as I prepared to give a testimony on the power of God and the wonderful things He has done in my life over the past year. I was supposed to speak for about fifteen to twenty minutes, yet I have a hard time stringing two sentences together! The previous year I had help from my friend. I'd pace, talking about my life and she translated that to paper. I gave her a list of my favorite scriptures and she interjected them into the testimony. It was a good collaboration—my thoughts, her words. I thought I could use that as a base and add to it, but it didn't work out. I got bogged down trying to shorten the original and I gave up after a week. So I tried a different track. I got in my car one morning, about four days before the testimony was to be given, turned off the radio, and turned on a voice recording device and spoke for an hour, as I drove to work. It sounded good but it was the hardest thing I've ever tried to transfer to paper.

Two days before the testimony I still had nothing on paper. My friend that had originally helped me was sympathetic and then asked the question, "Did you ask God to write the testimony?" *What in the world was she talking about,* I wondered. Of course the perplexed look on my face told the whole story. She went on to explain that it wasn't all about me, it was about God. What a novel idea—allowing God to work through me to write about Himself. Her favorite term for writing this way is called "throwing up on paper." You start with a blank sheet and ask God to give you the words to minister to His people. I asked God for help with His testimony and apologized in advance for assuming that it was about me. God gave me the words and the testimony went off without a hitch.

Thank you Lord for reminding me that it is all about You. Great is Your faithfulness to me even when I presume to try to do Your work. Let me be ever mindful of Your strength and power. Lord, I am weak and can't do a thing without You.

Carol Denson is a leader of Celebrate Recovery, a twelve-step Christ-centered program in Sadsburyville.

Lost and Found

"God is our refuge and strength, an ever-present help in trouble."
Psalm 46:1

My husband and I took a trip to Prince Edward Island, Nova Scotia, and Maine to celebrate our tenth wedding anniversary. We visited Fossil Cliff in Nova Scotia and walked down a set of wooden steps to the ocean. Tourists were forbidden to go to the right of the steps because of the rapid incoming tide.

We walked on the stony beach and took a few photos. We then went back up the steps to resume our journey, but on arrival at our van, we realized we did not have our keys. I searched my pockets and three fanny pack zippers several times. My husband searched his pockets to no avail. Being about 1,800 miles from home, what were we going to do? We had no spare key with us.

I began to pray, "Lord, please help us find our keys." We walked to the rear of the van and a visitor center employee walking toward us asked if we were looking for something. "Our keys," we replied.

Holding up a set of keys, he asked, "Would these be yours?"

I responded with upraised arms, "Thank you Jesus!" The keys were found by a man down on the fossil shore where the tide was coming in. Soon they could have been washed out to sea! God intervened. We worship and serve a God of miracles even in the midst of daily life events.

Dear God, You are an awesome God. Thank you for caring for us in the daily situations of our lives. Thank you that no matter what we face, You are with us. Amen.

Ginny Hoover is the wife of pastor Glenn Hoover and attends Carpenter Community Church.

Ultimately Perfect Answer

"...Your Father knows exactly what you need even before you ask him!" *Matthew 6:8 (New Living Translation)*

Have you ever thought it was your duty to be God's co-manager? Time after time, God lovingly affirms His Sovereignty to me.

Steps were set in motion for my husband, Jay, to have elective surgery. Achieving long-term success after surgery required implementing a major life-style change. I began to pray for a mentor, a Christian brother to walk beside Jay providing encouragement and accountability. Admittedly, I was also considering who I might prompt to fulfill this mentoring role. As Jay's surgery was fast approaching, I became discouraged as it appeared my prayer had not been answered. And, I could think of no one to fulfill this role.

Then it happened...a note arrived from a recently reconnected friend affirming Jay's decision for surgery and brimming with words of support. As Jay read, the last sentence was electrifying. His friend was scheduled for the same surgery one week prior to his!

Wow, how could I ever have pre-orchestrated that? My human mind certainly could not have conceived asking God to provide Jay with a friend having the same surgery one week apart. Only God foresaw the need of both men, providing perfectly, blessing them immeasurably.

Surmountable or trivial, our needs and troubled hearts can be fully entrusted to God. With our eyes intently focused on Him, pray in faith and know that God's timing and answer is always perfect.

Heavenly Father, I am in awe and humbled by how much You love me. Forgive me when I try to be Your co-manager. You continually exceed my wildest expectations, reminding me that You are God, the one in charge.

Nan Schock serves as a Stephen Minister at Manor Church, Lancaster.

Our Protector and Advocate

"...Let us run with endurance the race that is set before us."
Hebrews 12:1

"Did you slip and fall that you have those scars on your face and your arm?" the man asked frankly.

No, he may not have been very gracious with his question, but Bekah chose this opportunity to testify to God's hand in her auto accident. Waitressing at a local tea house, Bekah related her miraculous recovery to this customer. A nearby table of women also eavesdropped, and then Bekah returned to the kitchen.

A minute later another waitress, extremely upset, approached Bekah. She said the table of ladies had remarked, "So that's why that side of her face is so ugly."

Mary also dealt with an insensitive person following her brother Lazarus' traumatic death and resurrection. She sensed something "going down" with Jesus (He was soon going to the cross), and she anointed His feet with her costly perfume.

Judas, to cover up his own thievery, rebuked her action in front of the disciples. Judas didn't care that he had crushed Mary's spirit. He was focused on making himself look saintly. But Jesus quickly defended and protected Mary. "Let her alone," He told Judas. My daughter also has this same "white knight in shining armor" who comes to her rescue when her dad or I cannot be by her side.

We have the responsibility of "sitting at Jesus' feet," as did Mary. Notice it was her and not the disciples that discerned "Jesus' hour." Spending time in the presence of Jesus will give us the perseverance to finish the race well. Then when suffering comes, when insensitivity strikes, we won't quit. With our Protector and Advocate, we'll finish the race strong, together.

Dear Lord, help us to see beyond others' hurtful remarks to their own needs. Thank you for Your protection and Your defense. Help us to keep on keeping on even when hurdles rise on the horizon. Help us to maintain our focus on the finish line.

Tamalyn Jo Heim and her husband, Bob, are thankful for the Lord's protection upon their growing family of six adult children and one grandson.

An Ancient Historic Church

"For I am not ashamed of the gospel of Christ, for it is the power of God to salvation for everyone who believes...and also for the Greek."
Romans 1:16 (New King James)

Greek immigrants established the Annunciation Greek Orthodox Church in 1921. It has grown to a parish of 1,390 baptized individuals who adhere to the ancient and historic Orthodox Christian faith, with a continuous two thousand years' history. The Apostle Paul preached the gospel in Athens, Corinth, Thessalonica, Philippi, and Crete. People of Greek extraction have a continuous history of Orthodox Christianity since then. Doctrinally, Annunciation Church abides by the Nicene Creed, proclaims Jesus Christ as Lord, God and Savior and worships the Holy Trinity. The parish extols marriage and family, instills a Christian worldview, and provides opportunities for spiritual, social, educational and cultural growth. Orthodox Christian worship services on Sundays and feast days uphold the Divine Liturgy at the center.

Annunciation Church supports a vigorous social action ministry. It has chaired the Annual CROP HUNGER WALK in Lancaster for Church World Service for thirty-seven years, raising over four million dollars to reduce world hunger. For fifty years it has supported the outreach programs of the Lancaster County Council of Churches. Over 100 parishioners have served in long-term and short term Orthodox missions.

A popular Greek Food Bazaar at Annunciation Church draws 10,000 people annually on the first weekend of November. Parishioners of all ages participate to introduce the Orthodox Christian faith and segments of Greek-American culture to the public. Presently Orthodox Christians from twenty-five different ethnic groups worship at Annunciation Church, including people from Greece, America, Albania, Eritrea, Ethiopia, Egypt, Serbia, Bosnia, Korea, Vietnam, Russia, Croatia, Romania, Bulgaria, Poland, the Ukraine, Lebanon, among others.

Since the first century You have called people to faith, compassion, and service among all ethnic groups. Empower the church today to reach every ethnic group in our region. In the name of the Father, Son, and Holy Spirit. Amen.

Alexander Veronis, semi-retired, has served Annunciation Church for 48 years, 43 as pastor.

Gordonville, Lancaster County
Photo by Christina Riker

July

Still Speaking

"By faith Abel offered God a better sacrifice than Cain did. By faith he was commended as a righteous man, when God spoke well of his offerings. And by faith he still speaks, even though he is dead."
Hebrews 11:4

In the late nineteenth century, many in Lancaster County experienced a spiritual awakening. Out of that renewal, new ministries and congregations were born. Mennonites opened an industrial mission to improve the lives of people living on the Welsh Mountain and to offer them hope in Jesus Christ.

In 1913, twenty-two-year-old Arthur Moyer was appointed superintendent of the Welsh Mountain Mission. Under Arthur's leadership, a school was established on the Welsh Mountain, and Arthur himself served as a teacher in that school.

On January 24, 1924, Arthur came upon a thief stealing corn from the mission's corncrib. The surprised thief opened fire with a pistol before fleeing the scene. A shocked community gathered around the mortally wounded superintendent. In his pain, Arthur passionately called upon the unsaved by name, pleading with him to give his heart to the Lord. As he was lifted into a car, he said his farewells to those present. He was taken to the hospital in Lancaster.

Treatment at the hospital brought some relief, but Arthur continued to fail physically. Like the Lord Jesus and like Stephen, he prayed for the one who had harmed him. He also lifted his voice in praise and song. About twenty-four hours after arriving in the hospital, Arthur sang that great hymn "Rock of Ages," and then his soul passed into eternity. At the funeral service held at the Groffdale Mennonite Church, the scripture text was Hebrews 11:4 "By faith he still speaks, even though he is dead."(Based on an account by Noah H. Mack in the February 24, 1924 issue of the *Gospel Herald.*)

Lord, open my heart to be not only willing to die for You but also to live for You and to speak for You in the opportunities that You give to me today.

J. Carl Sensenig is a pastor of the Red Run Mennonite Church, bishop of the Bowmansville-Reading District of the Lancaster Mennonite Conference, and a middle school teacher at Gehmans Mennonite School.

Guided Along Unfamiliar Paths

"I will lead the blind by ways they have not known, along unfamiliar paths I will guide them; I will turn the darkness into light before them and make the rough places smooth. These are the things I will do; I will not forsake them." *Isaiah 42:16*

In July 2008 our 11-year-old son, Seth, was diagnosed with a cancerous brain tumor. Our lives took a twisting turn. Within six days of the diagnosis, Seth had brain surgery at Johns Hopkins Hospital in Baltimore, Maryland.

Although we were blessed to have one of the best pediatric brain surgeons in the world, it was extremely scary as we waited through the delicate surgery. As the hours crept by, I understood how Abraham may have felt when he laid his son on the sacrificial altar (Genesis 22) and gave all control to God.

I completely surrendered my son to God in the hospital corridor and He brought me peace that was beyond my comprehension. I realized that our son might not make it through the brain surgery alive, but knowing that God was still God and He would get me through everything I had to face was so comforting.

Thankfully Seth did make it through the surgery, but that was only the first part of the journey that continues to take us in directions over which we have no control. Seth had to undergo radiation and continues with long-term chemotherapy. He faces years of follow-up testing.

Sometimes our lives take a huge turn in directions that we do not want to go and over which we have no control. But God promises to lead and guide us along paths we do not know and He promises never to forsake us. That is the source of my peace.

Dear Father, I pray that You give us Your strength to make it through each day. Fill our hearts with peace beyond any human comprehension. May we hold onto Your promises and know that You are a faithful God even in our hard times.

Marie Good and her husband Todd have four children and are youth group leaders at DOVE-Newport.

Meet Him at the Cross

"And through him God reconciled everything to himself. He made peace with everything in heaven and on earth by means of Christ's blood on the cross." *Colossians 1:20 (New Living Translation)*

Jesus died on the cross because we were created to be His sons and daughters. When we don't feel like we belong anywhere or to anyone we can look to the cross and know He died so we may *belong* to Him. It was for *me and you* He died. What a revelation!

He died so we may be *reconciled* to Him—to be in fellowship with Him, to be identified with Him, to be His! He died to get sin out of the way. He died so we may have life. He created us in His image for the purpose of belonging to Him. He loved us so much He died to reconcile us back to Him. His shed blood washed my sins—sins which separated me from my Father.

Nothing we do can save us; it has already been done at the cross. Jesus came to redeem man! God doesn't come to us because we change; He comes to change us.

Walking with Christ leads us to freedom through the Spirit-filled life. The Holy Spirit is *all* that is able to transform lives, and the willingness to receive all the Holy Spirit wants to do.

Thank you, Lord Jesus, for Your love with Your outstretched arms to call all Your children back to You. May hearts be softened to hear Your voice speaking and to know You personally. Amen.

Julie Carroll Alexander is a missions director at Ephrata Church of the Nazarene.

Scattering Seeds of Time

"There is one who scatters, yet increases more...." *Proverbs 11:24*
(New King James version)

One of my favorite July 4th memories was when my husband, my son and I visited a local nursing home to hand out flags to the residents.

We were enjoying all of their smiles and handshakes, as we all had our patriotic décor on. We handed out the small flags and attached them to their wheelchairs. Little did we know that these small items, with their stars and stripes, would invade the doors that were chosen to be locked, regarding the memories of war.

We were so privileged to have met four WWII vets: Charlie #1, a decorated marine who was a gunner in a tank; Charlie #2, a pilot in the Air Force; Charlie #3, a Navy man who lived on a submarine for two and a half years; and then there was Harold, who was the only one in his unit to survive the beaches of Normandy.

We all sat around the table listening to their amazing stories that stirred our souls, with their memories of laughter and tears. It lasted over an hour, but it felt more like a military shower. As we said our goodbyes, a nurse came up to me and told me that Charlie #3 never talks and had never even mentioned anything about the war. It was the first time he smiled and opened up.

It hit me that all they really wanted was our time and that this is what we can give to each other and especially to this great generation—our gift of time and thanking them for their services to our country.

So if you see one of our service men or women, take the time to thank them and let your seeds of kindness be scattered.

Thank you, Lord, for the freedoms we enjoy today because of those who served.

Lisa M. Garvey is active in the Women's Ministry and Prayer Ministry at Hosanna Christian Fellowship in Lititz.

No Test Required

"Study to show thyself approved unto God, a workman that needeth not to be ashamed, rightly dividing the Word of God." *2 Timothy 2:15 (King James Version)*

My citizenship might be in question...at least if one considers the score I got on an American Civic Literacy Test.

The test, by the non-profit, non-partisan educational organization, Intercollegiate Studies Institute, appeared in a local paper. I sharpened my pencil feeling pretty good about taking this test. I expected to ace it. Hey, I'm a good citizen. I vote. I pay my taxes without complaining...well, I pay them. I keep myself educated as to the issues. I've written and called politicians. I complain about the government in letters-to-the-editors. I've been to political rallies, visited all three branches of government and even touched the Liberty Bell.

However, out of thirty-three questions, I got almost 20% wrong. Granted some of the questions were purposely tricky. I hesitate to cite any for fear that you might say, "He didn't know that?" But half of the questions I got wrong had to do with financial things (taxes, fiscal policy, profit).

I'm glad we're not given periodic tests to see if we should remain a citizen. Otherwise, we might be escorted to the closest border.

An even greater thought is that we do not have to take a biblical-knowledge test to see if we can remain a Christian. I'm pretty sure I'd score higher on this test unless it asked me to list the entire genealogy from Adam to David or put in order each victory the Israelites had under Joshua. I would hate to have my eternal security based on such things. Fortunately, the test was taken only once, on an old, rugged cross. And the test taker, Jesus, aced it for all time! Because of what He did, by dying and bearing our sin, He passed the test purchasing for us the gift of eternal life—for all those who believe.

That doesn't mean we should stop studying the Bible. We are exhorted to study hard so that we are approved.

Lord, thanks, first for taking the test for me. Now help me to be faithful to You as I study Your Word.

Dr. Dan Allen is a pastor, writer, conference speaker, radio commentator and Director of Pinebrook Bible Conference, East Stroudsburg.

Canoe Lesson

"For whoever exalts himself will be humbled, and whoever humbles himself will be exalted." *Matthew 23:12*

I was a true canoe veteran, having floated and canoed various rivers and streams for scores of miles often with a very weighted canoe. Never experiencing a tip really pronounced and trumpeted my river experience and seaworthiness. Safety, staying dry and caring for the valued gear was of the utmost importance. I had been there; done that.

My son was embarking on his first overnight waterfowl hunt with me on the Susquehanna River. I had prepped him for all the risks and really stressed the importance of weighted balance.

Why then, at 5:00 a.m. on this very cool October morning, did I find myself going head first into the cold, dark waters within seconds upon beginning this two-day voyage? It was like a movie in slow motion. I could not push the pause button as our weighted canoe began a slow starboard roll dumping me, and my pride out of the canoe. My son's incredulous stare from his front seat, while warm and dry, was priceless. I, gasping for air, wallowed toward shore with my waders filled to the brim. I knew the next two days were going to be wet and cold with little hope of drying out.

My pride and confidence went for a needed swim that morning. Pride can have a powerful stench to the nostrils of God. A bath may become necessary to wash us and awaken us. In this case, it accomplished both. My cold feet were a constant reminder of how quickly things correct themselves when out of balance. Pride was the original sin that cast Lucifer from heaven. Pride stands in the way of everything of who Jesus was and is. It will trip us up or tip us out.

Jesus, help me to express true humility in becoming like a child in Your eyes in all that I do today.

Brian E. Martin serves as lead pastor at Weaverland Mennonite Church in East Earl. He and his wife Shirley have two married and two young adult children, and one grandchild.

Pray it Forward

"The Lord is nigh unto them that are of a broken heart, and saveth such as be of a contrite spirit." *Psalm 34:18 (King James Version)*

Have you been praying for someone for a long time and it just seems to get worse? Well, I have great news, your prayers are working more than you'll ever know. I can tell you for sure because I'm proof of answered prayer.

I was a youth pastor for many years until I was hurt by a leader of the church. I quit and within months was drinking and drugging, trying to numb the pain. I was so hurt that when the kids from the youth department came to my house to beg me to come back, I said, "No way!"

As you can well imagine, my life spiraled downward fast! I had so much bitterness inside me. But God, in His infinite wisdom and great love for me, wouldn't let me stay that way. The worse I got, the more my mom prayed. One winter Sunday she left for church and I just broke down inside. I fell to my knees at her fireplace hearth and begged God to forgive me and to please take the filthy habits out of my life.

It wasn't easy to quit some of the habits I had. But God was faithful to help me day by day, sometimes minute by minute. So I encourage you to give all your hurt and pain to God and to never quit praying for those you love.

Father God, thank you so much for answered prayers.

Alton Alexander attends Ephrata Church of the Nazarene.

When Science Isn't Enough

"Jesus looked at them intently and said, 'Humanly speaking, it is impossible. But with God everything is possible.'" *Matthew 19:26* (*New Living Translation*)

Pregnant with her first child, Amy was feeling much joyful anticipation. This baby was wanted, hoped for, and planned. Then, seventeen weeks into her pregnancy in December 2002, her life as she knew it came to an abrupt halt. She was diagnosed with Acute Lymphocytic Leukemia and told she would probably lose the baby. A port was implanted for chemotherapy, an ultrasound was done to get a baseline on the baby's growth, and treatment began. In recalling this time Amy stated: "Everyone around me was freaking out. I felt this strange peace, this strange comfort. God was telling me that everything was going to be okay. I knew my baby was wrapped in a protective bubble."

While pregnant, Amy received countless dosages of chemotherapy, twelve shots of chemotherapy into her spinal column, and approximately fifty blood and platelet transfusions. In April 2003, at thirty-four weeks pregnant, Amy gave birth to a 4-pound, 10-ounce plump, pink baby girl, and her cancer treatment then continued for the next two years.

In April 2007, Amy and her husband decided to try to have a second child. Doctors told them to be prepared to be unable to conceive. In July 2007 they found out they were pregnant and in August found out that her womb held "three round, perfect egg sacks." Doctors were cautiously optimistic that all three babies would survive. They did survive, however, and in February '08 Amy gave birth to three healthy babies.

At the time of this writing, Amy is cancer-free and all four of her children are healthy, happy, and growing in God.

God, whenever we struggle with any kind of health problem, please help us to remember who the true Healer is. It is You who give health professionals their healing hands.

Mary Detweiler leads the Celebrate Recovery ministry at Manheim Brethren in Christ Church and is the author of *When Therapy Isn't Enough*.

Empty Lap, but Full Heart

"I came that they may have life, and have it abundantly." *John 10:10 (New American Standard Bible)*

As I stroked the kitten's fur, my heart ached as the tears flowed. Soon my lap would be empty again. My friend Linda had recently given me this stray kitten. Comical and loving, he was a welcome gift to our home. We never had the privilege of having children, so our pets are very special. In 2008 our "nest" became empty due to the death of our beloved Daffodil, a sweet Yellow Lab. Now we were hopeful of being "parents" again. Unfortunately, my husband had an allergic reaction to Tigger, so it became obvious that we needed to return him. Grief flooded my soul. However, I could *not* deny the indisputable fact that my heart is full because of God's love for me in Christ Jesus my Lord.

The blessings that I have received from my heavenly Father are too numerous to count. The foremost is the gift of my Savior, providing the forgiveness of all my sins, and adoption into God's family. Yet, as a beloved child of God, I enjoy the riches of His grace every day. One that is especially dear to me is His tender shepherding of my soul.

Because I am prone to depression and anxiety, life is a real struggle for me. The year 2008 was particularly bleak, primarily due to Daffodil's death, extended unemployment, and health issues. But my faithful Shepherd was always on duty. I recently came across a journal entry dated 06/23/08 which reminded me of God's loving-kindness. I was nervously getting ready for a job interview. I knocked over a metal sailboat decoration etched with the ending of the poem "Footprints" which caused the adjacent audio Easter card to sing "Halleluiah!" What a meaningful reminder of God's providential care, especially when my heart is troubled or hurting.

Abba Father, thank you for the new song that You gave to me simply because You chose to love me.

Susan Marie Davis is employed by Goodwill and is a member with her husband, Karl, at Calvary Church in Lancaster.

Self-Deception

"And why do you look at the speck in your brother's eye, but do not consider the plank in your own eye? Or how can you say to your brother, 'Let me remove the speck from your eye'; and look, a plank is in your own eye?" *Matthew 7:3–4 (New King James Version)*

In the short expanse of my lifetime, all 54 years, I have come to the realization that most problems that people grapple with regarding other people are relational in nature. *If only I can get them to see things my way, life would be so much less cumbersome.*

I recently read a book entitled *Leadership and Self Deception* written by the Arbinger Institute. Here's an example posed in the book: Think about a person from your work experience who's a big problem. Does the person you're thinking of believe that he's a problem like you believe he's a problem? Most likely he doesn't and will resist the idea that he has a problem. That is self-deception, or what we often call "blind spots." All of us have blind spots. However, in order for me to see my blind spots I have to trust someone else who can see the things that I cannot see.

Many people go through life struggling with situations and problems that keep reoccurring because of self-deception in their lives. They cannot see themselves as others see them. I read one time that women are never satisfied with the way they look physically but men think they look good all the time regardless of the way they look! In other words, men can be self-deceived into thinking that even though they are 25 pounds overweight, they carry it well!

I don't like being deceived. However, in order to not walk in self-deception I need to trust that those around me can see things that I cannot see. Then I need to receive their input without trying to defend myself. That takes real trust. Make it easy for those whom you trust to speak into your life. Ask them, "What are some blind areas in my life? What do you see that I cannot see?" It may be difficult and maybe even a little scary, but it is a great step in coming out of self-deception.

Lord, help each of us to trust our brothers and sisters to help us see those blind spots we may have.

Ron Myer serves as assistant international director of DOVE Christian Fellowship International.

God's Favor

"For whoever finds me [Wisdom] finds life and draws forth and obtains favor from the Lord." *Proverbs 8:35 (Amplified)*

For over twenty years we had prayed for a vacation house at the New Jersey shore. The Lord finally provided for us to buy a place in Stone Harbor, New Jersey. We were so grateful for the favor of God in answer to our prayers.

Three years later 9/11 occurred and my husband lost all his business as a result and was not able to find any work at all for over a year.

A spiritual leader, whom I have listened to many times, said that 2002 was going to be a year of God's extreme, uncommon, unparalleled, unprecedented favor—if we claimed it. So I started claiming God's extreme favor out loud every day, as a statement of faith.

However, by 2002 we were getting deep in debt, so it seemed logical to sell our vacation house to get out of debt. Every week or so, we would ask the Lord if we should sell it, and we would hear "no." Then one day in September I heard "yes." We called a realtor at the shore and arranged to go there to sign papers to list the house for sale. When we arrived there two days later, to put the house up for sale, the realtor had a buyer lined up with an offer to buy our house for the asking price. It never got listed and was sold in an hour. We were shocked! We were so awed at God's favor and how He worked.

We were able to pay off all our big debts with the profit—whew! As I look back at the years of having a longtime desire to buy a house at the shore, I realize the desire was from God, because He knew what the future held for us. We praise God for the four years we did have the beach house, that wound up rescuing us from debt through God's favor.

Lord, You know our needs long before we do. Thank you for Your favor on our lives.

Betty Cowley is a member of Ephrata Community Church, Altar Ministry Team; member, HarvestNet Ministries; and vice president, Papa's New Generals (Outreach to Papua New Guinea).

Our Differences Were Glaring

"Our firm decision is to work from this focused center: One man died for everyone. That puts everyone in the same boat." *2 Corinthians 5:14 (The Message)*

I still think about her. She was someone I would have crossed the street, or changed direction, to avoid. She was high, hard, and hazardous. But the Lord gave me His love for her, and gave her a heart to trust me. I could no more have not loved her than I could have not loved Him. His love was all I had to rely on, for I was on ground that I had never walked on before. Even though she said she trusted no one, she trusted me but was not sure why. The hurt and anger spewed forth but I always felt safe with her.

We talked a lot about her faith. She had backslidden and could not believe that God would forgive her. She often reminded me of how God loved me and forgave me, but then she saw me as someone better than herself.

The Lord had given her to me to love to life. She was beautiful to me. I did not see her failures; I heard her heart's cries. I did not see her weakness apart from His strength. I saw life in her when she saw only death. She wanted to get right with God and tried everything she knew to do to get there, then she would start believing the lies again.

I often wondered why God chose me to be in her life. I felt so helpless at times. I held her like a child. I would feel her go limp and sleep when she had not been sleeping for days on end. It was during one of these times when she felt safe and loved that she recommitted her life to her heavenly Father.

With all my heart, I know she is with her Father Creator. I know, because her love is still alive in me. My heart senses that love, a love that knows no boundaries now.

Creator God and Savior, thank You for Your love. Thank you for not giving up on us, even when we give up on ourselves. May Your love so fill us that whomever You place in our lives may be drawn to it and be loved to life in Jesus.

Carol Sanchez is a follower of Jesus, loving Him and others and serving those He loves, as He appoints.

My Message

"…If someone asks about your Christian hope, always be ready to explain it." *1 Peter 3:15 (New Living Translation)*

It's been about seven years since the day I first walked into a program called Celebrate Recovery. The program is a 12-step Christ-centered recovery program that does not only deal with drugs or alcohol but all addictions.

As I worked through the steps the program required, I realized a lot about myself, especially how deep in denial I was about my identity. Growing up I suffered with the same peer pressure that most kids do, but I was one who would give into them. I abused drugs and alcohol, and for the most part followed the crowd to whatever happened to be "in" at the time. I was involved in a lot of abusive relationships that I thought were love.

For a long time I believed that my past defined who I was and I continued to walk in that way. After accepting Christ as my Savior, I understood that my past only "influenced" who I was and that Christ "defined" me.

A couple of years into the program, God began preparing me for leadership. He was going to do, as we say in Celebrate Recovery, turn my mess into my message. All the things that I had been involved in, suffered through and abused, God is now using to help others.

Who would have ever thought God could do that? I know I didn't. If you would have told me years ago that I would be doing something like this, I would have called you crazy. I love sharing my testimony now, whereas before I only carried shame and guilt. My hope now is in the healing power of Jesus Christ and the message He is creating for me to help others in their struggles. Jesus is in the business of healing. How can He help you today?

Thank You, Jesus, for Your grace. You met me where I was and it had nothing to do with me or my abilities. You have set me free and have given me the privilege to watch You set others free.

Eileen Christiansen is a leader of Celebrate Recovery in West Sadsburyville.

Wounded Healer

"...By His wounds we are healed...." *Isaiah 53:5*

Due to my fair complexion I scar easily. I don't remember some of the wounds that caused scarring. Others are quite noticeable and memorable like the fall on the blacktopped playground when I was in second grade or the C-section I had   years ago.

This past year I celebrated my twentieth year of following hard after God. Through these years I experienced much healing and growth. I felt for my twentieth "re-birthday" I should be scar free and I began despising my wounds, my brokenness and my invisible scars.

The more I identified with Christ, the less I wanted to identify with the part of me that has been abandoned, rejected, abused, traumatized, betrayed and hurt by people whom I loved and believed that I could trust. As much as I was despising the wounds that I have suffered, I despised even more what I considered weak in myself, my brokenness and continued need for healing.

I gave up denying or excusing the pain. I felt it. I cried. As I pressed in to Jesus, His grace was sufficient and His power made perfect in my weakness. I pressed my fresh wounds and my old wounds into Him. I embraced what was left behind. Scars on my soul.

Jesus poured compassion on me and I released my contempt. Jesus doesn't expect me to be without scars. After all, when He came back to His disciples after His death didn't He prove who He was by His scars?

Scar tissue is stronger than original tissue—no more denying or despising the part of me that has been wounded. My brokenness is a strength that gives me compassion to reach out to the hurting with an authentic experience of the healing power of Jesus. And that is why I have rededicated myself to being a wounded healer, just like Jesus.

Wounded Healer, thank you for Your grace, love, mercy, compassion and healing power. Help me to faithfully walk beside the broken and wounded with Your love and compassion.

Sharon Blantz serves as a regional pastor at The Worship Center.

Light

"This is the message which we have heard from Him and declare to you, that God is light and in Him is no darkness at all." *I John 1:5 (New King James Version)*

One of my e-mail messages contained the quip: "To conserve energy due to the financial downturn, the light at the end of the tunnel has been turned off."

Many times we hear people in distress say they see "light at the end of the tunnel" giving them hope. Now, according to my e-mail message, the "light" has been turned off! How incredibly insensitive for the "keeper of the light at the end of the tunnel" to do such a thing!

Fortunately God's light continues to shine brilliantly. The Word informs us that "You are all sons of light and sons of the day. We are not of the night nor of darkness (1 Thessalonians 5:5 NKJV)."

Knowing that Christ is the light of the world gives us hope beyond human comprehension. We, as carriers of light in the darkness, know the way home. Our path is well lit. So we can live with confidence! Our optimism should be engaging to those who stumble in the darkness. Aha! We are the light that others so desperately need.

With a good word spoken in the most negative of settings, we hold the possibility of drawing people out of darkness into the light. In essence, we are "the light at the end of the tunnel" for those seeking the way out. This is our time to shine! Chase the doom and gloom away by turning on our light. Don't hide it, rather "Let your light so shine before men, that they may see your good works and glorify your father in heaven (Matthew 5:16 NKJV)."

Now more than ever is the time for us to let our light shine. The darker the night, the brighter the light!

Jesus, fill us anew with the power of Your light to influence others to move toward acceptance of You as Savior.

Richard Armstrong serves as assistant director of The Worship Center Global Ministries in Lancaster.

God of Great Detail

"For My thoughts are not your thoughts, nor are your ways My ways, declares the Lord!" *Isaiah 55:8 (New American Standard Bible)*

One morning I arrived at work to hear the receptionist say, "Your daughter is really trying to get a hold of you. You need to call her!"

Immediately I dialed the number. In tears my daughter explained that she had locked her keys in the car and the car was running.

She was thirty-five minutes from where I work. Mentally, I ran through the list of options and decided to try to make it home and back before a business appointment scheduled in forty-five minutes.

I returned to the office about 10 minutes late for the appointment. My guest was chatting with staff members. We immediately launched into a detailed discussion about our different ministries. I assumed this individual was a Christian as I outlined the concepts of sexual integrity and talked about God's love, forgiveness and mercy. What I didn't know, was that she had revealed to my staff shortly after she arrived that her beliefs were not necessarily the same as ours.

My guest listened closely as I talked. Before she left, she shared secrets from her past. I realized the information I had shared wasn't merely a description of how our pregnancy center could minister to her clients, but my words were divinely chosen to help her receive healing and forgiveness.

Later, I reflected on my mad dash across the county to unlock my daughter's car. Because I was late, I delivered exactly the message God had for this lady. I think God locked my daughter's keys in her car: He shut the door and pushed the lock, so that I would be late and would boldly share what she needed to hear. His ways are not my ways! I am thankful that He is a God of great details!

Father, I am so thankful that You are a God of details. You love us and know exactly what we need. I love You!

Lisa Hildebrand works for Susquehanna Valley Pregnancy Services and ministers as a teacher and speaker in local churches.

God's Presence

"Because of the Lord's great love we are not consumed, for his compassions never fail. They are new every morning; great is your faithfulness." *Lamentations 3:22–23*

They are energetic, sometimes rambunctious boys. After all, God made nine- ten- and eleven-year-old boys that way, didn't He? My expectation for meaningful teaching time was low. So was my energy level as I prepared to teach Wednesday night "Boys Club."

I'd been sharing the teaching assignment for those boys for two years so I knew what to expect. Nevertheless, I was disappointed when I taught a well-prepared lesson on the "parable of the talents." I had studied the lesson, considered the age and understanding level of the boys, and thought of a couple of unique applications. But try as I might, I could not get their attention. I was a little discouraged.

So a couple of weeks later I trudged up to the second floor room somewhat ill-prepared to teach the lesson of David and the children of Israel transporting the Ark of the Covenant to Jerusalem. How was I going to get their attention for this obscure Old Testament story?

The boys arrived with their usual vim and vigor. As we gathered around the table and began the story, something happened. Nine-year-old Jonathan started it. "Why did God strike Uzzah down?" "What was in the Ark?" "Why didn't David obey God's rules?" "What if Jesus had been there?"

The curiosity built and the questions came spewing out, faster than I could respond! The boys tumbled out of the room with their usual energy as our hour together ended. As I gathered up my materials, God and I held a short debriefing session. What just happened? Why tonight? What did I learn?

Tears welled in my eyes as I walked slowly to my car. Once again, God caught me off guard with his gift of *presence*. It's a profound lesson I need to be taught again and again. When we least expect Him, God shows up!

Father, help me to be alert to Your continual presence today.

Roger S. North is president, board of directors, of Love In The Name of Christ (Love INC) of Lancaster County. He attends Neffsville Menonite Church.

Peace and Prosperity for the City

"And work for the peace and prosperity of the city where I sent you into exile. Pray to the LORD for it, for its welfare will determine your welfare." *Jeremiah 29:7*

A year or so ago during a Veritas House Church we were watching a video by author Michael Frost and he was talking about where our word "church" came from. He said back in biblical times older men would retire from their work, give their business to their sons, and then spend their days at the city gate talking, discussing, and having people come and ask questions about life and other important issues. Michael went on to say that if you were to somehow go back to that time, and remove the elders from the city gate, the city would go into a profound sense of mourning and loss. The elders gathered at the city gate brought value to their community. That gathering of elders at the city gate was called *ecclesia*, which is where we derive our word "church."

That got me thinking. If our *ecclesia* were removed from our community, would anyone grieve? Would anyone not connected to our church miss the *ecclesia*? If I were honest with myself, not only would the community not grieve the loss, they wouldn't even notice the difference. That sent me on a journey, which continues to this day, to be a church that brings so much value and blessing to a community, that if Veritas disappeared, the community would grieve.

Think about it. What kind of value has your *ecclesia* brought to your community and if you disappeared from that place would people mourn the loss for themselves and their community? What can your ecclesia do to bring value to our community? Can you "adopt" a local elementary school? Can you "adopt" a park and clean it up? Pray, be creative, and work for the peace and prosperity of your city.

Lord, You have blessed us. Help us to be a blessing.

Ryan Braught is a church planter of Veritas, a Missional Community of Authentic Worshipers.

Dependable Prayer

"And pray in the spirit on all occasions with all kinds of prayers and requests. With this in mind, be alert and always keep on praying for all saints." *Ephesians 6:18*

With the hundreds of people who have touched my life, how do I know when to pray for them? It is impossible to pray for everyone all the time. So here is where I depend on God. I find him to be so faithful in bringing people to my mind at the needed time.

Sometimes it seems strange that I suddenly think of someone I haven't thought of in a long time, and then, find out later it was a time of need for him or her. I depend on God to bring to my memory persons at the right time; and then, when He prompts me, He expects me to be dependable and pray. It is so rewarding to see the fruits of this kind of prayer.

Recently I was invited to accompany some family members on a one-day excursion. The weather prediction was not good. I could not accompany them, but I dedicated myself to pray for them. I rejoiced greatly that they had a wonderful time.

The fruits of depending on God to prompt us to pray, and in return being dependable to God, are so rewarding. To see a friend find victory and come through a difficult experience is so good.

How many times have we heard of someone who is going through a very hard experience say, "It was the prayers of the people who gave us courage." Recently my brother's death was one such experience where the prayers of the people gave us unbelievable strength.

God, may I always be ready to pray when You prompt me to pray.

Miriam Witmer is a wife, mother of two, grandmother of five and great grandmother of six. She enjoys quilting, visiting the elderly and volunteering.

Follow in His Footsteps

"Enter through the narrow gate. For wide is the gate and broad is the
road that leads to destruction, and many enter through it."
Matthew 7:13

I recently went over to the house of one of my friends. We didn't
know what to do, so we decided to go into the woods. My brother, one
of the older friends, and I went into the woods with sticks. We decided
to follow the creek and see where it ended. There were a lot of thorns in
the woods. We finally decided to stop and go back.

We had all started on one path, but my friend and I decided to go a
different way than my brother. We were thinking our way was perfect.
It looked like a clearer path than what my brother was taking, until we
ran into thorns blocking the path. The older friend decided to keep
fighting the thorns, but I decided to go back. That path worked better,
because my older brother had cleared it.

Later I decided to go on a path because it looked like it was clear,
while my brother and his friend decided to go up another path. Again,
I ran into thorns blocking my way. I decided I couldn't fight them, so I
decided to take the path where my brother went up. We made it to the
top.

A couple days later, when I was deciding to write this story, I said,
"Oh, this is a lot like following Jesus. Jesus goes on a path that doesn't
look clear, but He clears it as He goes. Unbelievers go on a path that
looks easier, but is not."

God, please help me to follow more in Your footsteps.

Simeon Schlicher is eleven years old and attends DOVE Christian Fellowship
Elizabethtown.

Ask in His Name

"...I tell you the truth, my Father will give you whatever you ask in my name. Until now you have not asked for anything in my name. Ask and you will receive, and your joy will be complete." *John 16:23–24*

Several years ago, I was a single parent struggling to pay my monthly bills. Living from paycheck to paycheck, God had always made a way for me to pay my bills. God was truly sufficient for my needs.

Friends of mine, who were newly married and had just joined me on a mission trip over the summer, were moving into an apartment and were starting new jobs, so their financial state was the same or even worse than mine. They confided in me that they had not been able to raise all their support for the mission trip and now were receiving pressure to pay their remaining balance. I wasn't sure how to help them. I knew there was no way I could give them money; I was barely hanging on myself.

They shared with me on a Sunday and I prayed that God would provide them money or show me what to do. I prayed again on Monday. On Tuesday, I opened the mailbox and saw what looked like a check. I immediately thought, "It must be one of those scams again." To my surprise, it was a rebate check for over $300.00. This check was completely unexpected: I was never informed that I would be receiving it. I knew the true source of the check, so without hesitation I wrote a note and included the check to my friends to pay their support.

It was an eye-opening experience for me to see how God provided, and the power of prayer in His name.

Lord, thank you for Your assurance in Your Word that we can ask for anything in Your Name. Teach us to ask so that we can see Your blessings.

Randy Wingenroth is vice president for E.F. Martzall, Inc. and serves on the Discovery Commission Team at Mohns Hill ECC.

Proving God

"...Put me to the test, says the Lord of hosts..." *Malachi 3:10*

I find that my heavenly Father wants to move me beyond seasoned theology into a deeper experiential understanding of His heart and plans for me. As a person trained in analytical methodologies, I value the role of testing and proving, while recognizing their limits. "Simple faith" is fine. Simplistic faith is another thing.

I am struck by the way God loves to "demonstrate His stuff" to His children, much like I did when my children were small, impression-able, and unaware of my limitations and weaknesses. So perhaps I am saying that my Father is a show off. This "show off" is One who is committed to nurturing confidence, hope, and faith in someone who is timid, hopeless, and fearful.

When our economy was imploding, the realities of being on a "fixed income" were sinking in, and revenue from coaching and consulting engagements was drying up. I sensed the Father saying, "Remember many years ago when, as a father of two small children, you trusted Me when you quit your job and invested everything you had into the work that you believed I had called you to? Now I want you to release your concerns about compensation as you consider the needs of those I send to you to serve. Will you trust Me in this season of your life to provide for your needs and also to have some left over to be generous with others?" The months since my "Yes" to that question have been ones of open doors, fruitful ministry, and personal joy and freedom.

This may not be what God is saying to you, but He has again proven Himself faithful, firmly in control, and full of fun—sort of the way I tried, though imperfectly, to be when I showed myself off to my children to build them up and knit them to my heart. He passes the test. He is the real deal. The show must go on.

Thank you not only for demonstrating Your faithfulness through care and provision, but for the way You challenge me to refresh my joy, retool my heart, and rebuild my faith.

Bruce Boydell and his wife, Joan, are members of Covenant Fellowship Church in Glen Mills. They encourage and build up leaders of businesses and ministries through Lifespan Coaching and Consulting Services, based in West Chester.

Lighten Up!

"A cheerful heart is good medicine...." *Proverbs 17:22*

Proofreading is serious business. A proofreader needs to be alert and read carefully, checking that every word is written and spelled correctly. Grammar, capitalization, punctuation, and word order can be important in communicating exactly what a writer intends to say. Then there is usually a deadline to meet, so one has to work quickly as well as carefully. For these reasons, my job usually involves hours of tedious, nose-to-the-grindstone reading, checking, and marking manuscripts. Occasionally, though, I find a typographical error that is downright humorous, and I find myself laughing out loud. What a difference just one letter can make! Consider the following examples:

Cash prize <u>sinners</u> will be announced at the end of the day. (winners)

This coin was given to me by a German <u>fried</u>. (friend)

Diners will feast on <u>over</u>-roasted turkey. (oven)

Teams can accomplish much by <u>suing</u> the principles of science and engineering. (using)

A rare coin was acquired from a long-time <u>con</u> collector in New York. (coin)

The senior center will hold a <u>Medicate</u> party. (Medicare)

The hospital provides a wide range of <u>impatient</u> care. (in patient)

A bronze <u>plague</u> listed the names of the donors. (plaque)

Finding something humorous to laugh about can lighten my mood and make a long day seem to go faster. In fact, that's true in any occupation or activity. Yes, it's a good thing that someone was paying attention so that these errors were not included in a serious publication. But, often we take ourselves and our jobs way too seriously. Lighten up! A good laugh and a cheerful heart is good medicine. It can make you and everyone around you feel better.

Lord, help me to lighten up. Give me a cheerful heart and a ready laugh as I go through this day.

Jane Nicholas lives in Elizabethtown with her husband, Bill. She does proofreading, writing, and editing for various publications.

Spiritual Discussions

"Do you think I came to bring peace on earth? No, I tell you, but division." *Luke 12:51*

Some families are privileged to have everyone in their family or their neighborhood knowing the Lord and being in harmony from a spiritual standpoint. This, however, is not the case with my extended family or my neighborhood.

I have relatives and friends who have either never known Jesus or who have moved in other spiritual directions. It is more than just cultural differences.

Discussions cross into the spiritual realm quickly and there can be friction or avoidance when spiritual matters become part of the conversation. It might have to do with moral values, child rearing, behavior toward others, or a general worldview.

I do not judge the person, but I do hold a boundary or establish a position for the Kingdom of God. Jesus did not back down. He followed the Father's direction and relied on the Holy Spirit for further direction.

Lord, help me to be courageous and fearless when it comes to defending your Kingdom. Holy Spirit, lead me into the truth in any given situation.

Joe Troncale is a small group leader at Petra Christian Fellowship in New Holland.

Pressing In To Press On

"For just as the body without the spirit is dead, so also faith without works is dead." *James 2:26 (New American Standard Bible)*

I have realized over the years that God just doesn't move based on the snap of my fingers—funny I would even think that. He hears every cry, prayer, and thought—and then I expect Him to move. I have all the faith and believe in all His power, so why wouldn't He? And, because He's God, He might actually do what I think should be done. Other times, there's nothing. And then I have to ask, "What do I need to do now?"

Faith is one thing, but as the Word clearly says, "…faith without action is dead" (my paraphrase). Even when I believe with all the faith, I can muster up that God can do just what He promised to do; I still have my part to do. Primarily, I have to be so in tune with Him and His plan for my life. That only comes through spending time with Him. Secondly, recognize it's not the quantity of time in the day but the quality of time spent with Him that is effective. Lastly, knowing that when I get up from that place, then I have to move, ending the conversation with, "What would you have me do now, Lord?"

If it were just about waiting on God to move, we'd be sadly missing out on our purpose in life. We can't look at it as having to do something, but getting to partner with God in something. What an honor and a privilege! What do you need to do today that will allow you to press on as you press into and partner with the One who can move mountains?

Lord, help me today to spend quality time with You, becoming more into Your will and ways, and then giving me the direction and strength to move out and partner with You!

Joy Ortega is an associate pastor of Living Word Fellowship, where their purpose is to "Reach people and change lives!"

Symphony of Worship

"If any of you lacks wisdom, he should ask God, who gives generously to all without finding fault, and it will be given to him."
James 1:5

Decisions, decisions, decisions! One of the lessons I've learned about being in full-time ministry is that I am required to make many decisions. Some are easy and do not require much thinking process. Some decisions will require answers that will not be very popular to those they affect. Others—well let's just say that other decisions require hours, days, weeks and sometimes longer to make the final determination.

Some decisions just affect me but some affect many other people. These can be the most grueling. Do I say yes or no? Do I go or stay? That's when I find myself crying out to the Lord, Maker of heaven and earth. My cries often sound like, "Father, I don't know what to do. I need wisdom!"

He always hears my cries and He always answers. Sometimes His answers come during my times of worship, sometimes by writing in my journal and sometimes through other people. Sometimes He answers quickly but other times I often wonder why He seems to be silent. His timing, not mine, is something I must always remember. I must remember that I am not the only person He is working with in this process. Many times I've learned of other situations He has orchestrated in His other children at the exact same time. Once everything and everyone is in its perfect place, we have the most beautiful worship song created by the Master Musician.

Father, thank you for giving wisdom generously to Your children. Lead us this day to expect Your presence and direction. We long to be part of Your symphony of worship!

Karen Pennell is the CEO of CCWS Medical in Chester County and President/CEO of Karen Pennell Consulting.

Clean Up on Aisle Four

"For who can eat and who can have enjoyment without Him?"
Ecclesiastes 2:25 (New American Standard Bible)

This week I would be victorious and my frustration would be assuaged. For three weeks, my coffee had spilled at church. The first week, I considered it an anomaly. The second week, I figured I needed a different cup. The third week, I realized that cup also leaked. This time it would be foolproof. I took my cup with me to the back of the church, tucked the cup in a corner, and I stood nearby to worship.

We were twenty minutes in when I heard a mom whispering harshly. I turned and saw a huge puddle and my cup on its side. In that momentary instant (that all toddlers seem to watch for of mom turning to find something) the girl walked to the cup and accidentally tipped it over.

Don't get mad. Stay calm. I found my tongue and tried to assure the embarrassed mother I understood.

But inside I was a mess. I was angry at my daughter for kicking it the first time. I was angry at my son for running the second time. I was angry at the stumbling foot the third time—all accidents. I had tried so hard. All I wanted was to be normal for once and drink coffee like the rest of the church. I was just asking for that simple thing. I gave so much during the week: we were pinching pennies, and that Turkey Hill coffee was such a treat. I rode home in tears and defeat.

I began the pity party and God interrupted with two words: "It happens." Coffee spills. No big theological argument here. I didn't have to understand. I'm His, and it's just coffee.

God, keep my perspective from Your viewpoint. Quell my frustration at things I won't remember in a month. When those things happen, help me utter a holy, "It happens."

Carolyn Schlicher still occasionally spills her coffee at Elizabethtown DOVE Christian Fellowship.

Be Still and Know That I Am God

"…Meditate within your heart on your bed, and be still. Offer the sacrifices of righteousness, and put your trust in the Lord." *Psalm 4:4-5 (New King James Version)*

Interruptions from restful sleep are frustrating and aggravating, with me tossing and turning only to end up being more awake than ever. Worrisome thoughts tend to come to mind, which only sink me deeper into insomnia. At these times, I have learned that applying the admonition in the verse above pays big dividends.

To be still is a call to be humble before God and to listen for His still, small voice. This is a call for repentance toward God, breaking me of my independence, a call to seek Him. It is a call to meekness, for increased strength and for the cry of surrender to His will and wisdom by having no agenda but God's. This is essential for hearing God. The only desire is to please Him.

Recently during a Bible Study of John 15 about "Living in the Vine," I was asked to answer the question, "How does the Lord want you to be more intimate with Him in the little details of life?"

Recalling how He had instructed me in the middle of another troubling situation, I answered, "Stay with Me on this, don't move out of the realm of absolute faith in My ability to accomplish for you what needs to happen here."

This instruction has helped me to be careful to listen to His voice, not allowing myself to wander in fleshly, faithless thinking. I believe this is offering the sacrifices of righteousness and putting my trust in the Lord.

Defend Your people, Lord; defend and bless Your chosen ones. Lead them like a shepherd and carry them forever in Your arms.

Naomi Sensenig and her husband LaMarr serve at Lancaster Evangelical Free Church in Lititz.

Parental Responsibility

"Train a child in the way he should go, and when he is old, he will not turn from it." *Proverbs 22:6*

While in a barber shop one day, the conversation became a little animated over the issue of prayer in school, and how its removal was the beginning of all the problems in our country.

I asked those gathered in the barber shop how many of them prayed with their children before they left for school. Silence fell over the room.

I believe the scripture in Proverbs is true; however, as parents, we're depending upon everyone else to do the training for us. Beginning with daycare and preschool and continuing all the way through college, other people have enormous input into our children's lives and great influence on their values. In addition, there is also the influence of television, video games, computers, sports and other activities.

Unless parents see the value in training their own children and accept it as a God-given responsibility, all these other influences will cause children to be confused about the "way they should go."

In our world today, there is widespread erosion of moral standards and ethics, spiritual bankruptcy and depletion of true character. Judges 21:25 records, "Everyone did what was right in his own eyes." Sadly, this is also the case today.

We are accountable to God. Children are gifts from Him, given to us to be carefully nurtured, loved and protected.

Lord, help us to take seriously the responsibility to raise up godly children—to not only teach but also model the image of Christ and His character. Help us to give them a healthy spiritual foundation on which to grow.

John W. Shantz is pastor of Spring City Fellowship Church, which is part of the Hopewell Network of Churches.

Sharing the Good News

"'...Sirs, what must I do to be saved?' And they said, 'Believe on the Lord Jesus Christ, and thou shalt be saved, and thy house.'" *Acts 16:30-31 (King James Version)*

I received word that my brother was in the hospital and not doing well. Due to my husband's health, I had not seen my brother for several years even though we only lived about forty-five minutes from each other. We had prayed for my brother's salvation since 1980, but he would not accept the Lord Jesus as his personal savior.

Since my husband was not able to accompany me, he suggested I ask one of my friends to go with me. My friend and I went to see my brother in the hospital. As we went to the hospital, my husband and my friend's husband and her son prayed that we would have an opportunity to speak to my brother about accepting the Lord.

We visited with my brother for quite awhile before I asked him if he would mind if we prayed for him. He said he would like that. My friend took his hand and asked him if he had ever asked Jesus to come into his heart. He said, "No, I did not."

She asked if he would like to ask Jesus to come into his heart and he answered, "Yes I would." We led him in the sinner's prayer.

All the way home, we praised the Lord for the opportunity to lead my brother to the Lord. The following week, my brother was informed that his cancer had returned. Previously, he had made up his mind that if the cancer returned, he would not take any more treatments. They sent him home from the hospital with the prediction that he had three months to live. About three weeks later, my brother went to be with the Lord.

Father, I thank You that You prepare hearts to receive what You have to offer, if we are willing to be obedient and share the Good News.

Doris Showalter is a wife, mother, grandmother and great-grandmother and attends Mission of Love Church in Ephrata.

An "In Season" Pastor

"...Preach the Word; be ready in season and out of season; reprove, rebuke, exhort, with great patience and instruction." *2 Timothy 4:2 (New American Standard Bible)*

The Rev. William Easton, D.D. (1804-1879) pastored Octorara United Presbyterian Church from 1827 to 1879. A tribute on the fiftieth year of his pastorate stated, "He rebuked sin in a manner calculated to give offense, but he was prompted to do so by a deep conviction of divine truth. He was unflinching in his fidelity to the cause of his Lord and Savior Jesus Christ."

He lived three miles from the church where he had a small farm. At that time, farmers would furnish liquor to their hired men during harvest. When the men asked the pastor for their "morning bitters," he refused them. The men promptly laid down their scythes refusing to work without drinks. Pastor Easton asked how much their liquor would cost him daily. He then gladly offered to add double that amount to their daily wages in preference to placing temptation in their way. His offer was accepted by the majority but some left, preferring their alcohol. When the next harvest season arrived, Dr. Easton had his pick of laborers. In a few years, the custom of providing liquor was done away with and the increased wages he paid became the rule in that neighborhood.

In another instance, Dr. Easton preached against slavery when, at that time, the majority of people in southern Lancaster County favored it. He "preached the word" and showed that the Bible did not approve of slavery. He weathered the storm of criticism and lived to see the eventual freeing of American slaves.

Our gracious heavenly Father, may You continue to supply our land with godly men who will "be strong in the Lord and in the strength of His might" and "will stand firm" for "the faith once delivered to the saints." Amen.

Ross I. Morrison, Sr. and his wife, June, are missionary associates with Village Missions. Ross researches religious history of Lancaster County. They attend Calvary Church, Lancaster.

St. Peter Village, Chester County
Photo by Mark Van Scyoc

August

Seeking First God's Kingdom

"But seek first his kingdom and his righteousness, and all these things will be given to you as well." *Matthew 6:33*

In the early nineteenth century, the Welsh Mountain Mission brought employment, education and hope to the impoverished residents of the mountain. The farmers in the valley below awoke to their spiritual responsibilities to their neighbors. A sewing factory and a broom-making business were established, and the Welsh Mountain congregation was begun.

Faithful families supported the witness of the congregation throughout the decades of the twentieth century. Up the mountains came these families to hold Sunday morning services, midweek prayer meetings, and home Bible studies. They came in the heat of summer and in the cold of winter, undaunted by snowstorms. At times this meant "Everybody out!" (except the driver of the car) to push the car up the hill on a snowy road.

These farmers knew that God's call to share the good news was the top priority of their lives. Yet at times they needed to balance their farm work with the outreach work. One farmer planted a final field of corn on a lovely evening in May instead of attending the prayer meeting. The seed planted in that field never sprouted, and the field needed to be replanted. Another farmer skipped an outreach activity in order to bring in that last load of hay. However, a spark from the tractor's exhaust ignited that load of hay. These farmers understood these events to be reminders from God to keep their priorities right.

Lord, give me a heart for those who need to come to saving faith in Jesus Christ. Amen.

J. Carl Sensenig is a pastor of the Red Run Mennonite Church, bishop of the Bowmansville-Reading District of the Lancaster Mennonite Conference, and a middle school teacher at Gehmans Mennonite School.

Alpha

"'I am the Alpha and the Omega,' says the Lord God, 'who is, and who was, and who is to come, the Almighty.'" *Revelation 1:8*

When I was a kid, one of the things I really enjoyed doing was hanging at the playground with my friends. We played everything there. Two guys would always be picked as captains and they would take turns choosing players for their teams. Each captain always tried his best to pick the best player available. Failure to choose wisely could have been the difference between winning and losing.

When I think about God, it's just awesome knowing that nobody made Him, created Him, or picked Him. They couldn't because, after all, He is the Alpha, the first, the beginning. He created everything and everyone and He stands in the heavens scanning the people of the earth calling all to be on His side. It's awesome that He would even want us or believe in us enough to call us, but He does.

He loves us and cares for us. He wants to be first in our lives and He will share that place with no one. The world can be a crazy place sometimes; people and things can get the best of you, but they will never get the best of the Alpha; He's the one that holds everything in place. He knew the end of all things back in the beginning. He knows what we are qualified to do and how much we can handle just like any good captain would. We don't always understand why we go through some of the stuff we are called to go through but we have to trust the captain. Right now we only see a small piece of the puzzle but some day we will see all things as they really are. Someday we will see Alpha as He really is, too. The true King of Kings, and Lord of Lords, the Alpha.

Praise the Lord all the earth, Praise the Alpha! Amen.

Rob Heverling is youth leader at Mount Aetna Bible Church, Mount Aetna.

Praying from a Distance

"…Yet not one of them will fall to the ground apart from the will of your Father." *Matthew* 10:29

Startled by the sound of the bird crashing into my window, compassion flooded my heart. I looked at the defeated bird lying in a heap. "Father, in the name of Jesus, I ask you to heal this bird. Restore it to good health and help it to fly away. Amen."

I knew if *I* tried to help the bird I could actually harm it. It would be afraid of me. If it wasn't ready to fly, flapping its wings and fluttering to get away from *me* could cause more damage. But to walk away? Leaving it alone in its pain? It seemed somehow, well, cruel.

Jesus is the sustainer and lifter of my soul. I know He and He alone can help hurting people. But, as I try to help them sometimes they *flap* and *flutter* and hurt themselves more trying to get away from *me*—but to walk away? Leaving them alone and in their pain? Yes, it seems cruel.

Sometimes, when I'm feeling helpless and all I can do is pray, from a distance, it feels awful. I want to *do* something. God then gently taps me on the shoulder and reminds me He is in control and He loves this dear one more than I ever could.

Hopeful, I went out on my porch one more time to look at the bird. The bird's eyes were open. While I watched from a distance the bird lifted its head and then flew away!

Lord, please help me look to You for my help and to allow others to help me with their prayers, and with their touch. Help me not to be afraid. And help me to discern when to reach out and help someone who's hurting and when to back off, pray and trust that You, and You alone, will help them.

Lisa Dorr is a wife, mother, public speaker, writer and editor.

Welcome Home

"Reverence for God gives a man deep strength; his children have a place of refuge and security." *Proverbs 14:26 (The Living Bible)*

I'll never forget it. It was July, 1985, when my family and I left Lancaster County. It was like pulling teeth and dragging my heels to get into that U-Haul and head down south. A deep sadness enveloped me. Not for a week, or a month or two, but for several years I would think about my dear, sweet family in Christ.

I was born-again in 1979, through a cell group meeting of DOVE Christian Fellowship in Litiz. This small band of 25 people is now DOVE Christian Fellowship International with churches all over the world and it started right here in Lancaster County. Looking back on it now, in the 24 years we had been gone, we moved and moved and left church after church to establish our family in Christ over and over again. Yes, God blessed me and my family as we will never forget or eternally leave the precious Christians we had grown to love, but my heart was always in Lancaster County.

When we finally retired, the question was, "Where do we settle down?" One thing I knew for sure: I didn't want to start all over again! Every time we came back to Lancaster County to visit friends, I fell in love with it all over again: the rolling hills, the fresh produce, the endless rows of corn, and the feeling that Christ has His footprints all over the many churches and meeting places Lancaster countians are a part of.

God blessed us by being able to purchase a home at auction in Ephrata Township, but the ultimate blessing was the countless ways He brought all my brothers and sisters back into my life so I could feel right at home. We are so very glad to be back!

Lord, may I help all the strangers I meet here to feel as welcome as I did when I finally came back home.

Jan Dorward is a Messianic Jew who resides in Ephrata where she attends DOVE Christian Fellowship, Westgate. Jan loves to write and she presents Messianic Passovers.

Working Smarter

"Whatever you do in word or in deed, do it all in the name of the Lord...." Colossians 3:17

I am not always the most efficient worker. Sometimes it takes me twice as long to get something done as I think it should. Many years ago I decided to replace the faucet in our kitchen sink. It had been leaking, much to mt wife Dianne's annoyance. It didn't annoy me all that much—but when she told me we were wasting money—that motivated me. As a homeowner with little money, I thought, "Go to Sears, buy a faucet, and put it in." So off to Sears I went.

The salesman assured me it would be a simple task. It would take me maybe 30-45 minutes to accomplish. Since I am not much of a handyman, I decided to wait until I had nothing better to do. So one night around nine o'clock I decided to tackle it. First problem—I had to find the wrench needed. Then I found that the depth of our sink did not accommodate my short-handled wrench. I needed a long-handled one. Since I did not own one, I went next door to my neighbor's house. Dick is a handy man and he has almost every tool imaginable. He had the needed tool. Dick followed me home. There I discovered that no amount of effort would budge the old faucet. "Let's just take the whole sink out," suggested Dick. That made sense, so we started—only to discover that the sink was anchored into the cabinetry. Whoever had put the sink in must have feared earthquakes or just had too much time on his hands. He had anchored it in more than 30 places!

Finally, after three hours—we got the sink out, the old faucet removed, the new one replaced and the sink back in place (this time with perhaps a dozen anchor points). Guess what? The new faucet leaked as well!

After that I determined that you can work or you can work smarter. There is little satisfaction in work that requires a lot of effort and produces minimal results. And there's no merit in working faster if the job still isn't done right. It's not about the work—it's about the results.

Jesus, thank you for reminding me that the best results for my work come when I work according to Your purposes, following Your plans.

Dr. Steve Dunn serves as the lead pastor for the Church of God of Landisville—home of the FLOW Center for maturing adults and the Agape Youth Center.

Love Found

"Ask and it shall be given you; seek, and ye shall find; knock, and it shall be opened unto you." *Luke 11:9 (King James Version)*

When I was young I did a lot of hunting. When I went with my brother-in-law and his father, who was a Christian, I would be annoyed because his dad would always be either singing or whistling Christian songs.

In 1980 my brother-in-law's dad passed away and I picked up my parents and went to the viewing. When viewing the body, I could not take my eyes off of him. He had a smile on his face and was so at peace. My father said he wanted to introduce me to someone. It was his pastor. We had a nice chat and the pastor invited me to come to church. I told him I would come, but really had no intention of going to church. On the way home, my dad asked me to attend church with them on Sunday. Because I respected my dad's wishes I told him we would go with them.

That Sunday morning we had a terrible ice storm and my parents said they were not going to church. I was so relieved. But they asked us to go the following Sunday. That Sunday was the best day of my life. It was the day I gave my heart and soul to Jesus Christ.

I was so in love with Jesus, that I wanted to learn more about what He had for me. I wanted everything that He was willing to give to me. Whenever the church doors were open, we would be there. Friday nights and Saturdays I would spend with my Christian brothers and sisters and we would study the Bible.

I prayed for the love of God in my life. He answered that prayer. I fell in love with everything. When I would see a tree I wanted to hug it. I am so thankful for the amazing ways God has changed me over the years.

Lord, I pray that every Christian experiences Your love in a greater way today than ever before.

Kenneth C. Showalter is husband, father, grandfather, and great-grandfather.

Embracing Christ

"Yes, all the things I once thought were so important are gone from my life. Compared to the high privilege of knowing Christ Jesus as my Master, firsthand, everything I once thought I had going for me is insignificant—dog dung. I've dumped it all in the trash so that I could embrace Christ" *Philippians 3:8 (The Message)*

I attended a funeral for my coworker's wife. I never met her. It was the most inspiring funeral, most joyous celebration of life I ever experienced. My friend explained his wife's influence on him, especially in his faith. She was benevolent. Even fighting cancer she would call her husband to discuss giving money to worthy causes and helping people. There were praise songs, hymns, and a sermon. I didn't even know her and I was crying. But I was not sad. She lives with Jesus—like you will too—if your heart belongs to Him.

Driving home, an urgency grew in me. What if I died before I had the chance to express what is really important. God loves you. Incredibly! I think that is the most important concept we can grasp. I'm glad my heart is still beating so I can try again to shake myself and everyone within my influence into reality.

In my ministry I talk and nag about all sorts of things all the time. Philippians says these things are worthless—dog dung in comparison to what is really important—God's love for you and your response to it.

May you fervently endeavor to know God, and never stop. Love the Lord your God with all your heart and strength and soul. You will go to the grave as happy as my friend's wife, who encouraged people in their faith and ministered to their broken hearts even on her very last day!

If you know God's love, you have the most important possession you will ever have, for free, because of God's grace through Jesus.

Thank you Jesus. Let us all turn into Jesus freaks. Amen.

Allen Keller serves as youth pastor at Olivet UMC in Coatesville.

Are You Convinced That God is Good?

"He died at a good old age, having enjoyed a good long life, wealth and honor. His son Solomon succeeded him as king." *1 Chronicles 29:28*

My daughter recently wrote me a note. It said, "Even though his work never ends he always has time to spend with us. I love you." I felt a little bad about being so busy working but what a great feeling to know that my daughter knew I always had time for her. She had a sense of security in knowing my love was real. As I have spoken with Christians I find that many times they are not totally convinced that God is good and that He desires good for them. A father always wants good for his children.

Let's consider the following three questions:

Who is your father? A good father will protect his kids. You can be convinced that your heavenly Father is looking out for you. He has you covered.

What has he said? A good father will honor his word to his kids. If your heavenly Father said something is going to happen He will follow through and see that it happens. If He says it—it is as good as gold. It is going to happen. It is settled.

Can you trust him? I love to read about King David at the end of his life. In spite of his mistakes and challenges he was able to say, "God is good and faithful." He found he could trust his Father. We, too, can be confident that at the end of our lives we will be able to say that God was good.

Father, we ask today that You would give us one hundred percent assurance that You are a good God and that You are working for our good. Give us a revelation of who You are and show us Your faithfulness to keep Your promises to us. Let us know today that we can trust You and that we will look back on our lives like King David did in wonder as we recall Your goodness to us and our families. Thank you that You are a good God. Amen.

Brian Sauder helps provide oversight and direction for DOVE Christian Fellowship International's network of churches.

Restoration

"…And I will restore to you the years that the locust hath eaten…."
Joel 2:25 (King James Version)

I made a decision to have an out-of-state abortion in the early 1980s, believing the lies of Satan that I would abuse my child, just as I had been abused. For years, I never really worked through the impact of having an abortion. I did not totally allow God to heal me from what I considered an unforgivable sin.

In 2002, while at a safe house for victims of abuse, I finally received God's forgiveness. At that time, I started to think seriously about how I always wanted children, and about how much I loved children.

Nine months, to the day, we were given the opportunity to provide a teenage girl with safe housing. It was only to be for a week; but within that week, we bonded, and God blessed me to be able to fill the role of a mother to this young girl. We are so much alike; people think she is my biological daughter. Even though we discussed legal adoption, I told her that I was praying (from the first day she moved in) that some day she and her biological mother would reconcile.

Approximately three years later, that happened. I struggled with the fear of losing her because I had allowed myself to love her so deeply. But God is so good, as He is in the business of family restoration and healing. He continues to reveal His truth (amidst the fierce attempt of Satan's lies) that there are no losers in healing…but there are seasons.

Oh, did I mention, she is the exact age of my daughter that I aborted?

Thank you, Lord, that You make up for all the losses in our lives. We believe in You for complete restoration in our lives today.

Darlene Adams has been involved with a prison pen pal ministry (L.O.V.E. Ministry) and street ministry since 1995. She currently has a prison lay ministry certificate at her church, The Ephrata Church of the Nazarene.

Conscience

"For I know my transgressions, and my sin is always before me."
Psalm 51:3

I think all of us can identify with the words of today's scripture text, because at one time or another we've been in the position where the word *"Guilty"* is written in large letters right across our foreheads! *And, until the matter is dealt with, our consciences won't allow us to forget!*

Years ago, following a morning worship service, a lady in our congregation whose tongue always seemed to get her into a lot of trouble, approached my mother and said, "Oh Naomi, I've said such terrible things about you. Will you forgive me?" My mother's response was, "Well, of course I'll forgive you!"

"But I can't stay long," the woman continued, "because I have two more people to catch!" And, off she went!

Why the hurry? Because the following morning this lady was going to the hospital for a serious operation, and she wanted everything to be cleared up between her and other people—just in case she didn't make it.

"I know how bad I've been; my sins are staring me down!" is how Eugene Peterson paraphrases Psalm 51:3, today's text. King David had committed horrendous sins—adultery with the wife of one of his soldiers, having Bathsheba's husband murdered, and deceit in attempting to cover up the sins committed. A whole year passed until God sent the Prophet Nathan to confront King David regarding his offenses. Day and night, the king's conscience was dogged by the One who wouldn't let David go. Thankfully, David confessed the enormity of his wickedness, and acknowledged that his transgressions were more than against humans—they were sin against God!

The point of today's scripture text is this: conscience has a way of not allowing us to forget!

Search me, O God, and know my heart; test my thoughts. Point out anything You find in me that makes You sad, and lead me along the path of everlasting life.

Paul Brubaker serves on the ministry team at the Middle Creek Church of the Brethren in Lititz.

Guess How Much?

"…The steadfast love of the Lord is from everlasting to everlasting…and his righteousness to children's children…."
Psalm 103:17

As she neared the end of first grade, it became apparent that my seven-year-old granddaughter, Abigail, had burst into bloom as a writer. She loved to write her own messages on brightly illustrated cards for those she loved. Mother's Day brought multiple cards for her mother, her grandmothers, and her great grandmother. The front of her card to her eighty-seven-year-old great grandmother asked this question. "Guess how much years I have loved you? Guess?" Inside was a multicolored heart surrounded by the number 87 written about a dozen times. It was followed by the word "tranclatid" (translated) and the declaration, "I have loved you for 87 years!"

Her exuberance captured an eternal principle about the everlasting love of God. Psalm 103 calls us to bless the Lord with all that is within us. He is the God who forgives, who heals, who redeems, and who crowns us with steadfast love and mercy. He remembers that we are dust and that our days are like the grass. He reminds us that we flourish like a flower that is soon blown away and is no longer known. But, the steadfast love of the Lord is from everlasting to everlasting to those who fear him. It began before we were born and it extends beyond our brief span on earth, sweeping up the generations to follow. It is not limited or bound by time, but surrounds and permeates our whole existence. Guess how "much years" God has loved you? Guess?

Dear Father, may we always remember all Your benefits, and bless You with all that is within us. Bless the Lord, O my soul!

Joan Boydell attends Covenant Fellowship Church in Glen Mills. She is a counselor and consultant, enjoying a new season of ministry.

Alarm Clock

"…It's impossible to please God apart from faith. And why? Because anyone who wants to approach God must believe both that he exists and that he cares enough to respond to those who seek him."
Hebrews 11:6

While in college, I spent the night at a friend's apartment, and she asked me what time I needed to be up for classes the next morning. I told her what time she should set the buzzer on her alarm clock, and she responded by saying, "I don't have an alarm clock. God wakes me up." I was a little taken aback, but the conversation struck me in such a way that I thought back to it now and then as time went by.

Years later, I felt the Holy Spirit prompting me to give up using my alarm clock just as my friend had done. I was challenged to have faith that the One who holds the universe in His hands could surely have the power to wake me up at the right time. I obeyed, but not wholeheartedly. Before going to bed, I would ask God to wake me up at a certain time. However, if there was something important the next morning, I would set an alarm clock. A few times, I brought my cell phone to bed with me since I had an early morning meeting hoping someone could get a hold of me if I had overslept. In each of those instances, however, I woke up before the alarm, and I was never late for those six o'clock meetings.

My faith increased. I knew that God was taking this seriously, and He was holding up His end of the bargain. So I continued to pray before going to sleep that He would wake me up at the right time.

I have allowed God to be my alarm clock for over a year. I have never missed an event, nor have I awakened our son too late to get ready for school. One time I even asked God to wake me up between 5:30 and 5:45 and when I looked at the clock that morning, it was 5:37.

God, increase my faith! So often, I rely on things or people more than I rely on You. Forgive me, and please increase my trust in You.

Maria Buck is the wife of Gary Buck, worship pastor at Petra Christian Fellowship.

A Long-Awaited Reunion

"God did this so that men would seek him...and find him...." *Acts 17:27*

It had been twenty-one years since I had given birth to a daughter and lovingly placed her for adoption. Truly it was one of the hardest decisions I had ever made, yet in my heart I knew I had done what the Lord had told me was best for our situation. Leaving the hospital without her, I felt a huge ache in my heart. Not being able to see or hold her, I had placed her in God's hand and trusted Him to care for her.

Over the years, I prayed that she would want to find me. I longed to see her face and to hold her in my arms. How I loved her and desired a relationship with her. Eventually I found out that I could write her letters and place them in a file at the adoption agency. When she turned eighteen, she would have a legal right to the file. If she wanted to find me she could! As I sat down and wrote letters of love to her, I prayed that she would somehow find out about the file and read my letters. I visualized the long-awaited reunion and the joy that would be mine seeing her face for the first time.

Five years later I had the amazing privilege of meeting my daughter. As I reflected days later on our reunion, God reminded me that He too is longing for the day of our reunion in eternity. He has a File full of love letters, the Bible, and He longs for us to seek and find Him in preparation for our grand reunion in heaven!

Father, thank you for the amazing gift of Your written Word. As I spend time getting to know You through Your letters, I look forward to seeing Your face for the first time in eternity.

Anita Keagy is founder of JoyShop Ministries and more of her story can be found in her book, *The File, a Mother and Daughter's Life-Changing Reunion.*

It's Not Dark Yet, But It's Getting There

"The night is about over, dawn is about to break. Be up and awake to what God is doing...!" *Romans 13:12 (The Message)*

Eight of our residential men have died in the last three and a half years. Some lived on this campus; others had moved out. Each had a degree of relationship with us, with the Lord and with recovery. Several relapsed, one committed suicide, all died deaths hastened by a long history of abuse and destructive choices. Their deaths brought sadness to our community.

I am hopeful that the reality of their deaths will also bring a sense of urgency to both staff and the residents still living here. Not an urgency springing from desperation, but a resolve to put aside anything that would distract us from what's vital.

Do our residents understand how fragile life is—how it could end at any time? Are our staff members willing to lay aside anything—agenda, theological non-essentials, ego, fear, personal comfort—in their desire to remove relational barriers with the people who live here? They should because hope for living and for heaven comes only from God, as He works through relationships with Himself and through others.

How easy it is to be diverted from the life-giving capacity of the gospel when its truth is blurred by arguments about non-essentials of the Christian life.

Death is real and should sober us. Bob Dylan's lyric, "It's not dark yet, but it's getting there," well describes the inevitable death that ends a difficult life. We are all moving toward physical death, the timing of which is truly in God's hands. And, it is only the gospel—shared by those who are also dying—that can bring life.

The night is progressing. But, the night will give way to the dawn! As Bruce Cockburn sings, "Joy will find a way." May we be fervent and urgent in our love for each other!

Lord, help me to lay aside my agenda and allow Your heart for others to grip me.

Steve Brubaker is the Chief Vision Officer for Water Street Ministries, Lancaster.

Awakening in the Middle of Prayer

"So what shall I do? I will pray with my spirit, but I will also pray with my mind...." *1 Corinthians 14:15*

One morning several years ago, I learned firsthand the reality and importance of praying, not only with my mind but also with my spirit. My husband had left very early—around 3 a.m.—to make a service call in his work truck. I "happened" to awaken very abruptly around 4:30 a.m., and somehow I was already in the middle of praying for him. I didn't know exactly why, or specifically what I was praying for, but I was fervently praying (just general things, including safety and protection).

When he returned home very late that night, he told me that he had fallen asleep at the wheel and had nearly driven off a bridge! He had awakened and was able to jerk the wheel just in time and ended up with merely a dented rear fender. I asked him what time this had happened; you guessed it—the exact time I had awakened mid-prayer.

I have often thought back to that experience and been encouraged that, although there are many times in life that I may not know with my intellect how to pray, and even situations that I am completely unaware of, if I am keeping my spirit connected to the Father, He is able to guide my prayers and give words to my unspoken intercessions.

Father, I ask that amid my busy day, You keep me in tune with Your heart. Let my spirit be sensitive to Yours, and direct my prayers so that they will be perfectly aligned with Your will.

Jessi Clemmer is a church planter at Koinonia House, Pottstown.

It's Not Your Time to Go

"Is anyone among you sick? Let him call for the elders of the church, and let them pray over him, anointing him with oil in the name of the Lord. And the prayer of faith will save the one who is sick, and the Lord will raise him up. And if he has committed sins, he will be forgiven." *James 5:14–15 (English Standard Version)*

In the fall of 2003, I started feeling sick. The doctors ran tests but nothing was showing up in the results. One day in April 2004, I was in bed and not able to get up. I had severe throat pain and felt like I would die. While lying in bed, I started to pray. Just then our phone rang and it was the pastor of the new church we had just started attending. He heard I was ill and asked if I could come to the church service the next day and have a group of people lay hands on me and pray for healing. At the service they gathered around me to pray and anoint me with oil.

The next morning, I woke up to get my children ready for school. I had very little strength to get them to the bus. As I returned to the house, I crawled up the steps to my bedroom. There I had an encounter with the Living God. I fell face down and God spoke to me. "I have a plan for you to fulfill; it's not your time to go." The next thing I remember was desperately calling my husband at work because I was choking and hardly able to breathe or swallow. We rushed to the doctor who took one look and saw a sizeable goiter on my thyroid gland. I was rushed to Hershey Medical Center where a team of endocrinologists recommended steroids immediately. The steroids reduced the swelling and by October 2004 I was completely healed with my thyroid functioning normally again.

Dear Lord, I thank You and praise You for Your healing power. You are an awesome God who loves Your children so very much.

Michele Apicella is a child of God, wife and mother.

My Father Listened to the Lord

"My son, if you accept my word and store up my commandments within you, turning your ear to wisdom and applying your heart to understanding, and if you call out for insight and cry out for understanding, and if you look for it as silver and search for it as a hidden treasure, then you will understand the fear if the Lord and find the knowledge of God." *Proverbs 2:1–5*

Many years ago there was trouble in the church where my father was a member. It was of a serious nature. My father was upset and was considering leaving for another church.

As he contemplated a move, he was stopped one day by seeing the Lord standing by him saying, "Don't." He was surprised and amazed and perhaps relieved that Jesus' Word gave him peace.

And he knew running away from the problem was not the answer, because it really was not his problem. He needed to stay in the church he was in for his family's sake. Pulling up their roots in their church would only confuse them. I am so thankful that my father listened to the Lord.

Lord, I thank you that we can turn our ear to wisdom and find the knowledge of God for everything in our lives.

Miriam Witmer is a mother, grandmother and great grandmother. She and her husband are retired and living at Landis Homes Retirement Community.

Faith Comes

"So then faith [comes] by hearing, and hearing by the word of God."
Romans 10:17 (New King James Version)

"So shall my word be that goes out from my mouth; it shall not return to me empty, but it shall accomplish that which I purpose, and shall succeed in the thing for which I sent it." *Isaiah 55:11 (English Standard Version)*

As a pastor I'm often asked to provide a Bible for someone who requests one, and I gladly provide them. Recently, once again, I was asked to provide a Bible to a young man named Juan (not his real name) whom, I was told, wanted to learn all he could about Jesus. I gladly provided the Bible and within two weeks I received a letter from Juan. I was overjoyed when I found out that he had been reading the Bible non-stop and had come to know Jesus and had made the decision to follow Him. Juan has been attending our Sunday teaching services every Sunday since he made his decision for Christ and it's been a pleasure to watch him grow in his new faith.

I also had the pleasure of baptizing Juan and to see the joy on his face as he made his public declaration that he was proudly a follower of Jesus. Juan's baptism was a spiritual high for me as well as for him.

Father, I thank you for Your Word that it does not "return to you empty, but always accomplishes the purpose you have for it." I pray today for all those seeking You who are reading Your Word today. May Your Holy Spirit draw them to Yourself and above all I pray that they will come to faith through the power of Your Word!

Dale Weaver is the pastor of Sandy Hill Community Church, Coatesville.

.

Will You Choose Me or Fear This Day?

"For God has not given us a spirit of fear but of power, love and a sound mind." *2 Timothy 1:7*

We just finished breakfast and my three sons were busy clearing the table and readying themselves for school. My husband had kissed the boys and me goodbye and headed off to work on his motorcycle. It had only been 10 minutes after he left when suddenly our oldest son told me he saw a picture of daddy on the side of the road in an accident. My heart started to pound.

Right then an ambulance raced passed our house. I ran to my phone to find a message and with trembling hands I held the phone up to my ears. There I heard what my heart was so desperately hoping not to hear: my husband had been in an accident. I froze.

My three sons gathered around me patiently waiting for the news of their father. Immediately I heard the Lord speak to my heart. He asked me, "Will you choose Me or will you choose fear? Your decision will impact how your children see Me and respond to Me in difficult situations." I wanted so much to give in to my fear, but as I looked into the eyes of my boys I knew the choice I had to make. I chose God. I chose to trust in Him and lean on Him in that moment instead of giving into my fear.

As I informed the boys of their father's situation immediately they rallied in faith. They began to pray and tell one another that God can heal and take care of their dad. Their faith infected me and I began to feel God's strength permeating every part of my being. My husband and I believe that their prayers and faith were instrumental in my husband's healing. Today we rejoice in God's faithfulness as a family. We are daily choosing God and not fear.

Thank you, Lord, that You have not given us a spirit of fear but of power, love and a sound mind.

Becky Walseman is a member of Christ Community Church and intern at Teaching The Word Ministries.

The Good Old Days

"Do not say, 'Why were the former days better than these?' For it is not wise to ask such questions." *Ecclesiastes 7:10*

I don't know if our generation is more nostalgic than others, but reference is often made to "The Good Old Days." We would do well to think about the difference between interest-in-the-past on the one hand, and nostalgia on the other.

I admit to having some affinity for lines in Henry Vaughan's poem "*Retreat*":

O how I long to travel back
And tread again the ancient track.
Some men a forward motion love,
But I by backward steps would move.

But the preacher (or teacher) in Ecclesiastes offers this word of caution: "Do not say, 'Why were the former days better than these?' For it is not wise to ask such questions' (Ecclesiastes 7:10)."

Vance Havner, one-time "preacher-boy" from rural North Carolina, in his straight-forward way, made these comments on that verse:

Distance lends enchantment to the view, and in retrospect we crown the past with a halo. Like Saul, we try to call up Samuel, and sigh, "If only Wesley or Finney or Moody were alive now!" Elisha did not pine for Elijah: he asked, "Where is the Lord God of Elijah?" We do not inquire wisely when we cast longing eyes in the direction of the past. The days of Elijah are gone but the God of Elijah lives today. There are no untarnished haloes in any generation, and looking at heroes of any era is disappointing. Look not to "the good old days" but to the God of all the days.

In summary, we should appreciate the past and learn from it. While we cherish many memories, we should not overly sentimentalize or idealize it.

Our Father, thank you for all past blessings—but because of Your love, and our sure hope in Your Son, we look steadfastly forward to our glorious future. In Jesus' name, amen.

Peter W. Teague, Ed.D., is president of Lancaster Bible College and Graduate School.

Love of God's Word

"My soul is starved and hungry, ravenous!—insatiable for your nourishing commands." *Psalm 119:20 (The Message)*

Do you love the word of God? Is it more precious than your newspaper? When you get up in the morning, which do you choose, the morning paper or the living Word?

"Oh, how I love your law! I meditate on it all day long (Psalm 119:97)." Is your mind focused on the news, or on the Good News? David was a man after God's own heart. He loved the Lord and he loved his word. He writes, "Your commands make me wiser than my enemies, for they are ever with me. I have more insight than all my teachers, for I meditate on your statutes. I have more understanding than the elders, for I obey your precepts (Psalm 119:97–100)."

I have found that I need to ask God to give me a love for His Word. If we cry out to Him He will answer that prayer. In answering that prayer, your life will be transformed. You will move from one degree of glory to another.

It is almost always something good that will keep us from the Word of God—something good, but not what is best. Beware of the barrenness of a busy life! God's Word is a lamp and light throughout the day.

In our love of God's Word, we must remember that it is the Word that points us to Jesus—the living Word. We don't worship the Word: we worship Jesus. "You diligently study the scriptures because you think that by them you possess eternal life. These are the scriptures that testify about me, yet you refuse to come to me to have life (John 5:39–40)."

Father, give me a fresh love for Your word so I can know You more intimately. Thank you. Amen.

David Eshleman is a church consultant for Lancaster Mennonite Conference and Eastern Mennonite Missions. He is author of *Now Go Forward: Reaching Out to Grow Your Congregation.*

Red Birds

"I will go before you and make the rough places smooth…"
Isaiah 45:2

When our family built our first home, we never considered moving out. It was an integral part of our future. When we realized we'd have to sell it and find another place to settle, it was heartbreaking.

During that season of searching for a place to move to, I was regularly visited by cardinals. I'd be driving along and suddenly see one swooping in front of my car, just short of a collision with my windshield.

Trust me, this was *no* coincidence. I saw more than thirty cardinals do this daredevil feat! And every time my heart would sense the Lord saying, "I go before you and make the way!" My heart was deeply comforted by His involvement in my life.

Once we secured a place to live, it was as if the cardinals had done their job. Not even *one* took a dive for my windshield again.

We lived in that place for just six months before the Lord sovereignly moved us to our current address, which is a lovely farmhouse situated on several acres. Our family recognizes this homestead as a great gift from the Father.

Interestingly enough, the first week we moved in, my youngest son summoned me into his room calling, "Mom! Come quick! Your red birds!" I scurried into his bedroom, joining him at the window.

To my absolute astonishment, six bright red cardinals were perched on a small tree in the side yard. There were *six* male cardinals hovering about this little tree as if it were as natural as can be. It was a completely ridiculous sight. "*Impossible!*" was my first thought. "There are *six* of us living here," was my next reflection. It was as if the Lord had sent them as a benediction. The sight seemed to imply, "I have made the way for you!" His message of love and care seemed to sing through the scene, "Be blessed!"

Indeed, we are.

Lord thank you for giving us this sign of Your hand guiding our lives.

Kathi Wilson and her husband, Mark, of Body Life Ministries, are trusting God for regional transformation.

Whose Voice Do I Hear?

"…And the sheep follow him, for they know his voice. Yet they will by no means follow a stranger, but will flee from him, for they do not know the voice of strangers." *John 10:4-5 (New King James Version)*

It was on a packed full bus in Nizhniy Novgorod that I heard the voice. "Take a seat!" Seats are so hard to find that if one becomes available I will definitely take the opportunity to sit down. The voice sounded like Pastor Ivan. Not giving it any thought, I allowed the person to help me into the seat behind me. Just as I was getting comfortable, I looked at the open door of the bus and saw my husband, Pastor Ivan and his wife Natasha, and the rest of our group, leaving the bus. I leaped from that seat and bounded for the open door. I was not about to be left behind!

When we were all safely off the bus, I asked, "Who told me to take a seat?" No one knew anything about it: they were all asking each other, "Where is Joyce?"

I began to think, how many times I have listened to the wrong voice.

Lord, it's Your voice I want to hear! Help me to hear You and only You. May I live so in tune with You, that I will quickly differentiate the voice of a stranger!

Joyce Henson is with Petra Christian fellowship and serves with her husband, Darryl, traveling throughout Russia and Eastern Europe, with InSTEP Ministries International.

What Language Do You Speak?

"Do not snatch the word of truth from my mouth, for I have put my hope in your laws." *Psalm 119:43*

Early in my ministry I befriended a Christian counselor who taught me something that has served me very well. In communicating with people, the type of language you use is sometimes as important as the content of what you say. And I'm not just referring to the tone of voice or body language.

What is this secret of effective communication?

It is the distinction between descriptive and prescriptive language. Here's an example to show you the difference between the two. Consider the interaction between patient and doctor. The doctor comes into the room and asks you to "describe" your symptoms. There will most likely be more questions raised by what you describe and at this point the doctor is mostly listening and asking questions for clarification. The doctor will then grow quiet and so should you as she or he listens to your heart and breathing and whatever else is needed. This is all descriptive in nature and is absolutely necessary to come up with a good "prescription" for healing.

Descriptive language clearly lays out what I am thinking or feeling. It is non-judgmental and is not telling the other person to do anything. It leaves room for discussion and give and take in the conversation. The prescription should only come after close examination of the information and facts at hand. Sometimes further testing is necessary before a prescription can be made. In conversations it is best to remain quiet until we have had time to examine all of the facts. Giving thoughtful words to our thoughts and feelings, which are shared in clear non-judgmental ways, is the best gift we can give ourselves and others.

Living God, enable me to give thoughtful expression to my thoughts and feelings in clear descriptive ways. Thank you for hearing me and helping me give healthy voice to my deepest desires.

Jeffrey Snyder is senior pastor of Columbia United Methodist Church and director of the Columbia Community Houses of Prayer.

Oneness - God's Bottom Line

"Blessed are the pure in heart, for they shall see God." *Matthew 5:8*

On January 28, 2009, our 18-year-old daughter survived a serious auto accident. On April 18, 2009, our first grandchild safely arrived with the help of modern medical technology.

Traumatic and milestone events confront us with the weight of history and our own insignificance. What, simply, do life and death, really boil down to?

Gary Thomas, author of *Sacred Parenting*, answers this question from the "Genealogy of Genesis 5" perspective. He says all the boring "begats" "collapse into nothing more than a litany of numbers and outdated names...All we know is that they had kids, and then they died. This simplistic view of life is shockingly honest."

We easily get caught up in the world's detailed complexities to "have it all." Like the man on a variety show who tries to maintain a dozen breakable plates spinning on sticks, we stress ourselves by juggling too many unnecessary priorities. Generations from now, our great, great grandchildren will most likely not know that my husband was a pilot or that I enjoyed interior decorating, or that we lived in a town named Willow Street and that we were high-school sweethearts. So what should we leave to our following generations?

God's Word focuses us on what is eternally significant. Stated simply, God's bottom line is to love God, to obey His commands, and to love others. God desires us to remain pure. Purity is simplicity; it's not contaminated with other impurities. So a pure heart is one that's undivided. It's a oneness of heart that is totally loyal to a jealous God. Our genuine Christianity is the godly heritage we are to leave our children and their children's children.

Dear Lord, we ask that it doesn't take traumatic situations to help us focus on You. Guide us into a purity of heart that is "God only," not "God and." Maintain our "generational" perspective, motivating us to pass on a godly heritage for our great-children.

Tamalyn Jo Heim, author of the up-and-coming parent/teen Bible study, *Purity: The Potter's Plan*, teaches with her husband Bob on marriage and parenting topics at Calvary Church.

For Your Name's Sake

"Yet he saved them for his name's sake, to make his mighty power known." *Psalm 106:8*

God speaks to us in many ways and by various experiences. He often speaks to me by giving me a word or phrase. His purpose for speaking is because He wants me to understand something: a direction, correction, promise, hope or an assurance. Recently He wanted to change, or direct my understanding. Give me a new paradigm. The phrase I received was, "for the sake of His name."

So I went on a search for what he wanted me to understand. He wanted me to know that what He does is done for His name's sake. At first this sounds like God is selfish. Which He most certainly is not! 2 Timothy 2:14 tells me that He must be true to who He is.

My next place to search was the meaning of the names of God. A familiar name is Jehovah Shalom—peace. He is our righteousness, banner, shepherd. He sanctifies, heals, provides. He is there. My understanding was opened to see that while He is these things for me, He does them for His name's sake not for my sake. He will uphold His name all the time because of who He is, not for my sake.

Now I ask myself why I do what I do. And to be honest, most of the time it is done for my sake, even the good that He helps me to do. I think He is saying to me, that this kind of motivation is not appropriate in the kingdom of Heaven. I must, and want to, live for His name's sake. To be a faithful witness to the meaning of Jesus' name, "Savior."

Lord, in Your grace, grant me the power of Your Spirit to live for the sake of Your name.

Kathleen Hollinger, ACTS Covenant Fellowship, is a leader of the prayer ministry.

Vacation

"And he carried me away in the Spirit to a mountain great and high, and showed me the Holy City, Jerusalem, coming down out of heaven from God. It shone with the glory of God, and its brilliance was like that of a very precious jewel, like a jasper, clear as crystal."
Revelation 21:10–11

Just a few years ago, we were going to bring our first child to the shore with us. I was just as excited to share this experience with Hannah as when my parents brought me as a child. The anticipation built until I was acting like a kid myself. Images danced in my mind of a little girl giggling and laughing and then falling asleep peacefully after each day's fun.

Here is what *really* happened on that trip. For twenty minutes that week, swimming in the pool was good. She didn't cry, but there wasn't much giggling either. The playground was fun until it got too hot. Hand-made ice cream was great—but someone couldn't wait patiently for Mommy to offer a bite, and so there were screaming fits. The beach was okay, but the water was toe-chilling—more tears. At night, well, let's just remember that no one can sleep well in a new environment, including toddlers. It really *was* a great vacation filled with family and memories; but it did not match the expectations that I had built up to castle-sized proportion in my home-every-day mind.

We often have expectations of this world that it was never meant to meet. When life is not flawless, we complain. But because of the sin in this world, it never can go perfectly. There is a place where sin cannot mar the smallest detail. And as high as my expectations can get of the perfect vacation, they have not reached the floor of where they can be when I picture heaven. So instead, let's focus on the house of our Heavenly Father.

Lord, thank you for preparing a mansion for me in Your glorious kingdom. Help me to put aside things of this world to focus on what You have for me. Amen

Tracy Slonaker is a wife, mother of three, and Director of Christian Education at Harvest Fellowship of Colebrookdale.

Lest We Forget

"He heals the broken in heart, and binds up their wounds." *Psalm 147:3*

I was filled with a whirlwind of negative emotions! I had sought the Lord for many years. According to His Word, I had honored my husband and learned to be submissive. Why, then, had my spouse abandoned me for another?

During the first part of that devastating season I was in denial, angry, and depressed. How could this be happening to me...to our daughters? What a negative testimony this was to other Christians and non-Christians who knew us and who were watching our lives! My begging and bargaining was to no avail. I was a divorced woman.

When I look back at that single-again season of my life, I marvel at how many adventures and life lessons the Lord allowed me to experience. I realize that there were many lessons that could only have been learned during that difficult, but enlightening, season of my life. I realize that what I had taken for granted—marriage and children—were not the experience of many other women. I have learned that the Lord chooses to use us *because* of our brokenness, our rejection, our losses, our failures. He desires forgiveness and healing for us—yes—but not so that we can forget. Rather, He desires that we come alongside others that they, too, may be healed.

Dear Abba, use us as a conduit of Your grace, mercy, and healing to others. Help us to be an encouragement to the brokenhearted, as we are reminded that You always use every one of our wounds for Your glory and our good.

Denise Colvin is now remarried after many years as a single woman. She and her husband, Rich, a volunteer pastor, minister in a residential assisted living setting at The Villa St. Elizabeth in West Reading.

The Gift of Prayer

"Is anyone among you suffering? Let him pray. Is anyone cheerful? Let him sing psalms. Is anyone among you sick? Let him call for the elders of the church, and let them pray over him, anointing him with oil in the name of the Lord." *James 5:13–14 (New King James Version)*

"We were wondering if we could come over. We have something we want to share with you and we would like to pray with you, if it is alright." The voice on the other end of the phone was a member of our church who has also become a dear friend during our years of ministry here at First Presbyterian Church. When they heard the news of Cherie's recurrence of breast cancer, they wanted to be with us and pray with us.

The thing they wanted to share with us was a meal, but not just one meal. They had brought with them ten meals: ten gift certificates to Carry Out Courier. They said, "We know that there are going to be times during the next months that neither Cherie nor you are going to feel like cooking, and we would gladly do that for you. However, we may not be available, and we wanted you to always have the option for a good meal on us."

We were speechless (yes, even a pastor is speechless from time to time). The generosity of the gift was overwhelming to us. We felt cared for, supported, and uplifted.

Equally important to the visit was the prayer that was offered. Their words lifted us into the presence of God, reminding us that all healing comes from God and that God still works miracles, holding up the medical team that would be working with Cherie, and praying for her peace and my strength.

Our friends did not anoint us physically, but they prayed for us and left behind a gift that was and is a constant reminder that we are not alone, and that was wonderful. Hope had a face for us, the face of friends.

Lord Jesus, thank you for the friends who embody Your love for us in the most difficult circumstances of our lives. Bless them even as they bless us. In Jesus' name. Amen.

The Rev. Dr. Randolph T. Riggs is pastor of First Presbyterian Church in downtown Lancaster.

Behind the Waterfall

"Deep calls to deep in the roar of your waterfalls…." *Psalm 42:7*

"Arise my beautiful one…in the clefts of the rock, in the hiding places…show me your face, let me hear your voice…." *Song of Solomon 2: 13–14*

About four years ago, awake, I saw in a vision lots of people playing, myself included, in the river. The river was fun and it had a waterfall. We were all laughing and splashing each other while having a good time of fellowship in the Lord. Then I heard the Lord say to me, "Come behind the waterfall." Slowly moving behind the waterfall, I was immediately in the chamber of the Lord. The room was beautiful. Jesus was in the room smiling at me. He beckoned for me to come and sit with Him. He fed me grapes and some wonderful white stuff. I said, "I should be serving You."

He smiled and I was humbled and honored all at the same time. He spoke things directly to my heart during this time, and put a ring on my finger. When it was time to leave, He said, "It is good to play in the river, but I desire that you come often behind the waterfall."

This vision impacted my life, and continues to do so to this day. Recently, I sense the Lord wanting me to share this more openly with others. Jesus' desire is to be alone with each of us. He wants to feed us and for us to receive from His hand, not just be content playing in the river.

Father, thank you for Jesus. May we come often behind the waterfall. Give us ears to hear in the midst of the river Your heart beckoning us. May our hearts cry be to go deeper—to know Jesus and to be known of Him.

Debbie Davenport serves as a leader interceding and equipping others for kingdom purposes in her varied roles in the body of Christ and at Cornerstone Pregnancy Care Services.

Land of the Free

"Under the old system, the blood of goats and bulls and the ashes of a young cow could cleanse people's bodies from ritual defilement. Just think how much more the blood of Christ will purify our hearts from deeds that lead to death so that we can worship the living God."
Hebrews 9:13–14 (New Living Translation)

As I reflect back over the years of my life, I recall too many experiences of carrying emotional loads related to worry, fear or other areas of sin that our bodies were not meant to carry. One situation as a teenager was on our family farm. I shot one of my dad's ducks with my small BB gun. While sharing lunch together as a family, of course it was dad who discovered the BB in his entrée of duck. The wrong was no longer a hidden weight as it was exposed and forgiveness was experienced.

The year 2010 is the 300th anniversary in Lancaster County of Europeans receiving the first land grants from William Penn, land originally inhabited by Native Americans. History reveals many injustices done by Europeans to the Natives throughout the early years in this county. While none of us had direct involvement in these injustices, forgiveness is essential for healthy and prosperous living. "Now" is always a right time to move in an attitude of forgiveness where forgiveness was needed but never pursued.

God never intended our bodies to have to carry the unnecessary loads on our backs due to wrong-doing and sin toward each other. Since the beginning of creation He made a way to be free. Jesus Christ gave his own blood so that we can receive cleansing of wrong, sin, and the very things that will eventually rob of the ability to live free from the things that can weigh us down and destroy us.

Father, I thank you that Jesus Christ died, rose again, and has thoroughly paid the price for our freedom. I ask You for forgiveness for wrongs that I have been carrying that have been weighing me down and please give me grace to move in an attitude of forgiveness toward others.

Lloyd Hoover, is a bishop in the Lancaster Conference of the Mennonite Church. He serves on the executive team of the Regional Church of Lancaster County, and is exec. director of The Potter's House and other Healing Ministries.

Mural in the city of Reading, Berks County
Photo by Mark Van Scyoc

September

READING
A CULTURALLY UNIFIED COMMUNITY

The Donegal Witness Tree

"Trust in the Lord and do good; dwell in the land and enjoy safe pasture. Delight yourself in the Lord and he will give you the desires of your heart. Commit your way to the Lord; trust in him and he will do this: He will make your righteousness shine like the dawn, the justice of your cause like the noonday sun." *Psalm 37:3–6*

About 1700, the English crown had declared the English Established Church as the only church to be tolerated in Ireland. Presbyterians were shut out by law from all civil, military, and municipal offices. Landed gentry was brought in, and the Scotch who lived there for many years were evicted or required to pay high rent in order to remain.[1]

Deprived of civil rights and freedom to worship, large numbers of Presbyterians made the dangerous trip to America and settled in Lancaster County. Many settled in the northwest part of the county and in 1721 they founded Donegal Presbyterian Church. This is one of the oldest continuously operating churches in Lancaster County. (www.donegalpc.org)

The Revolutionary War was important to the local Scot-Irish Presbyterians. They did not want to be oppressed by the British Empire any longer. Many Colonial colonels came out of the Donegal Church alone. On a Sunday in June 1777, the Donegal Church service was interrupted by orders for the battalion of Donegal men to come and join the fight against the British. The congregation immediately dismissed and circled around an old oak tree outside to bless the soldiers and renew their commitment to fight for freedom and independence. This tree came to be known as the "Witness Tree" and stood for over 300 years. A new tree, grown from an acorn from the original, now stands in its place.[2]

[1] *Scotch-Irish Presbyterians in Lancaster County, Pennsylvania* by Ross Morrison, 2004, pp. 4–5

[2] *Ibid.*, pp .7–8)

God of freedom, thank you for a country where we can live, work, and worship publicly without fear of oppression. We humbly seek You to guide our steps so we can work for justice in all places, for all people. In Christ, we pray, Amen.

Don Hackett is a Scots-Irish Presbyterian pastor in Lancaster.

Our Incredible Value to God

"Look at the birds of the air; they do not sow or reap or store away in barns, and yet your heavenly Father feeds them. Are you not much more valuable than they?" *Matthew 6:26*

As I write this, it's getting to be Fall. During this time of year, many birds are migrating south to their winter home. You may have seen geese flying together, especially if you are up early. It's amazing to see their formations. They can get to where they are going without MapQuest, a GPS, or the AAA. They get where they need to go, often thousands of miles away. They travel without hotel or restaurant reservations. Those that eat seeds, find seeds. Those that eat bugs, find insects. Those that eat worms...well I won't go there. God takes care of them all.

And in the same way, He knows the plans that He has for us and He will get us to the right place at the right time. In the last few months it certainly has been a time of uncertainty. Our country has been going through big financial crises. But as God cares for these birds over their long trip, He promises to care for us, too.

Lord, help us to keep our eyes on You and not on our circumstances, because as You have promised to take care of the birds, You have promised to take care of us.

Beth Holden is a wife, mother, grandmother, and a former nursing instructor. She and her husband, Bill, serve in various ways at Lancaster Alliance Church.

Going Not Knowing

"Therefore, since we are surrounded by such a great cloud of witnesses, let us throw off everything that hinders and the sin that so easily entangles, and let us run with perseverance the race marked out for us." *Hebrews 12:1*

"Do you see what this means—all these pioneers who blazed the way, all these veterans cheering us on? It means we'd better get on with it. Strip down, start running—and never quit! No extra spiritual fat, no parasitic sins." *Hebrews 12:1 (The Message)*

Tom Hanks played a character in the movie *Castaway* who had been in control of his life and moved other people to get things accomplished. "Time is everything" was his motto, since he was a manager of FedEx. Finding himself on a deserted island after his plane goes down, he goes through raw life and the gamut of emotions from surviving to giving up, deciding to continue to breathe in, breathe out, and taking one step after another. After four years on the island, he makes a raft and decides to head out to the ocean knowing that the chances of being found on a raft are slim. As he leaves the island, you watch the ripping and tearing of his being as he paddles his raft into the ocean. He continues to look at the island and you can almost hear him think, "at least I'll be safe." He was leaving the familiar, albeit hopeless, circumstances to chance the unknown.

Isn't this human nature? God calls us forth into new territory and how difficult it is to leave what's familiar even if it is barren and empty. But just like Joshua, God calls us forth with the command, "Be strong and of good courage. Do not be terrified; do not be discouraged for the Lord your God will be with you wherever you go (Joshua 1:9)."

Lord, increase our faith and give us vision. Amen.

Christina Ricker, daughter of the King, is a wife, mother and nana.

Name Carved in Stone

"...And rejoice that [our] names are written in Heaven." *Luke 10:20 (English Standard Version)*

We slowly drove the Blue Ridge Parkway as we appreciated the kaleidoscope of color from the Fall leaves and tried to locate a special tree.Years ago, my girlfriend (now my wife) and I, along with best friends, took a drive from Lynchburg, VA, where we were all studying at the time, to this scenic parkway. And I had chosen a special tree, easy to find, to bear our heart, arrow and initials. It was a fairly young tree back then and was near the top of a tunnel on the north-east side. I know the exact spot. In fact, we stopped on this journey, but aborted the mission. Either the side of the tunnel grew steeper or I was much more agile in the mid-seventies. I'm hoping for the former but willing to concede to the latter.

There's a good chance the initials are still there unless they've been rutted away by a buck, struck by lightning or nibbled into sawdust by hungry termites. Our love remains. But I don't need initials in a tree to secure that promise.

Our initials, rather names, have been etched in stone, so to speak and will last forever not only in the heart of our heavenly Father, but also in the Lamb's Book of Life. In Revelation, John observes what he sees in heaven. At least twice he mentions the Lamb's book of Life which contains names. Scattered throughout the Old and New Testament are verses that reference this book as well. It's a good thing to have your name in the book, bad not to, and just as bad or worse if it is blotted out. I don't choose to get into the theological discussion of the latter circumstance, but I do wish to follow what our Lord said as recorded in Luke 10:20 and "rejoice that [our] names are written in Heaven."

No one can erase it, rub it off, white it out, delete it or rip out the page on which it is written. My name is in the book!

Thank you, Jesus, for inscribing my name in Your book. May it be the case with my friends who read this as well. May we rejoice in You together.

Dr. Dan Allen is a pastor, writer, conference speaker, radio commentator and Director of Pinebrook Bible Conference, East Stroudsburg.

Honor Our Veterans in Christ Jesus

"Stand up in the presence of a person with gray hair, show respect for the old; you are to fear your God; I am the Lord." *Leviticus 19:32 (The Complete Jewish Bible)*

Edna Gingrich was born in 1914 and lived an ordinary life. She worked on the family farm, cleaned houses, and quietly shared her faith. But it was an extraordinary life to her because she had a personal relationship with the Lord Jesus Christ.

Edna was seeking the Lord "because I knew I was a sinner." He found her in 1932 as she knelt at her church altar. She heard a small voice telling her to stand up. She obeyed, and then "something happened to me. It was between the floor and the ceiling, and it was between me and my Jesus. That was my starting place. Ever since that time I've been calling on my Jesus. I've made many, many mistakes, but every time I called, I always found Him there."

In 2000, Edna was living at the United Zion Home in Lititz. Doctors told her four times she would soon be gone. One night she awoke suddenly. Someone was touching her arm. No one was in the room with her. She thought it must be an angel coming to take her home. Then a small voice told her, "You've got to witness." But who would listen to an elderly woman cooped up in a retirement home?

The next day the Lord sent me to interview Edna for a column in the Lititz Record-Express, called "My secret of a good, long life." And so Edna became salt and light to an entire community, as she bore witness to Jesus' power to fill ordinary people's lives with blessing, joy and hope.

Lord Jesus, I lift up the witnesses and prayer warriors. May we always honor them for the wisdom You have given them and the difference they make in our nation.

Norman Saville, along with his wife, Joyce, worship at Hope of the Nations Christian Center in Reading, and work with Ken and Betty Eberly at Behold Your God Ministries.

Reproduce Yourself

"Therefore do not cast away your confidence, which has great reward. For you have need of endurance, so that after you have done the will of God, you may receive the promise: 'For yet a little while, And He who is coming will come and will not tarry. Now the just shall live by faith; But if anyone draws back, My soul has no pleasure in him.'" *Hebrews 10:35–38*

Everything the Lord created with life has the ability to reproduce. Inside of every apple is an orchard. Inside every cow is a herd, inside every bird is a flock, inside every fish a school. And, most importantly, inside every person is a legacy to live and leave for others to follow.

I can take an apple and put it in cold storage and it will be preserved for months or I can put it in the ground and it will grow and reproduce. The only difference between preserving and reproducing is the environment that I placed the apple in.

You and I are like that apple. We can place ourselves in safe environments that preserve us—safe places that we learn to function in, places that seem secure and do not require change or growth on our parts. Alternatively, we can take risks, step outside of our comfort zones, and place ourselves in environments that force us to grow. Placing the apple in the ground does not require the apple to do anything; the course of nature and the impact of the environment around it force it to grow. It's kind of like stepping out of my comfort zone and doing something different than before. Just the dynamics of the circumstances will force me to grow. Do I need more training? Do I need to take a step of faith? Do I need to be mentored in someway? Whatever it is, I take a bold step forward knowing that unless I position myself to grow, I will only be preserved. There is no reproduction in preservation.

Take a step in confidence and ask yourself this question. What environment do I need to be in to be able to grow and reproduce? Then take steps to place yourself in that environment. Do not draw back, for the Lord has pleasure in those who press into His plans and purposes for their lives. Reproduce! It is a biblical principle.

Lord, help us to take risks so we can reproduce!

Ron Myer serves as assistant international director of DOVE Christian Fellowship International.

Suffering that Brings Comfort to Others

"...Who comforts us in all our troubles, so that we can comfort those in any trouble with the comfort we ourselves have received from God." *2 Corinthians 1:4*

As a child, I was a delayed learner and did not learn to read until I was 8 and a half years old. That humiliating experience helps me to identify with the students I teach who struggle with learning difficulties.

Through an amazing set of circumstances, which can only be explained by God's guidance, God enabled me to develop a reading program that has helped many children who "learn differently."

One of the many things God has given me insight to incorporate and expand is a program using letter people, which help children understand letters and sounds. Each child is unique, so God often gives me ideas to help concrete and visual learners. For example, one child excelled in making things with Legos but could make no sense of words. God helped me think of a novel way to use Legos to teach reading concepts that he could grasp.

I've been privileged to see non-readers advance two to three grade levels within a school year. I also tutor students in math. This past year, one seventh grader entered my program testing at third-grade level math. Within the year, she advanced to sixth-grade math.

It is a great joy to see my students' self esteem and confidences soar as they experience success in learning. What a thrill to see how God's plan in allowing me to be a delayed learner worked together for good for both my students and me.

God, I'm amazed how You can take the troubles in our lives, comfort us and use those experiences to comfort others.

Sandra Kirkpatrick is a member of Ephrata-Lititz DOVE Christian Fellowship. She tutors students in reading, grammar and math.

"Me" Perspective

"But God said to Jonah, 'Do you have a right to be angry about the vine?'" *Jonah 4:9*

I've traveled to many vacation sites, but from my perspective, the best relaxation spot is available in my backyard. There, we have a spacious hammock stretched between a purple plum tree and a sturdy oak tree.

In recent years the trees have grown tall and branched out until their leaves mingle together. Lying on the hammock, I bask in the sunlight filtering through the leafy canopy. The slight breeze wards off summer's humidity and with it the daily stress of everyday living. The quietness of the countryside calms my spirit. Problems fade away and I'm content to let time slip away instead of facing chores that need to be tackled.

Sometimes as I lay there, I think of Jonah and how much pleasure he took in the vine that shaded him from life's harsh realities. Most people criticize Jonah for becoming angry when his vine was destroyed, but I understand Jonah's perspective. Underneath his vine, his discomfort with dealing with reality eased. Relaxing in the shade he almost forgot about the scorching sun, being thrown overboard into an angry ocean, his rough ride in the belly of the whale before being vomited on to dry land and his disappointment in God not holding up his end of the bargain. Hidden by the leaves, Jonah felt sheltered from the public's scorn that he was a false prophet because God had changed His mind and would not destroy the city after all. When the vine was destroyed, Jonah could no longer ignore reality. He was so upset: he wanted to die.

And that's why God reprimanded him. Jonah was preoccupied with the "me" perspective. God took away the vine to demonstrate the foolishness of being consumed with personal comfort and reputation instead of God's merciful compassion.

God, give me balance and perspective to discern when "me" concerns infringe on the time that should be spent in caring for others.

Lou Ann Good attends DOVE Christian Fellowship-Westgate and is a freelance writer.

Trust Me, I Will Provide

"The Lord is my strength; He will make my feet like deer's feet, And He will make me walk on my high hills." *Habakkuk 3:19*

Several years ago I gave up my job because I felt God's calling to write. I wondered how God would provide for the lost income, but I wanted to be faithful to His call. My husband had a good job at the time, so I was confident we would be okay.

When my husband's job ended, I questioned if it was truly God's will that I write and not work? This haunting question constantly lurked in the back of my mind. Doubt often tormented me and with my husband home, it became difficult to concentrate on the writing. We were challenged as never before, yet I still believed God would provide.

When I developed a painful condition in my feet, walking became difficult and I was unable to go about my normal activities. I was "forced" to be still. In that stillness, I found the time to write and discovered a deeper understanding of what it means to let God be in control of my life.

Still, the pain in my feet increased and eventually my doctor recommended a treatment that our insurance would not cover. Financially strapped, this therapy seemed beyond my reach. Then came a phone call from a longtime friend to whom I had not spoken for months. In our conversation I mentioned the problem with my feet. Later that evening my friend called saying it was critical that I come to her home that evening. As we visited, she handed me a check in the exact amount needed for the foot procedure. Her husband had overheard our conversation. God had laid it on his heart to provide for this need.

God is showing me that He will take care of me. I must not count on my husband's provision nor seek employment. I must look only to my heavenly Father. I must not doubt His will for my life, but walk obediently in it. As I trust Him, He enables me to climb over the hard places, see beyond the pain of this physical existence, and walk out of the valleys of discouragement onto the heights of His calling.

Thank you, Father, for Your provision for my every need. You have held me up when I stumbled in doubt and unbelief.

Nancy Magargle is a member of Lancaster Christian Writers and a speaker for Stonecroft Ministries.

Second Chance Together

"For it is by grace you have been saved, through faith—and this is not from yourselves, it is the gift of God." *Ephesians 2:8*

It was one of those days when everything I had planned was rearranged, unknown to me, for good reason. As you will read, there are many "God moments" in this story.

My mom had called me and asked if I would go to the store and get her some Tylenol. She was having really bad pains in her back and didn't want to drive. When I got there, she told me she thought she was having a heart attack, so off to the hospital we went. When the doctor examined her, he told her that if she didn't have stents put in immediately she would have a full blown heart attack.

First off, the surgical team had "nothing to do" at that moment and could take my mom right away! Secondly, one of the girls who was on the team happened to be my sister's best friend's daughter. She told us she would trust that doctor with her own mother's life.

Everyone left the room and I was alone with mom, and I knew that the Lord wanted me to talk to her about Him. I went to her, held her hand and asked her what her fear was, and of course it was the fear of dying. My mom was not a believer so I talked to her about Jesus and the reasons why He died for us and explained that if she believed she would live with Him forever.

She accepted the work He did for her on the cross and spoke aloud her belief in Him. Later, we talked about how everything fell into place. She told me that she didn't remember that she told me she was having a heart attack. I told her that it was God speaking to her.

She has since gone on to be with Him and I am thankful for that day when I was able to lead her to the Truth, for now I know beyond a shadow of a doubt that she is with Him.

Lord, thank you for rearranging "our" plans so they fit Your perfect will for our lives. Help us to live our every moment for the kingdom.

Eileen Christiansen is a leader for Celebrate Recovery, a Christ centered 12 step programs in West Sadsburyville.

I Declare!

"Because he hath set his love upon me, therefore I will deliver him. I will set him on high because he hath known my name. He shall call upon me, and I will answer him, I will be with him in trouble, I will deliver him and honor him." *Psalm 91:14–15 (King James Version)*

It took me a while, but I memorized Psalm 91. The thought crossed my mind there might be something really difficult coming up. Only a couple of months later I landed at the bottom of the stairs where I live. A cracking sound and intense pain told me I was not going to be able to help myself. I called on Psalm 91. The Lord not only knew what I was going to go through, but His word alive in me was helping me through it. The declaration that came out of me rang through the house, "I declare this is for God's glory and my good!" Sometimes it rang softly: other times it sounded more like a war chant. I sensed an inner confidence I did not feel on the outside. It wasn't long before I was discovered lying on the floor; 911 was called, and I was whisked away to the hospital with a broken femur.

During and after the hospital stay, my beautiful family and friends watched over me. Some friends took me into their home for a month. I was nearly helpless. They went above and beyond in helping me to adjust to my new pace and keep a positive outlook for the future. Rick and Jess, the friends I stayed with have a little dog that stayed by my side. I called her Nurse Scruffy. Maybe angels sometimes come in fur.

I was overwhelmed with the love shown by my employer and co-workers. They pulled together and carried the weight of my responsibilities until I could return. And they continue to encourage and support my healing path. I have learned that my faith is not built on my comfort, or understanding. It is built on His promises, and His strength. What I am called to do is trust Him with all my heart, lean not on my own understanding, acknowledge Him in everything I do, and wait for Him to direct me.

Thank you Father for Your Word that is alive in us. Thank you for Your presence and Your promises.

Carol Sanchez is a follower of Jesus, loving Him and others and serving those He loves, as He appoints.

Spiritual Gifts

"We have different gifts according to the grace given us." *Romans 12:6*

Paul reminds us in Romans 12:4-8 that we all have spiritual gifts whether it be prophesying, serving, teaching, encouraging, contributing to needs of others, leadership, showing mercy—and adds that all are to be offered cheerfully! Discerning our spiritual gifts is always a lively and much returned-to topic whether in Sunday School, small groups, home Bible studies or just among close friends over a cup of coffee. Having finally reached retirement age, I was still puzzling over just what my gift might be—surely I should have discovered it many years ago?

While visiting with residents in a local nursing home recently, it suddenly dawned on me—my "gift" is that proverbial gift-of-gab! That may not sound too spiritual, but I believe it truly comes from God, fitting smoothly into the category of "encouraging." I rejoice now in the knowledge that I'm not *just* a chatterbox, but a chatterbox with *purpose*. Responding to any subject at a moment's notice does not require in-depth conversation, but it does require a mind that is tuned in to 'seeing' what is needed at that particular moment, to help that particular person, in that particular situation.

God rewards us daily by strengthening both us and our gifts the more we put them into practice, even if the gift seems as silly as being a perpetual small-talker. No gift is too small or too unusual to be put to work for our Lord. When you think about it, He truly does have a magnificent sense of humor, doesn't He? Praise God for our vast differences and our sometimes comical, individual abilities!

Dear Lord, thank you for giving Your children such diverse gifts, all to Your glory and to Your use. We praise Your name because we are so wonderfully and fearfully made! Amen.

Janet Medrow works with Scripture Union in Valley Forge, and is a deacon at Great Valley Presbyterian Church.

Shalom Makers

"Blessed are the peacemakers for they will be called the Sons of God." *Matthew 5:9*

Historians speak of the Roman age of peace—the Pax Romana. However, Rome was one of the most brutal empires that ruled the face of the earth. Romans brought peace by causing people to submit in fear of their mighty sword. This wasn't real peace. It was the absence of war. There is a big difference. The Hebrew word used in the Bible for peace was *shalom*. Shalom was a blessing that people exchanged with one another. It meant so much more than the absence of war.

It meant the presence of everything good—health, prosperity, long life, joy and fulfillment. When a person actively engages in work that helps to bring health and wholeness or feeds the hungry or extends the hand of welcome to the alien, he or she is making shalom. They are peacemakers!

Jesus says in Matthew 5 that His followers were people who created shalom. When we visit an elderly neighbor we create shalom. When we volunteer at Water Street Ministries or the Salvation Army we create shalom. When we support clean water initiatives through Mennonite Central Committee we are doing the work of peace. When we serve with Habitat for Humanity or Mennonite Disaster Service to build homes for the poor, we are shalom makers! When we sit down and listen to an angry child, spouse, neighbor or church member and try to resolve the conflict, we are doing the work of God.

There's a human tendency to use the "forget and avoid" approach to conflict resolution. For peace-making we substitute peace-faking. We say, "Oh, just forget it" and then avoid the unpleasant person or situation. What results is a false peace—a counterfeit peace that is achieved by absence. We absent ourselves from the struggle. The unhappy partner leaves the marriage. The unhappy member leaves the church. The unhappy employee avoids his quarreling coworkers. God's brand of peace is a genuine peace. It is shalom!

Our Father, we ask for Your help to be like You in the effort to create shalom in our world.

Dan Houck, has been a pastor in the Brethren in Christ Church since 1978. Currently he is the pastor of the Table Community Church in Lancaster.

He's My Provision

"Day by day the Lord takes care of the innocent, and they will receive a reward that lasts forever. They will survive through hard times; even in famine they will have more than enough." *Psalm 37:18–19 (New Living Translation)*

Coming home from work I walked into the garage. I noticed that my husband's work tools were there, but his work truck was not in the driveway. I wondered why, and asked him, "Hey, did you have an accident on the icy roads this morning or did you get laid off?" He confirmed he had lost his job that morning.

Being a practical person, I drove right back to work and started the process of putting him on my insurance. I saw that as our first step of "survival" and I wanted to take care of it right away. I didn't forget about God, but just now He was coming along on my ride.

Shortly upon returning home, I realized the truth. This lay-off blindsided us but the Lord was not one bit surprised. We could make plans and adjustments, but only God sees the whole picture. He spoke sweetly to me the entire evening, telling me not to worry; tomorrow will take care of itself. He's taking care of me—I can depend on Him because He gave His life for me. These are words of truth—words that I've spent most of my lifetime putting into my heart. Peace came over me and I knew I was loved and provided for no matter what our situation was.

Father, thank you for who You are and that nothing is out of Your control. Help me to completely trust You, especially when I am afraid of the future. You are always faithful and You will provide everything we need. Amen.

Belinda Fry attends DOVE Elizabethtown Celebration and is the leader of the ladies' Heart Connection group that meets in her home.

Everything We Need

"And without faith it is impossible to please God, because anyone who comes to him must believe that he exists and that he rewards those who earnestly seek him." *Hebrews 11:6*

"Now faith is being sure of what we hope for and certain of what we do not see." *Hebrews 11:1*

The Lord spoke to my heart recently and said, "If it's in My Word, it's yours!" A short time later, during a time of worship, He said, "You must believe that I am a rewarder...." I looked the verse up and read it. Then I inquired of the Lord why He was speaking just that part of the verse.

The Lord took me to Hebrews 11:1, "Now faith is the substance of things hoped for, the evidence of things not [yet] seen (KJV)." He said, "Look at the words *substance* and *evidence;* faith sees the substance, faith sees the evidence, so that what you are asking for (or decreeing) is made a reality. It is no longer a hope; it is seen; it becomes a tangible substance—something you can say, 'I saw the evidence for myself.'"

So, the Lord said, "If it is truly faith, it will see the substance; it will see the evidence of what is being asked of Me. To go from hope, to go beyond saying 'I believe' into the faith that sees the results, you must understand that I am a rewarder, rewarding those who diligently seek Me."

God is no respecter of persons: what He has done for one person, He will do for another. He has given us everything we need. If it's in His Word, it is ours! We are heirs and joint heirs with God, through Christ! If you really want to move into the faith realm that sees the substance of things hoped for, the evidence of things not seen, open your heart to receive the revelation of who you are in Christ. You are seated in heavenly places for the purpose of bringing heaven to earth!

Father God, we love You and we receive a greater measure of Your divine love and Your very nature that opens our hearts to receive the fuller revelation of who we are in You.

Sandra Bernhardt is the founder and president of Joy Celebration Ministries, and laid foundation with two other pastors for The Apostolic Church that meets in Lancaster.

Boy, Have I Learned About Pain and Being a Receiver

"By faith we understand that the universe was formed at God's command, so that what is seen was not made out of what was visible." *Hebrews 11:3*

The Word teaches us in Hebrews 11:1-3 that Christian hope causes us to live a certain way.

This springtime, I planted nine tomato plants in a different area where I believed there would be more sunlight. During this planting I pinched a nerve in my lower back. For months, I have been in and out of the hospital, prayed for by many and anointed with oil. I learned throughout this time just how pain feels and how it takes over your body, but I also learned the importance of how to receive from others.

Since I was saved 66 years ago, I have served in a number of roles and responsibilities as pastor, shepherd, teacher, and on a number of church and denominational boards. I have mostly been a server. For over 50 years I have visited the ill, prayed for them, and led a team of men and women visiting local hospitals, nursing homes, rehabilitation centers and private homes. I keep a record of my visits for renewing my ministry license each year, and I usually have visited local hospitals 100 times each year. I just love to serve.

But since I have been ill, I have been receiving visits in the hospital and at my home. Believe it or not, it was hard for me to receive. But the Lord has taught me to receive with a loving heart. I've learned to let God take care of me through other people and be a receiver as well as a giver.

Lord, thank you for hope in Christ, and for learning to receive from the hearts of others.

Robert A. Burns is a pastor, shepherd and leader of the Glad Tidings Assembly of God Pastoral Care Team, West Lawn.

Bow Down to God Only

"You shall not make for yourself an idol in the form of anything in heaven above or on the earth beneath or in the waters below. You shall not bow down to them or worship them; for I, the Lord your God, am a jealous God, punishing the children for the sin of the fathers to the third and fourth generation of those who hate me."
Exodus 20:4–5

My grandfather was a 32nd degree Mason. He died young, at the age of 57. Several years after he died, I received a tape from a family member, who attended a meeting where insight was given on how families associated with freemasonry should repent and renounce confessions that were made in the mason rituals.

I stuck the tape in and proceeded to listen as I cleaned my house. I didn't realize it, but I was about to have a spiritual house cleaning of my own. At the end of the tape, there was a prayer that we could agree with. To my surprise, I physically felt something leave my body as I prayed. I had no idea I was cursed in some areas, because of what my grandfather opened himself and his family to. I know he would never curse himself or his family on purpose, but that is the whole idea behind hoodwinking.

Proverbs 18:21 tells us that "death and life are in the power of the tongue" and God says in Deuteronomy 30:19 that He has "set before you life and death, blessings and curses. Now choose life, so that you and your children may live." It is so important to watch our words and agree with God's Word by putting His Word in our mouth.

Father, thank you for Your compassion to heal and restore people from any and all curses by repenting and renouncing them. In Jesus' name, Amen.

Dorinda Kaylor is a regional intercessor and minister at Gateway House of Prayer and Lancaster Prison.

Angels in My Bedroom

"Even angels long to look into these things." *1 Peter 1:12*

It was 3:30 a.m. when I felt my water break. I had been anxiously awaiting the arrival of my seventh child, and the time had finally come! I lay in bed trying to get some much needed rest before my contractions started. I was hoping for a supernatural, pain-free homebirth in this very room! All of a sudden a picture flashed into my mind. Angels were crowding into our little bedroom. There were so many of them, that they stood wing pressed against wing, powerful and majestic. The room felt electrified with their excitement. They wanted front row seats to this amazing event, the birth of a human child—a child of destiny created in the very image of God.

The morning turned into afternoon and my labor became more and more painful. I totally forgot about the angels. I began to get so tired; my muscles quaked. I watched the hours tick by on the clock. Finally our beautiful baby boy came into this world at 6 p.m.

The next few days I tried to concentrate on the joy of this new life, but all my muscles were sore and after-contractions continued to rack my body with waves of pain. This was not the glorious experience I had been anticipating! Slowly by the third day the pain subsided, and I began to regain my strength. It was only then that I was reminded of the angels packed tightly into our room. Even though the event did not feel supernatural to me, God pulled back the veil of this life and allowed me to see into the spiritual realm. This birth was something that created shockwaves among hosts of heaven and changed the landscape of eternity! We go about our daily activities usually oblivious to the angels and the great cloud of witnesses cheering us on. But if we live for God, the seemingly normal, mundane, and even painful things bring glory to Him.

Lord, help me to see how my life today is changing the landscape of eternity!

Anne Brandenburg is a mother of six and the wife of Chris, a pastor at Life Center Ministries.

Eugene is Dying

"This is the day the Lord has made; let us rejoice and be glad in it."
Psalm 118:24

Eugene is dying. I don't know much about Eugene's life. I don't know how long he lived in Florida, or the name of his girlfriend. I don't know why he walked with a cane. I do know a little about his last days.

A week ago I stopped and talked to him as he waited for a ride to his radiation treatment. He wore a New England Seafood baseball cap and squinted in the sun. He told me he was feeling good and had determined to wake each morning remembering that this was the day the Lord had made and would rejoice and be glad in it. "I could just as easily have died on a sidewalk," he said. "I have everything I need at the Mission."

Several months earlier Eugene's cancer had started in his lungs. Now it was in his brain. He smiled as he spoke. He spoke—almost gratefully—about having the opportunity to walk in the shoes of his girlfriend who had died of cancer many years earlier.

A few weeks before our conversation in the parking lot, Eugene was with a group of us gathered around a long Amish dinner table. We ate a hearty meal and shared our stories. We were joined by an Italian photographer and his family from New York, retired missionaries from France and a basketball coach from Arizona. When I introduced myself, my voice cracked when I spoke of the honor of calling Eugene, Allen and Kenneth my friends. The sacredness of the moment had surprised me in the darkening farmhouse. We ended the evening singing "Amazing grace how sweet the sound that saved a wretch like me."

Today Eugene nears eternity. This is a sacred time. Eugene's life has been redeemed by the Saviour who knew him in life and will greet him in death. The last words Eugene said to me were, "Thank you for talking to me."

Thank you for talking to *me*, Eugene.

Lord help us to see the sacred moments in each day.

Debbi Miller is the executive secretary at Water Street Ministries. She lives with her husband, four teenagers and two dogs in Lititz.

Can You Hear a Twig Snap?

"Be self-controlled and alert. Your enemy the devil prowls around like a roaring lion looking for someone to devour. Resist him, standing firm in the faith...." *1 Peter 5:8*

Recently I was taking a much needed break and visiting the majestic Niagara Falls. My life had seemed to lack focus lately and I felt an increasing desire to get away for a time of prayer. As I listened to the roar of the falls it brought to mind a story I had heard about an eighteenth-century evangelist named John Whittier. Whittier was a mighty preacher who lived in the early colonies after coming to America from England. One day he and an Indian companion stood before the great Niagara Falls. As they were listening to the thunder of the water as it crashed below, his Indian companion said, "I hear an enemy coming." Whittier turned to him and asked in wonder, "How do you know there's an enemy coming?"

The Indian replied, "Because I just heard a twig snap." The Indian's alertness saved the two men that day from the attack of an enemy Whittier didn't even know was near. In this same way we must be listening attentively to what the Holy Spirit is saying to us. The enemy intends to do all that he can to distract us from the things of God. Therefore, we must focus on our God-given assignment pouring our time, energy, finances, and attention into that goal.

Nehemiah demonstrated this when he surveyed the broken down walls of Jerusalem. He had to continually resist the voice of Sanballat and Tobiah and keep the people focused on the task at hand. He protected his "God assignment" at all costs. He was firm in faith and refused to allow the enemy to blur his vision in any way.

I discovered that day that it is important to ignore those things that would distract us from our God-given mandate. We need to put to death every distraction and maintain focus as a way of life. Success will only come when we keep our minds clear and focus on the things of God.

Father, help us to stay clear and focused today. Keep us sensitive to the move of Your Spirit despite the "noise" around us. Amen.

Pat Denlinger is founder of Forerunner Ministries, prayer leader at Teaching The Word Ministries and is involved in the worship and prayer ministry at Church of The Word International.

God's Command to Loving Parents

"Train a child in the way he should go, and when he is old he will not turn from it." *Proverbs 22:6*

Several years ago we took our children camping on an island at Raystown Lake. Since the only access to the island was by boat, our friends met us and took us to the island on their boat. We planned to spend the weekend tenting on the island and sharing in special times on the lake. Though water depths go much deeper than 150 feet at places, all of us wore our life preservers and felt the assurance of safety they provided. We had so much fun tubing and swimming that weekend. As they say *all good things must come to an end.* The morning we were to leave we decided to go out one more time. We put on our life preservers and went out to enjoy one more splash in the water. We went back to camp and cleaned up, put on dry clothes, crawled into the boat and started out across the lake. The rough ride across the wakes caused by other boats added to the thrill of our last boat ride.

While sitting in the back of the boat the thrill quickly turned to fear and helplessness when I realized my two small children sitting in the front of the boat were without their life preservers. We were very fortunate that day because God protected them.

Ever since that day God has made me very aware of how important it is for parents to spiritually equip their children for the life that lies ahead of them. The day is coming when we as parents will only be able to watch our children's lives from a distance and then and only then will we be able to see how we prepared them.

Father, help us to now begin to prepare our children so we will be able to look back and say, "I'm glad I did." Instead of, "I wish I would have."

Ted Andrew is an adult Sunday School leader at New Holland Church of The Nazarene.

Do You Have a Right to be Angry About the Vine?

"Then the Lord provided a vine and made it grow up over Jonah to give shade for his head to ease his discomfort, and Jonah was very happy about the vine. But at dawn the next day God provided a worm which chewed the view so that it withered. But God said to Jonah 'Do you have a right to be angry about the vine?' 'I do,' he said. 'I am angry enough to die.' But the Lord said, 'You have been concerned about this vine, though you did not tend it or make it grow.'" *Jonah 4:6–7, 9–10*

All we have is from the Lord. He blesses us with rain to grow crops, health to work, the intimacy of relationship with a spouse, a family to love, wisdom with which to make decisions, capital to invest for increase, and on it goes. It's easy to accept blessings of "the vine" the Lord provides for us, but when "our vine" dies, we may be tempted to question the goodness of God. All of a sudden we feel entitled to the fruits of these blessings—after all, we worked hard to get where we are. We earned them by the sweat of our brow and the knowledge acquired. How dare God take away what is ours?

Jonah grumbled toward God, angry enough to die. But in the face of extreme loss, Job got it right! "Naked I came from my mother's womb, and naked I will depart. The Lord gave and the Lord has taken away, may the name of the Lord be praised (Job 1:21)." Job understood God was sovereign in His decision to bless and in his allowance of those blessings to be taken. Paul takes it one step further telling us to rejoice in all things (Philippians 4:4). As Christians we have the opportunity to model the way for our neighbors just as Job did, blessing the name of the Lord in richness and adversity.

Oh Lord, grant me the grace to rejoice always in all circumstances. May Your name be praised!

Kent Martin, is President/CEO of Signature Custom Cabinetry, Inc.

God Met Me in Singapore

"My soul thirsts for God, for the living God. When can I go and meet with God?" *Psalm 42:2*

I don't remember exactly what the speaker was saying. I know that I did not think it was relevant to me. In fact, very little of the conference had been helpful to me, and I was wondering why I was there.

I had traveled halfway around the world to attend a ministry conference. I didn't go because of the theme or for any desire to visit Singapore. It was because of a pervasive, gnawing sense that I was *supposed* to go—that God wanted me there.

It was not the most convenient time to do this. Money was very tight. But wouldn't you know? Just in time, just enough unexpected money (yes, it's one of those stories!) showed up in my mailbox. So I went, hoping to meet with God.

But I was so disappointed! The conference was boring, even distasteful at times. But in that meeting room, that afternoon, God showed up. At the end of the session there was an invitation to pursue God boldly. Suddenly I found myself at the front of the room, kneeling on the floor, crying my eyes out.

The tears and sobs kept coming as I poured out decades of grief, pain, fear, and guilt. All the while God soaked me in His love until every tear was shed and I was exhausted. But I was at peace. That day began a spiritual journey that continues to deepen in love and wonder.

Why God chose to meet me in Singapore rather than at home, I don't know. But I'm glad I went, and so very glad He met me there, halfway around the world.

Father, thank you for calling us to unexpected places—burning bushes, high mountains, and Asian cities—to meet with you. Thanks for showing up and changing our lives in profound ways. Amen.

Tony Blair is one of the senior pastors of Hosanna! A Fellowship of Christians in Lititz. He also teaches for Eastern University.

Everyone!

"The Lord is good to all and His compassion is over [rests on] all He has made." *Psalm 145:9 (New Revised Standard Version)*

My mind grapples with the question, "How could He be good to *everyone*?" Does this include every believer, every non-believer, every "cruel" person like murderers, thiefs, adulterers, angry men in traffic, vengeful family members, etc.? I believe the answer lies in the second part of this verse—His compassion *rests* on *all* He has made.

I think of Olivia: barely two-months old; precious, innocent, totally dependent. She has just awakened. I lean over her crib. Her eyes latch onto mine and my sing-songy voice is as involuntary as breathing. "Well, good morning, honey!" The smile that follows as she turns her head, draws up her legs, and clenches tiny fists next to her cheeks completely melts my heart. I think to myself, *we all begin this way.*

We often tend to relate in the moment, don't we? An offense has the power to create emotions that if followed can instantaneously cause us to relate to another as if they have no past, no childhood, no trials and tribulations, no joy or sadness…no goodness. We judge based on the moment of pain that's been inflicted.

I'm reminded that one of God's titles is The Ancient of Days. I embrace the reality that His eyes have not only witnessed the beginning of world history, but mine and everyone else's included. We are all His baby girls and boys: whether we believe or not—whether we choose good or evil *because He has made us*. He is Father in Heaven and His compassion rests on *all* He has made.

Abba Father, help me to embrace a life of compassion realizing that all people have a history that has resulted in where they are today. Help me to trust in Your leading, for You are sovereign. I praise You, for You are holy and just and vengeance is Yours…not mine. In Jesus' name. Amen.

Amy Grumbling is author of *Only for a Season* and resides in Willow Street with her husband and two daughters.

God Does Not Have Coincidences

"And my God shall supply all your need according to His riches in glory by Christ Jesus." *Philippians 4:19 (New King James Version)*

While vacationing out west, the handle on the harness for my service dog broke. I am greatly dependent upon my dog (with harness intact) for a myriad of tasks including transferring in and out of my wheelchair. Since my dog and I were going to be on our own while my husband was in school, I desperately needed the unruly handle to be reattached. The wonderful lady at a local saddle shop performed temporary surgery to restore it to workable condition. It would need parts to be fully functional.

When we got home I called the organization where I had received my dog and harness to order the parts. I was informed the harness was beyond repair. My choices were to either buy a new harness, which was very expensive, or try a used harness that *coincidentally* was just donated to them. They didn't even know anything about the company that made it or what dog had used it. Doubtingly I agreed to try out the used one.

Later that evening my husband presented me with a harness that looked too small for my dog to use without harming her back. The handle looked much too tall and the supply bags on the side looked like they had barely made it through military basic training.

God was waiting for me to get over my pessimism so I would open my eyes to His exceptional provision. The harness fit as though it was custom made for her. The handle was the perfect height and the bags from her old harness fit. I started praising God for His extraordinary blessing.

Thank you, Father, for Your unspeakable gifts. You shower us with blessings above what we could hope for. Your provisions are never a coincidence. You provide for us before we even know we have a need. Amen.

Joan Patterson is a member of Lancaster Christian Writer's Group and representative for Canine Partners for Life.

A Lesson in Faith

"'Have faith in God,' Jesus answered." *Mark 11:22 (New International Version Study Bible)*

"It started a few weeks ago," I informed the mechanic. "Whenever I press the brake to slow down, my car sputters and chokes. Sometimes it even quits running!" I stated. As I handed him my car keys, I requested an estimate before he made any repairs.

"Sure, no problem," he said.

Sliding into the passenger seat of a friend's vehicle I hung my head and pleaded with God for a miracle, but not really expecting one. As a college student, finances were always tight, but with only $ 20.00 to my name, I had no idea how I was going to pay someone to fix my car. Honestly at that moment, my faith in God to provide was very small, and my problem seemed very big!

Later in the day the mechanic called to tell me that my car was ready.

"You fixed it without calling me first?" I blurted.

"Yes, Ma'am," he replied.

Inwardly I groaned as dollar signs floated around in my brain. Finally I asked, "How much is the bill?"

"Twelve ninety-eight," he stated.

Thinking that couldn't be possible I questioned him, "Do you mean twelve dollars and ninety eight cents?"

"Yes, Ma'am!"

"To repair my car?"

"Yes, Ma'am!

Completely dumbfound I listened as he explained, "It was just a coil wire that needed to be replaced. We didn't charge for the labor, only the part."

As I hung up the phone I chuckled. *How like God,* I thought. All day long I had been doubting Him and telling Him about my big problem. He just reminded me to place my faith in Him—that He's much bigger than anything I will ever face!

Lord, You never cease to amaze me. Thank you for always providing, and for teaching me more about placing my faith in You.

Jill Printzenhoff is an earth science teacher at Lititz Christian School.

Teach Us, God

"O Lord, you have searched me and you know me. You know when I sit and when I rise; you perceive my thoughts from afar. You discern my going out and my lying down; you are familiar with all my ways. Before a word is on my tongue you know it completely, O Lord. Where can I go from your Spirit? Where can I flee from your presence?" *Psalm 139:1–4, 7*

As a teacher I answered hundreds of questions a day—that is—those questions that had answers. I couldn't answer them all at once except when talking to the whole class.

And then each student heard the answer according to their level of learning. So there were more questions.

Think what God must be like hearing thousands, yea, millions of prayers at one time, and being able to discern who prayed and what they prayed. God knows how sincere and honest or selfish we are. Since God knit us together in our mother's womb, the knowledge of every hair, bone and brain cell, thought, good or negative are God's knowledge. We can never flee from God's presence, even when we are unaware of it.

So I ask a question. What is your answer?

How can I come to this God, above all gods, who knows *all*—without falling on my knees in reverent worship, begging for mercy, asking for forgiveness for my sins, while seeking to know more about what this relationship means in every aspect of my life?

O Most Holy God, search me, know my heart, test me, know my thoughts, and lead me in the way everlasting. Amen.

Ruth Rudy is God's child, teacher, wife, mother, grandmother and volunteer.

Today I Saw the Gospel in the Flesh

"Do not forget to entertain strangers, for by so doing some have unwittingly entertained angels." *Hebrews 13:2 (New King James Version)*

We decided that instead of having a yard sale, and earning a buck, we would open a one-day free clothing store, and give out clothing. It caught on! We had donations from friends, family and stores. As the store opened, we saw many homeless and down on their luck come in and find the treasure of a coat for winter, a new suit for the interview, shoes or a pretty dress that just makes you feel good. I kept hearing the word of God answering the age old question, "What would Jesus do?"

Today's verse kept coming alive with what was happening. When a homeless man who towers over you, holding a small bag of "new" clothes, bends down and says, "Thank you, mom. Bless you. I didn't know where I would get a coat," it can bring you to your knees in grateful thanks.

Sharing the love of Jesus is more than just telling someone you love them: it is really giving them shoes, shirts...a hug. We thank God for that day when we were able to be God's hands, His feet, His heart— and to give a hug. It was so thrilling to say, "Take what you need." And it truly brings you to a place of surrender from which you can never go back!

God, help us be Your hands, Your feet, Your eyes and Your heart every day of our lives.

Kim Zimmerman, and her husband Brian, are the founders and directors of City Gate Lancaster and attend The Lord's House of Prayer.

Hearing, Listening, Answering

"Before they call I will answer, while they are still speaking I will hear." *Isaiah 65:24*

Usually the school calendar works for me. All the events for the school year are already marked; days off and half days are marked too. It's very informative.

The problem is it ends in July and those of you who also use this calendar know there is a very small section at the bottom right hand corner with the dates for the month of August.

Well, I don't want to start another calendar for August because a new one will arrive before school starts and it will have all the information on it needed for the new school year.

I began to circle dates and write in the very small margin the events for that date in August. However, when I looked at it later, I couldn't read what I had written. I was stuck! As friends started asking if I was free to plan something with them, the dates circled, with words beside them that I couldn't read, became a problem.

"Lord, I messed up." That is as far as I got in my prayer when the Holy Spirit brought to my mind the events for those circled dates. It was amazing! I was going to ask Him to reveal to me what I had written, but *before* I could ask with my words—God answered!

Lord, thank you for knowing what is on my mind and what I am in need of before I ask.

Lisa Dorr is a wife, mother, writer, editor and public speaker.

Full Access

"…If we ask anything according to His will, He hears us." *1 John 5:14*

The Beverly Hillbilly's story goes something like this: a poor mountaineer barely kept his family fed, but one day as he was shooting at some food for his family's table, some bubbling crude came to the surface. Old Jed became a millionaire as he hit the mother lode of oil. All his life, that oil was beneath the surface of his property. For generations he and his ancestors were rich and didn't even know it. They lived in poverty and sat on an oil reserve that eventually gave them a mansion in Beverly Hills, California. (Or, so the story goes.)

In Exodus we are given the story of Israel leaving Egypt and bitterly grumbling to Moses that there wasn't any meat on the menu. They longed for the pots of meat they had in Egypt while in slavery. Funny how the children of Israel forgot about the torture, the plagues, the personal cost of slavery and bondage to their nation. But, God graciously provided all the manna and quail they could stomach day after day. They hit the mother lode, so to speak, of provision directly from God.

What is it that you and I have access to? Some of us have ATM bank access. Some of us know the combination to a safe. Some of us have access to a secret family recipe. But, how many of us realize that day after day and hour after hour we have access to God. Hebrews four says, "Let us approach the throne of grace with confidence…." We can come to God boldly! Israel's high priest could come to God once a year and hope he didn't die in the process.

Access your Father today for the soul or healing of another. He's waiting.

Father, there is no other god that gives us such free access than our God. May we with every breath take advantage of that access.

Steve Prokopchak helps provide oversight and direction for DOVE Christian Fellowship International's network of churches.

October

A Place of Light

"In a very short time, will not Lebanon be turned into a fertile field and the fertile field seem like a forest? In that day the deaf will hear the words of the scroll, and out of gloom and darkness the eyes of the blind will see. Once more the humble will rejoice in the Lord; the needy will rejoice in the Holy One of Israel." *Isaiah 29:17–19*

On December 19, 1737, George Adam Steitz laid claim to 313 acres of land along the Quittapahilla Creek in what is now Lebanon County. In today's monetary markets, the price would have been $2.30 per acre. Through the next decade and a half, Steitz and his family worked the land, traded very successfully with neighbors, and many settlers were drawn to the area. In the mid-1750's Steitz began to organize his land into sixty acre plots, planning out the town that was to be known as Steitztown. By 1772, more than 200 well-built houses were present in Steitztown.[1]

Through this same time period, the Moravians began to show up in what is now Lebanon County, bringing with them a deep focus on prayer and missions. In 1740, Count Zinzendorf himself traveled through southern Berks county, along Pilger Ruh in Bethel, and down through Steitztown, issuing calls to prayer along the way. A strong Moravian community settled in Steitztown and as was customary with the Moravians, began to influence all spheres of culture. In their minds, this "Steitztown" just did not fit. This beautiful, lush agricultural land needed a biblical name worthy of its design. And so, in 1778, the land was officially deeded Lebanon.[2]

Lebanon's destiny is that for which she has been named. It's a place of healing, light and worship—a place where the glory of God shines. Lebanon has been named well.

[1] Carmean, Edna J. *Lebanon County, Pennsylvania: A History.* Lebanon County Historical Society: 1976.

[2] *Ibid.*

Father, today we rejoice in the Holy One of Israel.

Jay McCumber serves as lead pastor of Cornerstone Christian Fellowship and president of the Lebanon222 Team in Lebanon.

Fallsville Seminary, Chester County
Photo by Mark Van Scyoc

Salvation History

"Great is the Lord, and greatly to be praised; his greatness is unsearchable. One generation shall laud your works to another, and shall declare your mighty acts." *Psalm 145:3–4*

It was common practice in Jewish families and gatherings to recite the stories of great works and wonders that God had performed for His people. These stories of our spiritual ancestors make up our *Heilsgeshichte,* or *Salvation History.* It is also important that we recite our *Heilsgeshichte* to each other, and to our children.

A migration of Mennonites from Pennsylvania to Upper Canada began in the late 18th century. When compulsory enrollment for military service came during the Revolutionary War, many Mennonites were not ready. The previous sixty years had been spent clearing the forests and establishing farms and homes in Pennsylvania. They neglected the telling of their history of *nonresistance* or *defenselessness* to their children. So, when war came, rather than allow their boys to serve in the continental army, they did what their ancestors had done. They left their homes and went to a new land rather than appeal to the government for non-military status.

Had they told these stories to their children, things might have been different. What better way to pass on our faith and values to our children than through the stories of our ancestors? In so doing, we make a connection to those who prepared the way for us, for indeed their story often becomes our story.

God has performed mighty acts in our personal lives, as well as in those of our ancestors. Let's recite those stories to our children and to our grandchildren, and pass on our *Heilsgeshichte* from one generation to another.

God of history, we praise You for all Your mighty acts. Help us to remember our Heilsgeshichte and make it a living story, or like the Mennonites of old, we will be bound to relive our history. Amen.

Jay D. Weaver grew up in the Ephrata Mennonite Church, Ephrata, and is now a member of the Lancaster Church of the Brethren, Lancaster. He is Professor Emeritus of Mathematics at Millersville University.

How's Your Oil?

"The kingdom of heaven shall be likened to ten virgins who took their lamps and went out to meet the bridegroom. Now five of them were wise, and five were foolish." *Matthew 25:1–2*

When I was a young girl, I loved to watch "Let's Make a Deal." I really wanted to meet Monty Hall and go on his show. Little did I know that the show was in California and not at WGAL's studio in Lancaster, where Percy Platypus was. I would dream of what costume I'd wear and jump up and down as he asked, "What's behind curtain number one?" I even went as far as getting a purse and stuffing it with everything from an aspirin to bobby pins to a piece of lint and putting it in a Sucrets tin can. I wanted to be *ready*, as he handed out prizes for having the item he would mention. Yep, I was a Monty Hall groupie, and I was prepared to meet him.

Jesus says the kingdom of heaven is likened to ten virgins, five of them wise and five foolish. The wise ones were prepared to go out and meet the Bridegroom with their oil lamps that contained enough oil, even enough while they waited for the Bridegroom because he was delayed. They were wise enough to say "no" to the foolish ones who didn't have enough oil. The foolish ones were not ready when the Bridegroom showed up. They were left out.

Are we really *ready* to meet God if it were to happen today? I ask myself, "Did I procrastinate in things that I know God put on my heart to do? Did I make things right with that certain person? Did I finish those legal documents I keep putting off?" Foolishly, I have been guilty of procrastinating in certain areas. Now is a good time to make those things right...and put more oil in my lamp.

Lord, forgive us for any procrastination or foolish habits that we haven't dealt with yet and give us strength to do so. Help us to make wise decisions and plan ahead for important circumstances. Amen.

Lisa M. Garvey serves at Hosanna Christian Fellowship, Lititz, with the Women's and Prayer Ministries.

Costs and Privileges

"And anyone who gives up his home, brothers, sisters, father, mother, wife, children, or property, to follow me, shall receive a hundred times as much in return, and shall have eternal life." *Matthew 19:29 (The Living Bible)*

Being a Messianic Jew has its privileges and its costs. I had no idea who Jesus was. His name was used in vain and He was the reason for the persecution of Jews for centuries...or so I was taught. In fact, I had no idea that Jesus was Jewish! God took me out of my anti-Semitic environment and brought me to Lancaster County where people told me I was privileged to have been born from the seed of Abraham. I was hugged almost as a celebrity to have come from the line of David. And, did I know how fortunate I was to be part of the roots of Jesus?

Oh, it didn't happen overnight accepting Jesus as my Messiah; the Lord brought many devoted Christians who loved me, cultivated me, taught me about the beautiful connection between the Old Testament and the New and then showed me how privileged I was to be a Messianic Jew.

It took two years of nurturing before I prayed the sinner's prayer in the living room of my dear friends, Larry and LaVerne Kreider, of Lititz, but as soon as I did, I became thirsty for the knowledge of God and zealous to bring anyone to Him. *Oh certainly they'll understand*, I thought as I prepared to tell my parents. But I was chastised and rejected, then finally disowned.

God had clearly showed me the truth by then and I stood by it. But, Jesus blessed me through my obedience. I felt the love of Christ which was far deeper than my blood family. I now had a family in Christ through DOVE Christian Fellowship and anyone else who lived the Word of God. He promised me one-hundred fold in return for my sacrifice and eternal life. I concede that His blessings have far exceeded His promise to me.

Dear Heavenly Father, let us all reach out to those who have a misunderstanding of who Your precious Son really is.

Jan Dorward is a Messianic Jew who resides in Ephrata where she attends DOVE Christian Fellowship, Westgate. Jan loves to write and she presents Messianic Passovers.

Still Believing

"…If thou canst believe, all things are possible to him that believeth." *Mark 9:23 (King James Version)*

"Bear ye one another's burdens, and so fulfill the law of Christ." *Galatians 6:2 (King James Version)*

For twenty-nine years my husband and I have been praying for my nearly eighty-year-old brother to accept the Lord. Many years ago my husband had a vision of my brother wearing a white suit going to the altar and getting saved, but he did not recognize the church. Years later my brother sold some land and a church was built on it.

Recently, he was mowing his lawn and as he was coming up a hill in his yard the front of the lawn mower came up around and overturned. Thank God he did not land underneath the mower. His wife is in a nursing home so he is at home alone. Sitting on the bank he looked toward the church that is next to his property and saw some cars there. He walked down to see if someone would help him lift the mower on the wheels again and of course they did. He had lots of aches and pains but nothing was broken. He told me he felt like a tractor trailer truck ran over him. A few days later he said it was more like a motorcycle ran over him. He has a great sense of humor.

For the past two years we have been getting together with some friends and having "Praise and Prayer Time" in our home. In talking with my friend that attends the "Prayer and Praise Time," she informed me that she had a burden for my brother and went to God in prayer for him. We discovered she prayed at the same time that my brother was mowing grass. God is so good.

He still has not given his heart to the Lord, but we are praying for the day he will accept the Lord and he really doesn't have to be wearing a white suit.

Father God, we are so thankful that Jesus was willing to die on the cross for us. You have been so good to us and our family, even those that do not serve You. We thank you for Your love, the many times You brought healing to our bodies and the many times You supplied our needs and even our wants. We are so grateful. Amen.

Doris Showalter is a wife, mother, grandmother and great-grandmother, and attends Mission of Love Church in Ephrata.

Jesus and Weed Killer

"The kingdom of heaven is like a man who sowed good seed in his field." *Matthew 13:24*

I've been battling weeds in the flower beds. Not just a few weeds, but trash cans full of weeds. I found weeds where I didn't think there could be weeds. While I was pulling weeds a few days after giving them a good spray with industrial strength weed killer, I found I still had to dig down deep and make sure the root came up with the visible part of the plant.

Beautiful as some were, they were weeds. Ugly as some were, they were weeds. It's kind of like sin. Sometimes there are things in our lives that are blatantly ugly. Some sin we know is there and we ignore it without "weeding." There are also "beautiful" weeds—ones that seem harmless. We rationalize by saying they produce flowers, saying they beautify. But as they grow, their true nature is revealed: they're weeds. They become larger and more entrenched than if they'd have been eliminated first.

How are weeds remedied? Some pull the tops: they figure if they rid the view of the surface leaves, there won't be sin below. Some avoid looking at weeds by simply passing by. Others realize that only a good "spraying" of scripture, prayer and walking with Christ will get those deep roots. They let the weed killer sink into their souls and fend off sin that has become entwined into their lives. It doesn't happen in a day or a week. It takes a lifetime of tending with the right weed killer. I'm envisioning Jesus with a jug of spray going at my weed-infested heart. It's kind of funny actually, metaphorically of course. Spray 'em down and pull 'em out.

Who would've thought weeds and sin were alike? That's right, Jesus did.

Jesus, we pray that You would help us to use that daily weed killer that helps Your beauty to grow in us.

Beth Smith attends Living Word Community Church and enjoys reaching out to her church and community with the love of Christ.

Climb

"I was right on the cliff edge ready to fall, when God grabbed me and held me. God is my strength, He's also my song, and my salvation." *Psalm 118:13–14 (The Message)*

"It is better to take refuge in God than trust in people." *Psalm 118:8*

When my husband and I did a VBS in an orphanage in Ghana, West Africa, we had no idea how important the subject of the 23rd Psalm would be to us. While I was preparing and praying the Lord impressed the fact that we don't stay in the valley. Soon after returning from Africa, I was diagnosed with cancer. What the Lord had revealed to me in Africa had deeper meaning now. The scripture says, "Though I walk through the Valley of the Shadow of Death, I will fear no evil." We walk *through*, or sometimes climb up.

Some days it's hard work to climb out of the valley, the valley of weeping, the valley of "what ifs," hopelessness. But I needed to climb— climb to clear air, to hope-filled air, to Jesus' arms.

He's with you in the valley; His strength helps you to climb. Climb you must. Climb to the air of hope and a new day. Hope brings life. Hope brings healing.

Resting on a cliff can be slippery; it would be easy to fall back into the "what ifs" into the dark. But listen...

Hear the shouts, hear the triumph songs in the camp of the saved?
The hand of God has turned the tide!
The hand of God is raised in victory!
The hand of God has turned the tide!
Psalm 118:14-20

I thank you, Lord, that we can rest and take refuge in You.

Christina Ricker is a walker and climber, cancer survivor, wife, mom and nana who worships at Petra Christian Fellowship.

You are Chosen

"But you are a chosen people, a royal priesthood, a holy nation, a people belonging to God….." *1 Peter 2:9*

Recently, I have been meditating on the goodness of God. What does it really mean to be His chosen generation—to be joint-heirs of the Great King?

Picture with me a beautiful property. The land around the house has gorgeous landscaping. There are pretty flower gardens in every corner. It is breathtaking. It is a house that has valuable things in it. It is almost as though God has opened the gates of heaven ahead of time.

This is a picture of a property that belongs to God. When we accepted Christ as our Savior, the land is automatically transferred to our name. What was His is also now ours.

All of these things belong to His children. The beautiful land and valuable things represent victory where there was once defeat, joy instead of sorrow, and healing where there was pain.

Some people sign the deed but are not quite sure how to receive and move onto their new land. I encourage you to walk to your new property and boldly receive all that God has for you.

Thank you, Father, that we can be born of your Spirit. Thank you that we are Your sons and daughters. Thank you for giving us the faith to believe in Your many promises.

Lydia Anne Miller is a wife and mother of two and attends Newport DOVE Christian Fellowship.

Footprints in the Snow

"...Your hand shall lead me, and your right hand shall hold me."
Psalm 139:10

My dog and I walk almost every day. Part of our route has me going up and down a rather steep hill twice.

After a dusting of snow, I was walking down the hill for the second time. I looked at my previous tracks, along with Cricket's paw prints. Even though we have trained her to heel, I was surprised to see that her prints were all over the place; they went off the sidewalk and crossed right and left as she sniffed and discovered new scents. They even showed where she stopped to "mark her territory."

I was reminded of the poem, *Footprints in the Sand* by Mary Stevenson. It followed a believer as he and God walked together along the beach. When troubles came, he only saw one set of prints. As he questioned God, the Lord assured him that he hadn't been alone. During those times, God was carrying him.

Cricket's tracks made me realize her prints could represent mine as I walked with the Lord. He is my Master, but sometimes I walk ahead. Sometimes I'm distracted by things I find delightful. He even pulls me along when I try to claim land that isn't even mine.

During my walk with Cricket, my prints never faltered. My love for Cricket hadn't waned when I had to tug a little to get her back on the sidewalk. In fact, it amused me that a route we walk so frequently would seem new to her. And I never once thought I should let go and let her indulge in wandering around. That would put her in danger of injury or worse.

Too many of us think that God is standing by and waiting to zap us with lightning for any infraction of His laws. He is not. He is walking with us, steady on, loving our companionship, gently correcting our missteps, and leading us home.

My precious Leader, let me walk in Your way today.

Carolyn Schlicher walks around Elizabethtown. Her favorite walking buddy is actually her husband, Darryl.

Denial Has Many Forms

"Therefore, my beloved, as you have always obeyed, so now, not only in my presence but much more in my absence work out your own salvation with fear and trembling." *Philippians 2:12*

Most of us only understand the kind of denial that affects our thinking capacity in the realm of drug and alcohol addiction or some type of addiction such as food. This denial often leads to making poor choices. But denial also restricts our capacity to see other issues in our life such as anger or bitterness. Because of a false belief that when we come to Jesus there is nothing else to deal with, we believe our sin issue is now taken care of.

When I came to Water Street Ministries in March of 2002, I realized there was a major flaw in my understanding of issues in my life which had never been dealt with. This led to sin in my life. I had sought relationships in all the wrong places, such as inappropriate relationships with women. I also sought relationships through alcohol and drugs, which led me to the wrong crowd because of a desire to belong. Instead of trusting and seeking an appropriate relationship with God, I used these relationships with women, alcohol, and crack cocaine to medicate the pain that I was felling inside of me. I chose to ignore God, my Father; His Son, Jesus; and the Holy Spirit, who was given to me as my Comforter, Counselor, and Teacher.

Because of my denial of these issues in my life and choosing to allow anger and bitterness to control me, I had landed at Water Street Ministries. It was here in transition and later through the program with my chaplain and others' help, that I began to realize what the Apostle Paul was speaking about in Philippians, "Therefore, my beloved, as you have always obeyed, so now, not only in my presence but much more in my absence work out your own salvation with fear and trembling."

Lord, help me to seek after a relationship with You as my Comforter, Counselor and Teacher.

Philip Wrightstone is the Resident Assistant at Water Street Ministries.

Is Your Foundation Solid?

"Therefore everyone who hears these words of mine and puts them into practice is like a wise man who built his house on the rock. The rain came down, the streams rose, and the winds blew and beat against that house; yet it did not fall, because it had its foundation on the rock." *Matthew 7:24–25*

As a young thirteen year old, I remember well how hard we had worked at preparing our farmette for the open house and upcoming property sale. We cleaned, scrubbed, mowed, trimmed, and attempted to have the property looking immaculate for interested buyers. Finally, the day of the first open house arrived. I waited in eager anticipation for people to come. No one came.

Finally mid-day, a well-known and respected neighbor came in his horse and buggy. I was bursting to show him our entire property. He quickly commented that he only wanted to see one thing, our dirt cellar. Of all things to show, he wanted to see our musty cellar. I remember well the man of few words descending our creaky steps into our dimly lit cellar. He quietly reached into his pocket, pulled out a small flashlight and penknife, and began gently probing the logs that carried the frame of our house.

He left our home as quietly as he had come. He saw all that was needed. The value of the property was not the nicely mowed lawn, or brightly washed exteriors. What mattered was the integrity of the logs that bore the weight of the house.

A sobering life long lesson took place for me that day. Jesus speaks very clearly to examining the foundation we are building on. The rock or the sand, which is it? It makes all the difference between spiritual life and spiritual death.

Lord, may my life today be a reflection of building on Your solid foundation in all I do.

Brian E. Martin serves as lead pastor at Weaverland Mennonite Church in East Earl. He and his wife Shirley have two married and two young adult children, and one grandchild.

Sunrise

"Yes, the day will come, says the Lord, when I will do for Israel and Judah all the good I promised them." *Jeremiah 33:14 (The Living Bible)*

I was reading this during my morning quiet time. I got up from the kitchen table to walk with my husband to his car as he was leaving for work. I lingered outside to watch the beautiful sunrise. I was struck by the faithfulness of God in causing the sun to rise each morning. No matter how badly I had lived yesterday, no matter how much sin had occurred in the earth the day before, today the sun was rising on humanity again. Along with the sun came God's promise of his new mercies. What a good God we have!

I sat down and continued to read in my Bible. "If you can break my covenant with the day and with the night so that day and night don't come on their usual schedule, only then will my covenant with David, my servant be broken… (verses 20, 21)." Then I heard God say, "Anne, if you are able to keep the sun from rising this morning, then you will be able to mess up badly enough to break My promises to you." Sometimes I believe the lie that I will disqualify myself from receiving God's promises. But God reminds me that it was He who made the covenant in the first place. He cannot lie, and He knows all things. He already took my weaknesses and mistakes into account when He made those promises. So I can rest in the knowledge that it is God's job to bring His words to pass, and it is my job to simply believe.

Lord, help me to rest in Your faithfulness.

Anne Brandenburg is a mother of six and the wife of Chris, a pastor at Life Center Ministries.

At Last...

"I took you from the ends of the earth; from its farthest corners I called you. I said, 'You are my servant'; I have chosen you and have not rejected you. So do not fear, for I am with you; do not be dismayed, for I am your God." *Isaiah 41:9–10*

As I sit here in my seminary's library, my eyes are drawn to a picture tacked onto the office bulletin board. It is a picture of Jesus with His arms wrapped securely around a young woman wearing jeans and a long-sleeved tee shirt. Her arms are wrapped around Him as well. His eyes are closed and there is a broad smile on His face. The young woman's eyes are closed, but she is not smiling. The look on her face is one of immense relief and gratitude. As I ponder the woman's expression, I sense that she has finally found Someone to trust—someone who will not reject her—and she is hanging onto Him for dear life.

It is a beautiful picture that brings unbidden tears to my eyes every time I see it.

How desperately our human hearts long for Someone who can be completely trusted. How desperately our human hearts long for Someone who will never reject us. That Someone exists and He is God the Father, God the Son, and God the Holy Spirit! Perhaps, you have been rejected by a spouse, a family member, a friend, or a coworker. Do not lose heart! He has chosen you and will never, ever reject you!

Dear Lord, You are so much more than we could have ever asked for—so much more than we could have ever imagined! Help us to remember that You will never reject us as You were rejected.

Ellen Dooley serves as assistant pastor at Crossroads Wesleyan Church in Lancaster, and is a M.Div. candidate at Evangelical Theological Seminary in Myerstown.

Finishing Well

"Even though I walk through the valley of the shadow of death, I will fear no evil...." *Psalm 23:4*

My casual question, "Hi Lenny, how are you?" was greeted with a sigh. Lenny's roommate, Matt, had died the previous day of cancer. It was proving to be a tough day for Lenny as he reminisced over those final hours spent with his friend.

However, within those memories, tinged with sadness, was a ray of hope. Lenny was deeply impacted by Matt's courage. He remarked that he had learned a great deal from Matt that had strengthened him in his own journey of faith. He was impressed that Matt read his Bible every night right up to the day he died. He was surprised that, discovering the cancer was terminal, Matt had not resorted to complaining, doubting or losing faith. Fear did not appear to be a word in Matt's dictionary.

Lenny became a caregiver for his friend as the disease quickly began to take its toll on Matt's body. As Lenny reflected on this, he smiled and commented that God had surely intended for him to have Matt as a roommate. It seems Lenny had run from a previous and similar situation when his own father had developed cancer and died. He believed God was giving him a second chance to "do it right" and for Lenny, this was a healing time.

I never met Matt personally during his battle against cancer, but I knew of him through my students in the Water Street Learning Center who often asked that we pray for Matt in our devotion time.

I finally got to meet Matt, but only after he had gone home to Jesus. I met him in the treasured memories of Lenny as he shared how much he had grown in his faith and in his understanding of what it means to be at peace and to have a hope that anchors the soul.

Matt, thank you: you finished well.

Thank you, Lord, for allowing us to see You through Matt's life and through the eyes of those who loved him. May I finish well so others can see You.

Sue Pearce worships at Landis Valley Christian Fellowship and is the instructor in the Water Street Ministries Learning Center.

Expectation

"Rejoice in our confident hope...." *Romans 12:12 (New Living Translation)*

The parking space said "Stork Parking...Expectant Mothers Only" and I jubilantly pulled my car into the front row spot. My passenger, my beautiful and very pregnant daughter-in-law, was bemused at my over-the-top-grandmother-to-be-enthusiasm.

I'll admit: I've been absolutely giddy about the prospect of being a grandparent for the first time. I don't just *hope* for a grandchild; I fully rejoice in the *expectation* that it will happen. Just to hope has no feeling of certainty at all; it is only a pie-in-the-sky dream. I know for sure that the baby bump I see is not just wishful thinking. That's what today's scripture is saying: we can rejoice in a *confident hope*.

I grew up on a farm so I know that if you plow the field and put your energy into planting the seed—you do not just hope for—you absolutely expect a harvest. I absolutely expect a grandchild, and I am joyful in that expectation.

Sometimes life throws some stuff at us and we begin to expect the worst to happen. We start to think, "What's going to go wrong today? The washer has broken down, the car needs repairs; uh oh, things come in threes—there must be a third disaster lurking somewhere!" And yet God says we should be expecting the best and have a confident hope because He is a God of expectation (Romans 15:13).

Are you expecting God to do something in your life today? Are you trusting in joyful and confident expectation? Your confident hope will sustain you through any adversity because you are recognizing your continuous need for the Lord's help. This allows you to be patient, which in turn makes you steadfast and confident.

By the time you read this, I will be a grandparent. I am confident of it, and I will be patient.

Thank you, Lord, for filling me with all joy and peace as I trust in You today, so that I may overflow with hope by the power of the Holy Spirit.

Karen Ruiz is editor of House to House Publications, an expectant grandmother and the mother of three grown children.

Own It!

"…From whom the whole body, joined and knit together by what every joint supplies, according to the effective working by which every part does its share, causes growth of the body for the edifying of itself in love." *Ephesians 4:16*

I recently contemplated the thought, "What makes a good family?" Immediately I thought of things like love, relationship, respect, honor and forgiveness—things that I would normally think of when I visualize a family functioning in a healthy family setting.

Then I thought of another key ingredient—healthy ownership. I thought back over the times when the children were growing up. I remember more than once saying something like this, "Go and clean up your room!" Now, was the room really their room? Did they take it with them when they eventually went off to college or got married? No, but we still considered it their room while they were living with mom and dad.

What we were doing was giving healthy ownership to them. They were accepting responsibility for a specific area in the family domain. We were teaching them that they should not be looking to mom and dad to do everything for them. We were teaching them to take responsibility for the betterment of the family.

I think we can apply the same thing to the church family. There needs to be healthy ownership by everyone involved—in other words—people taking healthy responsibility for their part that will bring about the success of the whole. When everyone can see their part as important to the success of the whole, I believe they will give themselves to that responsibility and fulfill it. When each one does his share, the family is encouraged and empowered.

Lord, help us to do what Paul describes in today's scripture verse— take healthy ownership and do our share for the benefit of those in the body of Christ and our local church family.

Ron Myer serves as assistant international director of DOVE Christian Fellowship International, Lititz.

Our Lifeblood

"In him we have redemption through his blood, the forgiveness of sins…." *Ephesians 1:7*

The word, hypertension, took on a personal meaning when my husband did not pass his CDL renewal because his systolic blood pressure number was too high. Bryan's daily routine suddenly included new medications, frequent blood work, heart tests, and doctor visits. After weeks of experiencing negative side effects from different medications, and a late night trip to the emergency room, he got an appointment with a Hypertension and Kidney Specialist.

We learned that 90% of people with normal blood pressure at age 55 would develop high blood pressure as they age. What a poignant reminder of the progressive deterioration of humanity. Hypertension is a common, but dangerous condition as it increases your risk of stroke, kidney damage, and damage to the blood vessels in your eyes. While genetics, diet, exercise, and our life-style all play a role, we were surprised to learn that sleep apnea can also cause hypertension.

Still in the process of walking through the maze of evaluation, testing, and treatment options, the Lord reminded us of the importance of "the blood." Literally our physical life is in our blood. Spiritually, the Bible says that our eternal life is through Jesus' shed blood at Calvary—personally believing God's diagnosis of our condition and receiving His prescription for that life. We experience daily the symptoms and effects of our spiritual health and can choose to follow the Great Physician's advice. Alternatively, we can choose to be in denial and similar to hypertension (the silent killer), the long-term effects will be deadly.

Making life-style changes in our diet and exercise is a test of our motivation and our will. Physically and spiritually, our daily choices and habits speak volumes about us, and whom we serve (God or self). Are we motivated to make the necessary changes? Are we as diligent in pursuing our spiritual health as we are with our physical health?

Father, You are my lifeblood. Help me to be purposeful in my choices and habits as I pursue You daily.

Coleen Gehman enjoys being a wife and mother serving with her husband, Bryan, at Lancaster Evangelical Free Church.

The Safe House

"Thou art my hiding place and my shield: I hope in thy Word."
Psalm 119:114 (King James Version)

Once I was an avid spy novel reader. Whether the agent was CIA or from his Majesty's Secret Service, while he was in a foreign country, he could seek shelter at a safe house. At this house, he was hidden from the enemy. Fed and given a bed to rest, he could recover from wounds if needed; and if required, he could contact his agency for further instructions on his mission.

For the last seven years on our walk across America, my wife, Nadine, and I slept in cheap motels, a caboose, and a charming state park lodge. I slept in my car and in a tent on a mountaintop only to be awakened by a black bear that was meandering through the campground. The times that I adore the most were the times that our Lord provided a safe house for me: Steve and Jeanne's in Maryland and Alan and Monika's in West Virginia. Beside the delicious home-cooked meals, they do contain one amenity that can be missing with the accommodations of many luxurious hotels. That item is the love of Jesus Christ.

In 2007, Nadine and I slept in a new safe house, a church in Logan, Ohio, aptly named the Father's House, where one can run during times of trial. Pastors Mike and Cheryl gracefully invited us to use the room in the church, when we were in the area. That year Nadine and I, along with Pastors Mike and Cheryl, led a multi-church prayer walk in the streets and around the schools of Logan.

There is one other safe house that I go to during the storms of life: the Word of God—the Bible.

Hear my cry, O God; attend unto my prayer. For Thou has been a shelter for me, and a strong tower from the enemy.

Jim Shaner is a board member of Chester County Women's Services Medical and founder of One Nation Under God–Walk Across America.

Toward Resolving Racism

"Your Father knows what you need before you ask him." *Matthew 6:8*

On my way home from seminary classes, a young man from another college often waits at the train station with me. I gave Hussein my business card once. We are friendly but I keep my distance to avoid pressuring him. When the train arrives we rush off in different directions to find a seat.

When philosopher Cornel West was to visit the seminary, a friend of mine suggested a provocative question to ask, "Is it possible to be completely non-racist?" I could not resist struggling with this and spent a fair amount of effort thinking and discussing the topic with my friend, as well as attending the lecture itself, but never had the opportunity to ask questions.

After the lecture I got on my train. I sat down and got organized. I looked up to see I had taken the seat right behind Hussein, for the first time. Thinking Hussein might be "put off" by the business card I'd given him, I purposely avoided a conversation. I had never mentioned Cornel West or anything about what I was doing that evening to Hussein, and he had no idea what happens at seminary.

He turned and asked, "Are you reading?"

"Not really, just notes on my PDA," I said.

Hussein looked at me very seriously and then blew me away with a question, "Do you think that everyone has a little racism in them?"

Recovering from my shock at the "coincidence," our conversation continued until I got off the train, based in great part on all the thought I had given the subject as a result of my friend's question. We finished by discussing how society might work toward resolving issues of racial persecution.

It is both comforting and scary to undeniably come to the realization that God's footprints are very close in front of you.

Lord, how carefully You weave the events of our lives, even as we are clueless. Thank you for Your intricate loving care. Amen.

Allen Keller serves as youth pastor at Olivet UMC in Coatesville and attends Palmer Seminary in Wynnewood.

In the Neighborhood

"You have heard that it was said. 'Love your neighbor....'" *Matthew 5:43*

The wreath hung on the door as a beautiful "Welcome." Many of my guests would comment on the pretty yellow, white and purple flowers that wrapped around the grapevine.

Soon, however, the comments were about the birds' nests! Yes, there were birds' nests in my wreath. A robin diligently built a nest for her young and then only about six inches from the robin's nest a house finch built a nest for her young.

My family and guests coming and going marveled at the event. We watched how they built their nests. We watched the eggs of each bird as the days and weeks went by and the "moms" sat patiently—beside each other—waiting for their precious young to be born.

I had never before seen two different types of birds so close to one another. It made me think of the scripture, "Love thy neighbor as thyself."

How often do we squawk and squabble with our neighbors? Maybe we can learn from the birds.

It was fun to watch the eggs hatch, the birds grow and then fly away. Hmm...not squawking, not squabbling.

Lord, please help me to love my neighbor as You do.

Lisa Dorr is a wife, mother, writer, editor and public speaker.

Lord, Help Me!

"Do not be far from me, for trouble is near…come quickly to help me." *Psalm 22:11, 19*

Even though this event happened some thirty years ago, I could still take you to the place. Our family was living in Pottsville, Pennsylvania where we owned a Christian bookstore. We befriended John during that time, who had a troubled marriage and dysfunctional family. John had interest in spiritual things, loved to talk, and was a gentleman when sober. But, alcohol often controlled his life and he got angry and irrational. Early signs of palsy made John shaky and unsteady.

One day after a fight with his wife, he came to talk to me. He was upset. As I drove him home, he suddenly pulled a pistol out of his pocket, brandished it around in the car and said, "When I get home, I'm showing my wife who is boss."

I don't remember what I prayed but it was short. It was probably, "Lord help me," and maybe, "Lord, come quickly." John showed me later, as we sat in the car, talked, and prayed together, that the gun was not loaded and he only intended to scare his wife. I tried to explain how that was not a good idea.

I was protected that day, for which I am grateful. I recently found that David, in Psalm writings, used that, "Lord, help me" phrase over 40 times in various settings. His life was often threatened and in danger. He often felt forsaken. He often felt surrounded by enemies. But, David knew where to call for help. I too am thankful that our God is near, He hears our prayers, even if they are only a few words like, "Lord, help me!"

God, thank you for Your protection and guidance as we journey through life. And, may You especially be near those today who have troubles, illness or special needs. Amen.

Nelson W. Martin and his wife Anna Mae live near Lititz. Nelson is director of Support for Prison Ministries, a Lancaster County based prison ministry and prison chaplain program.

Wild Goose Chase

"The wind blows wherever it pleases. You hear its sound, but you cannot tell where it comes from or where it is going. So it is with everyone born of the Spirit." *John 3:8*

Once a year, snow geese usually descend, by the thousands, upon a local wildlife reserve. No one knows when they will come, how long they will stay or even if they will show up. Upon hearing of this phenomenon, I just had to take my family to see them. By the time we left, I realized that after our forty-five minute drive we would only have ten minutes to watch before sunset. To my usually practical nature, this seemed ridiculous, but still I plowed ahead, feeling compelled on by an unseen force.

Upon arrival, we encountered thousands of these magical creatures, resting on the waters. I soaked in the peace and wonderment of this sacred moment. Even my two-year-old was awestruck and silent. That night, before going to bed, the Lord gave me revelation about our trek. God reminded me that the Celts used to refer to the Holy Spirit as the "Wild Goose" and that this "wild goose chase" that I found myself on was not simply my crazy notion but the leading of His Holy Spirit.

God brought confirmation that He is leading this family on our unconventional journey to missions. We had changed direction and were in a season of waiting that felt very uncomfortable. I too often worried what people were thinking, wondering if they saw us as crazy. God spoke to my heart that what may appear to be a "wild goose chase," is really our journey of chasing after His Holy Spirit. What comfort and courage these words bring to our family as we seek to follow the course of the Spirit, no matter how wild it appears.

Lord, help me to obediently follow the wild leading of Your Holy Spirit today.

Deb Muenstermann, ACTS Covenant Fellowship, is headed to the mission field with her husband, Ralph and their children.

Fear Not!

"Casting all your anxieties on Him, because He cares for you."
1 Peter 5:7 (English Standard Version)

She's afraid of a paper bag.

Vonnie and I were amused at the fright our 7-month-old puppy displayed when she accidentally knocked over a small paper bag. While we were eating dinner she jumped on something near the sink when she tipped a bag. It fell over, not far, but just enough to startle. Five minutes later, after barking, sneaking up on, sniffing, staring down, with hair raised before, she realized it was not going to attack her and began to eat it.

This incident reminds me of the fear we often display over ridiculous things, especially in the light of a Sovereign God. God must be sadly amused when He observes His children hiding under a bed about things which may have little or no impact on us and are eternally of absolutely no consequences. It's a wonder He doesn't shout out, "I can't believe you're worried about that again!"

As I write, I carry the burden of my ministry's finances at the same time seeing the entire nation struggling—banks closing and insurance companies going belly-up. I wonder what is going to happen next. Will we survive? Will I be able to feed my family? When does the next shoe drop?

Somehow all of this works in God's plan and none of it has any bearing on my relationship with Him. I'm still saved. I'm still going to Heaven. My God will never leave or forsake me. He's the same yesterday, today and forever. Yet, it's the paper bags that have my stomach in knots, hair on end and barking at way too many people.

Lord, may my undivided trust be in You and Your provision. May I not allow circumstances to rob me of my joy in You. May I be reminded that You are in absolute control and are totally faithful, all the time, everyday, in every circumstance, no matter what. Amen and Amen!

Dr. Dan Allen is a pastor, writer, conference speaker, radio commentator and Director of Pinebrook Bible Conference, East Stroudsburg.

Restoration

"Give back everything that belonged to her, including all the income from her land from the day she left the country until now."
2 Kings 8:6

Have you ever felt like you suffered loss after having obeyed the Lord? Life can take on a Joseph moment like when Joseph in his obedience ended up in prison. I know I can identify with those feelings, but the truth is, I really don't have an answer for you. Perhaps a story from the scripture will help.

The story of the Shunammite woman mentioned in 2 Kings, chapter eight, and verses one through six is pretty interesting. This is the woman who received a son and then the gift of resurrection of that son through Elisha the prophet. She and her family did not do a whole lot to gain this favor other than provide hospitality for the man of God. It seems that a famine was on its way and Elisha once again was watching out for this woman and her family. He told them to leave the country for seven years. She obeyed and went to the land of the Philistines.

When seven years had concluded, they returned and somehow she had the audience of the king who at the time just happened to be speaking with Gehazi, Elisha's servant. Timing is everything. Gehazi told the king that this is the woman whose son was restored to life by the prophet. The king heard her plight and immediately assigned an official to her case and then proceeded to return her land and her house to her. But, that's not all. He also ordered the restoration of the income she would have gained from her land from the time she had left. In her obedience (after seven years), she experienced full restoration.

I know we don't like waiting seven years for something, but God is the God of restoration. He will not allow the devourer to win. What or whom in your life needs to be restored? Ask Him today for their return with interest.

Thank you, Father, that even when we obey and the outcome is not as expected or when expected, we can still trust You for a great return and complete restoration.

Steve Prokopchak helps provide oversight and direction for DOVE Christian Fellowship International's network of churches.

Chasing Leaves

"And now these three remain: faith, hope and love...." *1 Corinthians 13:13*

The trees were just beginning to lose their glorious crowns to the blowing winds on this autumn day. As we hiked, my husband chased after a few of the vibrant leaves to catch them as they floated by from gray sky to forest floor. No easy task! Neither the trees, nor my husband, could seem to hold onto that which was meant to fall.

I've been thinking about what I try so hard to grasp and hold onto: my time, agenda, and plans; my stuff, my way, my rights. Is this what I spend my life chasing after? I've been wondering if I'm holding onto what I should let go of and vice versa. To hold onto what really doesn't matter and let the most important things slip through my fingers without an attempt to grasp them would be tragic, like one of those glorious forest trees holding onto its leaves while allowing its roots to rot.

There are some things worth holding onto when the winds blow and our lives are shaken. Some things are meant to endure the winds, but not the leaves. As beautiful and glorious as they are, they are temporary. The roots are what should warrant our attention. Roots of faith, hope, and love. We must resolve not to give these over to the uprooting power of the wind. Let everything else fall and fade, but let these three remain. For if they do, the glory of life will never be permanently lost.

Everlasting God, may I be more concerned about my roots than any fluttering leaf I've been found chasing. O God, forgive me for letting go of what gives me life to chase after what I think brings me glory. Strengthen my resolve to hold onto, pursue and care for that which is really life!

Jenny Gehman, founder of LiveWell! Ministries, loses her leaves and tends her roots in Millersville.

Maintenance Required

"But if we walk in the light, as he is in the light, we have fellowship with one another, and the blood of Jesus, his Son, purifies us from all sin." *1 John 1:7*

When you start a garden you realize that there is a big difference between starting something and maintaining it. Earlier this season, I planted six strawberry plants. I tilled my soil with additives and made sure to water them regularly. I added in the right amount of fertilizer and a friend even brought me a tomato plant for my budding garden.

Everything was going well. Then, the slugs, weeds, ants, and field critters found my little plot. The tomato plants disappeared one day and something left only a sliver of my one ripe strawberry which was just enough to attract the ants.

Reading up on strawberries, I learned several steps to a healthy garden but knew it would take some serious maintenance to keep such a treasure going. They would need to be protected and watched closely. In some cases, they would have to be thinned out.

I couldn't help but think of this scenario as a wonderful parallel to our lives. Time together with other Christians is so precious. We learn and grow from each other. We encourage each other. But, there is much competition for our time, and when we start Bible studies and events, they can fizzle without maintenance and some serious hoeing of those things that pull us away.

Like my organic experiment, it is easy to let things slide and think, "Oh, I'll get back to that," but in my little gardening book and in the Bible, we learn that now is the time to act when problems crop up or the plants won't produce fruit next year and our lives will be dried up and empty without the light of Jesus and fellow Christians.

Lord, help me to read my Bible, Your instruction book for my "gardening" skills and to actively pursue Christian fellowship as Your Word commands.

Sarah Peppel is president of women's ministries in the Philadelphia Metro-West Presbytery.

God's Ways

"As the heavens are higher than the earth, so are my ways higher than your ways, and my thoughts than your thoughts." *Isaiah 55:9*

In the summer of 2000, my husband and I led a short-term missions team to Ecuador, South America. Our team worked alongside a small church in the suburban community of Guamani outside of Quito. We were helping to construct a larger building because of the growth they were experiencing, including the growing Compassion program that was operating out of the church.

While constructing the building, we built special relationships with the Ecuadorians with whom we worked. My husband and Oswaldo, who we lovingly nicknamed "yellow hat" because he always wore a yellow hard hat, struck up a friendship.

Years later, in 2006, my husband and I decided to support two children (one boy and one girl) in the Compassion program in Guamani. When I called Compassion, I specifically asked for a boy and a girl in a certain age bracket from the Guamani project who were awaiting sponsors. Then I prayed and ask God to give us the children of His choice.

We received our packet in the mail with pictures and names of the children designated to us. As I looked at the last name of the little girl we would sponsor, I recognized it as Oswaldo's last name. Could it be that we actually had been given a child of Oswaldo's to sponsor? We knew that in 2000, Oswaldo did not have a child that was this young, but maybe his family had grown.

In my first letter to Elizabeth, the little girl, I sent a picture of Joe and Oswaldo that we had taken and asked if the man on the picture was her father. If he was, Joe and I were her sponsors. Because Elizabeth was only three-years-old, her tutor wrote back for her and said that Oswaldo was, indeed, her father, and the family was so happy to learn that we were her sponsors.

What joy to discover that God had given us Oswaldo's youngest child to sponsor, who was not even born when we were in Ecuador!

Father, I give You praise that Your ways are so much higher than mine, and that it gives You great joy to give us sweet surprises.

Dawn Nolt attends DOVE E-town and delights in worshiping her Savior and King, Jesus.

The Antidote

"Do not let your hearts be troubled. Trust in God; trust also in me."
John 14:1

One of the most amazing characteristics of God is His compassion, and of course, that flows out of the fact that He is love. Jesus has just told the disciples some disturbing news, that He will only be with them a little while longer and that where He is going, they cannot follow. They have followed him for three years. Their hearts are troubled. Then, knowing the content of their hearts, He says, "Do not let your hearts be troubled. Trust in God; trust also in me (John 14:1)." My study Bible defines *trust* as "the antidote for a troubled heart."

When first invited to the Ukraine to give my testimony at a women's conference in Kharkov, I had several fears. Would I be alone? No, I can't go unless someone else goes with me. I prayed for the Lord to provide someone, but those who came to mind couldn't go. Gradually, the Lord gave me the courage and peace about going alone, so I did.

The day before the conference, several women, including me, walked the streets of the church neighborhood passing out invitations to women to come to the church the next day. I walked with two other women, but as it grew colder, they thought I should go back. I thought that I knew the way, but soon all the streets began to look alike. I allowed my heart to become troubled. If I saw a man walking alone ahead of me, I prayed for safety. Then I prayed, "Lord, You know where I am. Please help me find my way back." Eventually, I looked up and saw the cross-shaped windows that graced the back of the sanctuary and I knew that I was safe. Yes, I am safe at the foot of the cross.

Trust was the antidote (a relief, prevention, or counteraction) for my troubled heart.

Father, whenever I am afraid or troubled, I know that I can go to You at that moment and find relief, the perfect peace that You have for me.

Sharon Neal serves in Women's Bible Fellowship, children's education, and on the Shepherding Team of Lancaster Evangelical Free Church, Lititz.

314   *God Stories 5*

We Are What We Say

"Do not let any unwholesome talk come out of your mouths, but only what is helpful for building others up according to their needs, that it may benefit those who listen." *Ephesians 4:29*

We love to get away to our little cabin in the woods, where it is so peaceful. One thing we especially enjoy is watching all the beautiful birds and hearing their individual songs. We know the Canadian geese are coming when we hear their distinct honking sounds.

My grandson, Kade, was on a walk with me, and I said, "Hear that Kade? That sound is a red cardinal bird. We found him with our ears; now let's try to find him with our eyes." We played that game for a while and then Kade started to act "silly." I said, lovingly, "You are a silly bird today!" Then we laughed and tickled.

About that time, my neighbor walked by and we started to chat. He began to grumble and complain about many things with his loud voice. After a while he left and Kade said, "Grammy, that man sounds like he is a grumpy-bird."

"Yes," I said, "Sometimes he sounds like that."

This made me wonder what I sound like. Do I gripe and complain to others, or to God? Or, do I praise God with a thankful heart? Do I encourage others or am I negative most of the time? Do I repeat things without thinking, like a parrot? Do I pick on every little speck, like a crow? Or, do I soar like an eagle, with my confidence in the Lord? What kind of bird am I? What sound am I known by?

Lord, I want to be known by the distinct sound of praising You, and glorifying You, with my words, and deeds. Give me open ears to hear Your wonderful Good News of hope, and a sweet voice to share it.

Shirley Ann Bivens serves at Christ Community Church as a preschool teacher, and is a Christian clown (CoCo). She is also a full time grammy.

God's Creation

"Delight thyself also in the Lord and He will give thee the desires of.thine heart." *Psalm37:4 (King James Version)*

From a very young age, I have been a lover of God's creation. I recently joked that I was born in a tree. This love of God's creatures and His creation caused me to spend a great deal of my childhood in the forest exploring trees, rocks, streams, making paths and dams, and finding new things to show anyone who would pay attention.

God gave me a desire to be outside as much as possible. The things I have enjoyed most in life have been working as a camp counselor, trips to national and state parks, and cruises with my parents. The joy and contentment these things bring cause me to worship and praise the great, awesome God, whom I know made all of it for us to enjoy.

After the death of our precious daughter six years ago, my heart was so deeply broken that I felt it would never heal. So I spent much time outside in gardens, near streams and ponds until I learned to bask in His love again.

This year God has given us an incredible answer to my heart's desire by allowing us to be chaplains at Crater Lake National Park in Oregon. Praise God who gives us all good things to enjoy. We leave in two weeks and will spend four months in this amazingly beautiful part of God's creation. I believe if we delight in our Lord, He will give us the desires of our hearts.

Precious Father thank you for answering my heart's desire. In Jesus' name, Amen.

Jeannette Taylor serves in Coatesville with REST Ministries and the Navigators with husband Dick Taylor.

Skeletons in the Closet

"At this, the administrators and the satraps tried to find grounds for charges against Daniel in his conduct of government affairs, but they were unable to do so. They could find no corruption in him, because he was trustworthy and neither corrupt nor negligent." *Daniel 6:4*

Most of us have at least one skeleton in our closet. You know, it's that one thing we did in the past that we don't want anyone knowing about.

What's really sad is that the more popular you become in life the better your chances are of something from your past leaking out. Take politicians for example: every election year the media likes to play in the mud. They like to go digging for bones that people buried a long time ago just so they can ruin the reputations of the people running for office. We are told they do it because the people have a right to know, but we all know it's about ratings and who they want in office.

The sad truth is that there are people out there who actually care about what others did twenty years ago—like somehow a decision that was made so long ago only means you're incapable of making one today. Daniel had a similar problem back in his day. He did his best in office and served with integrity and honor. He lived his life in such a way that when the people around him became jealous and wanted him kicked out of office they could find no wrong in him. There were no skeletons in his closet. As Christians we need to be very careful of the choices we make every day because they can come back and harm us. So protect your integrity today and you will have no regrets tomorrow.

We know that in order to keep the skeletons out of our closet we have to guard the door. Help us walk in integrity, Lord!

Rob Heverling is youth leader at Mount Aetna Bible Church, Mount Aetna.

November

Dear Young Hearts

"Do not love the world or anything in the world. If anyone loves the world, the love of the Father is not in him. For everything in the world—the cravings of sinful man, the lust of his eyes and the boasting of what he has and does—comes not from the Father but from the world. The world and its desires pass away, but the man who does the will of God lives forever." *1 John 2:15-17*

In 1754, nine-year-old Christian Burkholder, his five siblings, and their widowed mother arrived in Philadelphia aboard the ship Phoenix. They had traveled from Switzerland in hopes of a better life and religious freedom. The Burkholder family settled near Groffdale.

Later in life, Christian Burkholder became a prominent leader in the Christian community. As a pastor and bishop, he traveled from place to place to teach the good news of Jesus. He carried a deep concern for all the young people. Out of this concern, in 1792 Christian Burkholder wrote, "Addresses to Youth." Originally in German, this booklet has also been translated into English and is still available today. Christian Burkholder taught the scriptures to young people. Eternal life means knowing God and Jesus Christ, who has been sent by God. Genuine repentance means turning to God and experiencing a substantive change of life. True love for God expresses itself in a wholehearted obedience to Jesus Christ and a caring for our fellow human beings.

"Now, my dear young hearts," wrote Christian, "if the Word of God binds us so closely to love Him as our Creator with all our hearts, and with all our strength, there remains nothing of our hearts to love the vanities and pleasures of this world."

Dear Lord, show me that part of my life and heart that I have not yet submitted to Your lordship. Let me, by Your grace, love You with all of my being.

J. Carl Sensenig is a pastor of the Red Run Mennonite Church, bishop of the Bowmansville-Reading District of the Lancaster Mennonite Conference, and a middle school teacher at Gehmans Mennonite School.

Cornwall Manor, Lebanon County
Photo by Mark Van Scyoc

"I Want to Pray"

"Plant your seeds early in the morning and keep working until dark.
Who knows? Your work might pay off and your seeds produce."
Ecclesiastes 11:6 (Contemporary English Version)

Watching from my window, I observed the three neighborhood boys playing roughly. Already there were signs of behavioral problems. I sighed to myself and feared for their futures.

"So what are you going to do about it?" the voice asked.

With sudden inspiration, I found myself inviting the boys to my home. We read Bible stories and played games. We had craft activities and snacks. And they kept coming throughout the next year.

One day I used a Jack-o-lantern to illustrate how Jesus wants to clean up our hearts and live inside of us. I explained that knowing this gives us a choice. It is like someone knocking at the door. We decide if we will invite them in or tell them to go away. Then we continued with our other activities until it was time for the boys to go home. Before they left we paused to pray.

"I want to pray," said the first boy. Taken by surprise, I watched as he folded his hands, bowed his head and said "Jesus, I say *yes*. Come in."

Then the second boy wanted to pray. Earnestly he invited Jesus to "clean up my heart and help me to grow up to be a good man."

The third boy wanted to pray but didn't know how. Lying prostrate on the floor he repeated after me his desire for Jesus to come into his heart too.

Just three little boys and a story time. Why should I have been surprised at their response? Seeds cannot produce until they are planted. But when they are planted, God can bring them to life.

Forgive me, Lord, for underestimating the power of Your truth.
Help me to seize opportunities to sow the seeds of eternal life.

Martha Mellinger lives in Paradise and attends Lancaster C&MA Church where she is involved with mentoring and missions.

What's Your Anchor?

"Do not remember the former things, nor consider the things of old. Behold, I will do a new thing. Now it shall spring forth; shall you not know it? I will even make a road in the wilderness and rivers in the desert." *Isaiah 43:18–19*

It was the summer of 1980 at Muddy Run Park. I was on a date with my "now" husband and we decided to go fishing. We rented a rowboat. We weren't even getting a bite, so we tried to go to another spot. It was my turn to row. I was getting a nice workout when all of a sudden an elderly man passed us. He must have been in his eighties, and might have weighed 100 pounds soaking wet. We thought, "Wow, he is in good shape," as we were looking for his boat motor. He didn't have one. He had the same kind of boat and oars that we did, but no motor. It took us a few minutes to figure out that we forgot to bring in the anchor. We were stuck and didn't even know it. I thought this lake seemed longer than it looked and I was thinking that the scenery all looked the same...now I knew why!

Some of us have anchors in our lives and we don't even know it. They keep us stuck. These anchors can be in forms such as regret from a wrong decision, unforgiveness toward someone who may have hurt you or holding onto something from your past. These anchors prevent us from rowing our boat of life forward and preventing us from changing the scenery in our lives.

Let's stopping dragging our anchors with us, and reel in the "keepers" of life instead.

Thank you, God, for Your patience with us as we work on getting free from the "anchors" we drag with us in our lives. Give us the courage and the strength to face them, knowing that You are with us in every step. Amen.

Lisa M. Garvey serves with Hosanna Christian Fellowship in Lititz with the Women's and Prayer Ministries.

Pa's Most Valuable Lesson

"Let my soul live that it may praise You, and let Your ordinances help me. I have gone astray like a lost sheep; seek Your servant, for I do not forget Your commandments." *Psalm 119:175–176 (New American Standard Bible)*

My number one spiritual hero in my life was my paternal grandfather or "Pa" as we called him. Pa loved the Lord with all his heart and he loved God's Word. He liked hearing his only grandson (that would be me) read from the Bible to him before he went to bed anytime I was visiting. He always said to read, "Anything that Paul wrote…he's my favorite." After reading 3 or 4 verses, he would fall asleep. One evening in 1982, Gayle and I were busy getting ready for a trip the next day. Gayle recommended making a quick stop at my grandparents that evening even though I didn't think we had time. Pa was headed for bed and asked me to come back and read to him. I started flipping through the Bible and asked Pa which of Paul's writings he wanted to hear. He said, "I think tonight I'd like to hear the 119th Psalm." As you probably know, that is the longest chapter in the Bible…*a hundred and seventy-six verses*! I didn't panic because I knew Pa would be asleep shortly.

Wrong! He stayed awake and kept his eyes focused on me the whole time. When I got to the last two verses, Pa looked at me and said, "Son, those last two verses are what I wanted you to hear. But more importantly than hearing them, I want you to *remember* them." I promised him that I would and kissed.him on the forehead. The next morning, after we had loaded up the car, I took one last trip back to the apartment and the phone was ringing. It was my grandmother. "Mike, your Pa is gone." God had given me one last chance to read to my Pa. Those eleven words have rung true in my ears every day since that August day in 1982. "I have gone astray like a lost sheep; seek Your servant…" What a loving grandfather I had and what a loving heavenly Father I *had*. Thank you, Pa, I miss you terribly.

Lord, thank you for a grandfather who showed me Your love in the midst of his love.

Mike Stike is operations manager and morning show host at 94.5 FM, The Voice Of Christian Radio, WDAC, Lancaster.

God's Kingdom is Within Me!

"The time has come...the kingdom of God is near. Repent and believe the good news!" *Mark 1:15*

Our God is a king who is building His kingdom in our lives and in our communities. He transforms whole societies as people come to know Him by receiving His good news. I recently witnessed God's kingdom influence in amazing ways during a visit to a new church near Kisumu, Kenya, the birthplace of our president's father. At Restoration Church, in the village of Kadawa, I saw first-hand a village of ten thousand being transformed by the kingdom of God! The church is less than two years old and already has over five hundred people coming together each Sunday as hundreds have received Christ. In fact, they have already planted two new churches from this newly established church.

But the most amazing thing is the way the entire community is being transformed by the kingdom of God. Believers are starting new businesses, the swamp in the region has become a banana plantation, the main government leader of the village and his whole family is now transformed by Christ. He told me that his job is now easy because violence and mugging have stopped. Hope has been restored. This is the first year that they can remember that no one has contracted cholera in their community. Last year the community was dying of AIDS, this year there are signs of kingdom influence everywhere!

The kingdom of God is good news! *Religion* places rules and regulations on people and brings them into bondage. The kingdom of God transforms families and towns and cities and nations. God wants to use each of us as His tools to accomplish His purposes. The kingdom of God is within you (Luke 17:21) and it is like a mustard seed, which is the smallest seed you plant in the ground. Yet when planted, it grows and becomes the largest of all garden plants, with such big branches that the birds of the air can perch in its shade (Mark 4:30–32). No matter how small you may feel, His kingdom is within you! Start where you are at, and watch His kingdom grow through you.

Help me to realize anew that the kingdom of God is within me, and that wherever I go, You desire to release Your kingdom through me!

Larry Kreider is the international director of DOVE Christian Fellowship International.

Who Said That?

"You will know the truth and the truth will set you free." *John 8:32*

Our pastor had been teaching us to recognize and identify the "voices" we hear—the "voices" that create filters through which we process life. It may be "true," but is it "truth"?

It was Sunday morning; the body of Christ was invited to pray for Brian's healing. His oncologist had recently told him he was concerned about some of the "numbers" in his last test. As we gathered to pray, the first thought that came to my mind was, "Why should God heal Brian when He chose not to heal my husband?" My husband had died four and a half years earlier from pancreatic cancer in spite of many prayers for his healing.

Without asking, "Who said that?" I knew it was the enemy. I immediately shut him up! I choose to acknowledge that God is good, He is in control and loves me (and Brian) and what he chooses to do is well done!

I can pray for Brian's healing (and anyone else's) with faith and joy. The devil is defeated!

Father God, sharpen our listening hearts and give us wisdom to discern the voices we hear. We want to listen only to Your voice!

Esther Helmuth was involved with her husband in church planting in Costa Rica and Texas for more than thirty-five years. She finds fulfillment as a part of the body of ACTS, as a mother of three and grandmother of six, as well as in her work as a hospice nurse.

Everyone Counts!

"And we urge you, brothers...help the weak, be patient with everyone." *1 Thessalonians 5:14*

Kevin was one of the first young fellows I took into the group home I founded for the deaf-mentally retarded. Though he was profoundly deaf and classified as moderately to severely mentally retarded, he had an outstanding smile and a pleasant personality that seemed to win the hearts of everyone around him. Kevin was a hard worker and loved to please.

My first experience with facing prejudice happened just before I took Kevin into my home. The lady I was renting from was concerned about her neighbors and property values—especially after she saw Kevin. At first, I thought it was because of his deafness, but then I realized it was because the neighborhood was all white—and Kevin was black. We moved Kevin in anyway, and slowly, the neighbors began to warm up to him.

The next challenge was with the school system—they couldn't accommodate the four young men in my group home. Kevin was tested by a psychologist who unfortunately did not know any sign language. The test results came back showing that Kevin was moderately to severely mentally retarded. Gratefully, the local United Cerebral Palsy training center was willing to work with Kevin with some job training along with some basic academic skills.

A few months later, I was able to find a psychologist who knew sign language. Kevin's IQ score immediately jumped up by twenty points —in the mild to moderate range of mental retardation.

Kevin is still in the group home, and doing very well.

Thank you, God, that You love and care about everyone—even those whomsome consider unfit.

Jim Schneck is a free-lance interpreter for the deaf, an advocate for the multi-disabled and and a doctoral student.

Fix Your Gaze

"And Stephen, full of faith and power did great wonders and signs among the people." *Acts 6:8*

Autumn had begun! My fall schedule was more intense than I had ever experienced. With school, full-time employment and my daughter's (and her four small toddlers) recent move to Pennsylvania there was hardly any time left for prayer or study of the Word. As I was reading through my Bible, the Lord captured my attention with the example of Stephen.

Stephen, an ordinary man, became extraordinary under the Holy Spirit's anointing. Initially chosen to serve tables, Stephen's faithfulness took him to a larger responsibility in service for the Lord.

Smith Wigglesworth tells us that Stephen "became lost in the power of God." He lost sight of everything in the natural and steadfastly fixed his gaze on Jesus, "the author and finisher of our faith (Hebrews 12:2)" until he was transformed into a shining light in the kingdom of God.

Stephen was an example to the early church to "fix their gaze" on the power of the Almighty God through challenging times. As they did, the Father favored their work, demonstrated His power, and used them to change the world around them.

While Stephen was an ordinary person he allowed the Lord to move him to a place where he could be used to affect many. He began in a humble place and became a man mighty for God.

Lord help us today to remember: wherever we are serving and in whatever we do, to do all for the glory of God (1 Corinthians 10:31).

Pat Denlinger is founder of Forerunner Ministries and a prayer leader at Teaching The Word Ministries.

Humility Comes Before Honor

"The fear of the Lord teaches a man wisdom, and humility comes before honor." *Proverbs 15:33*

With a unanimous vote our local school board elected me as President of the Board. What a turn of events! This was proof that God can redeem any situation. Only a year and a half earlier the same board had voted me out of the position of board president by a 5-4 vote. The events leading up to my very public ousting as the board president were some of the most humbling and difficult of my life. As I would read Proverbs over this difficult time, I would come across these words over and over again, "Humility comes before honor." This phrase appears numerous times in Proverbs. Well, I had the *humility* part for sure and later found the *honoring* part came to pass as well.

The timing of this turnaround was so perfect that as board president I was asked to sign all the diplomas of the graduating seniors, and my oldest son was graduating. What an honor and privilege to sign my own son's diploma as school board president. Only God could do something like that.

Maybe you have experienced something where events did not turn out as you expected or somehow you were disappointed with life's twists and turns. Your humbling experience may be the gateway to something great.

God, many times we do not have any idea how You could redeem things that have gone terribly wrong in our lives. We know that we make mistakes but sometimes the mistakes of others adversely affect us as well. We humbly ask that You would redeem these impossible situations in our lives in Jesus' name.

Brian Sauder helps provide oversight and direction for DOVE Christian Fellowship International's network of churches.

My Father Had a Conscience that Worked Well

"The man of integrity walks securely but he who takes crooked paths will be found out." *Proverbs 10:9*

One day, many years ago, when my father lived in Ephrata, the Main Street was a dirt road. There was a toll booth near the Cloisters that collected a nickel each time you passed through.

One day the road was so dusty that my father thought, "Why do I need to pay a nickel each time I go through with the road in such a bad state?" So he buzzed through without paying the nickel.

His conscience began to speak loudly to him and he decided to listen to it and go back and pay the nickel. He felt much better and did not make that mistake again.

Lord, help us to be people of integrity and walk securely in You.

Miriam Witmer is a mother, grandmother, great grandmother and a volunteer worker. She and her husband live at Landis Homes Retirement Community.

Choosing to Remember

"I thank my God every time I remember you." Philippians 1:3

I had the honor of joining my two older brothers in Las Vegas to celebrate my mother's eightieth birthday. My mom glowed in the attention and soaked up love we radiated her way as we talked around the dinner table. One of the activities we did together was remembering. My brother had brought a stack of old photos, yearbooks, letters, and even a Little League Baseball season batting summary sheet. With the video camera running, we sat around and discussed each item. We had a blast! We laughed as we recounted old stories and precious family memories. We chose as a family to remember the people and choices that had shaped our life together. We did not forget. We chose to remember.

One thing we did on our last visit together was especially powerful. We hopped in our cars and drove down to the Veterans Cemetery in Boulder City, Nevada. My father helped establish this beautiful memorial to men and women who have served our country. My father has been buried there for over sixteen years. In the midst of all this remembering I almost, though, forgot something very important. As I got out of the car and walked over to the place where my dad was buried, I started to cry. I had forgotten how much I missed him. My dad loved me well and was a key source of wisdom, hope, and encouragement in my life. I have missed him dearly. There has been a hole in my heart ever since he died. I have gotten used to living without him, but I still miss him dearly. Thank you, God, for helping me to remember how precious James Hackett is to me.

Thank you, God, that You give us the gift of remembering...the good, the beautiful, the true, the faithful and loving in our lives. They all remind us of You. We love You. In Jesus' name. Amen.

Don Hackett is a pastor at First Presbyterian Church in Lancaster.

Entitlement

"For by the grace given me I say to every one of you: Do not think of yourself more highly than you ought...." *Romans 12:3*

We are living in interesting times. Bailouts seem to be the approved method of action to any financial difficulty that we are experiencing. It seems that this is the answer to many bad decisions made over years of easy credit—bad business decisions that have paved the way to make it possible to finance cars we could not afford, houses that were beyond our means and then refinancing them and using the money to buy more.

With all the money being pumped into previous bad decisions, it can very easily lead to a spirit of entitlement that causes people to think, "I am entitled to a house that I cannot afford on my income; it is the responsibility of the government to make this possible; if I get into trouble, they can bail me out, that is what they are there for." While I am certainly not making light of any financial difficulty that anyone is going through, I do feel that a spirit of entitlement can carry over into the kingdom. When that happens, we lose sight of the grace of God. We begin to expect everything to be handed to us without a cost. It cost Christ greatly to extend the kingdom, and it should not surprise us that we will need to pay a price as well. We want intimacy without being willing to take the time to spend with the Father. We want to be healed without persevering to receive it. We want spiritual maturity without the very things that mature us—trials and difficulties.

A healthy understanding of the grace of God begins with an understanding that everything good and perfect come from Him. He is the author of it and lavishes it freely on us, but we need to have an understanding and appreciation from whom it comes. As a dad, I love to give gifts to each of my six children, but when they take it for granted and expect it and are not grateful, it takes some of the joy out of blessing them. I believe our heavenly Father can feel the same way.

God, You are a redeemer and God of a second chances. For the bad decisions we sometimes make, we ask You for another chance. Help us to come to You expectantly, along with a heart of thanks.

Ron Myer serves as assistant international director of DOVE Christian Fellowship International, Lititz.

Scarred

"Cast all your anxiety on him because he cares for you."
1 Peter 5:7

When Tim and I were on our honeymoon we did a paint-your-own pottery. I love the large platter I made because it's cute, but mostly because of the memories of that unique time in our life which can never be replaced and neither can the platter!

Skip ahead six years...our son decided to try his own version of the tablecloth trick. The result was a shattered platter, and a mother that cried endlessly...

Once I came to my senses, my mom assured me that we could glue it together as much as possible and it will still represent our honeymoon, but now it also has a little bit of Ryan in it: fixed, but scarred.

Through this life *we* are broken by harsh words, breakups, loss of job, infertility, loss of loved ones, disease.

God sheds tears for us when we are shattered. If we let Him, He slowly heals our wounds and they become scars. Jesus bears the ultimate scars.

Jesus is who He is, not in spite of His scars, but rather, they help define Him. And so do ours. They're a part of who we are, what we've been through.

We are broken through this life. God cries for us, loves us, carries us through and glues us back together.

Are *you* broken?

Have you allowed God to glue you back together?

God, thank you for weeping with us, picking up the pieces of our lives and, because of the crucifixion and resurrection of Your Son Jesus who bears the ultimate scars, you glue us back together and hold us tightly in Your everlasting and unconditional love. Amen.

Jen Manthey serves as a small group leader with her husband Tim at Keystone Evangelical Free Church in Paradise and is the owner of Diapers Naturally.

Keeping the Faith

"…I tell you the truth, if you have faith as small as a mustard seed, you can say to this mountain, 'Move from here to there' and it will move. Nothing will be impossible for you." Matthew 17:20

As I discussed the day's event with a coworker during lunch, a man placed his tray on the table and sat down next to me. We exchanged greetings at which time I found out his name was Geoff.

He was originally from Pennsylvania but had been living in Alabama until recently. Geoff said he had come to Pennsylvania in search of a job. In fact he had an interview that very afternoon. He spoke with confidence about finding employment.

His confidence was somewhat surprising to me. He was living in the emergency shelter at the mission after hitching a ride from Alabama. He had neither shaved nor was he neatly groomed.

Geoff had once lived the high life with a top-level job, great house, nice cars and a family. An addiction caused him to throw all that away. After seven years of drifting and doing whatever he could to survive, he was ready to change. He had been broken and now he was looking to make amends. He revealed the true reason he had come to Pennsylvania. He was indeed looking to land a job, but before he could start a new life he wanted to make restitution for his past. There were outstanding fines and other unpaid debts, which had resulted in Geoff spending some time in jail. It was a price he was willing to pay. After serving his time, Geoff tried to reconnect with his family and explain his new outlook on life.

With nowhere to go, Geoff came to the emergency shelter, where he was living when he answered an ad for a job. Despite his disheveled appearance, Geoff must have made a positive impression at his interview that day. Four days later Geoff was offered the job.

Lord, remind me that when I have little else, I can have faith to move mountains!

Keith Shetter is the director of Donor Relations at Water Street Ministries.

Opening the Door to Jesus

"Look! I stand at the door and knock. If you hear my voice and open the door, I will come in." *Revelation 3:20*

Yesterday afternoon Kyle stopped by Teen Haven to get some supplies for school. When he came in he asked about Arnie, one of our summer interns. He said with a smile, "I like Arnie, he's funny."

Arnie's friendship with Kyle started at day camp this past summer. We were involved in Operation Barnabas—a program helping the teens look for ways to encourage those in their communities. We were walking down to Water Street Mission for lunch when we stopped to talk to some kids playing in the playground at Carter McRae School. This is where we met Kyle and invited him and his friends to day camp scheduled to take place the very next day. He came, and since then we see Kyle all the time! He lives right down the street from Teen Haven and every time he sees our green van he gets excited and pulls us over to say hello.

Out of all the things we did those days, Kyle remembers Arnie. Did he remember the games, devotion, snack, activities? Maybe…maybe not. What he does remember is something that he may not even realize. It's more than laughing with Arnie. What he really remembers is Arnie's love for him. Kyle's smile made that clear. The love of Christ through Arnie made such an impression on 10-year-old Kyle that he not only asks for Arnie but he can't wait to go to camp! Now the door is open for Christ to make the biggest impact—to become Kyle's very own personal Savior. All because a teen dared to encourage a kid in his neighborhood.

Father, may our youth remember how essential they are to the Kingdom, how indispensible they are to our world and how valuable and loved they are to You.

Nina Maldonado is the Lancaster Girls Program Coordinator for Teen Haven. She lives in Lancaster.

The Greatest Among Us

Jesus told them, "In this world the kings and great men lord over their people yet they are called 'friends of the people.' But among you it will be different. Those who are the greatest among you should take the lowest rank and the leader should be like a servant."
Luke 22:25–26 (New Living Translation)

We celebrated communion today. We formed a circle around the church and passed loaves of bread tearing off pieces and serving the person to our left. *The body of Christ*, Tom said, as he handed me the loaf.

"And he took bread, gave thanks and broke it, and gave it to them, saying, 'This is my body given for you; do this in remembrance of me.'"

We took the bread—the bread of heaven. Near the back of the church one of our regular attenders from Friendship Community, George, swallowed, then sighed a little too loud. His caretaker leaned into him.

We began to pass the cup. *The cup of salvation*, I hear Tom quietly murmuring to others. I held the small cup steady waiting for all to be served. George held his with both hands. He never took his eyes off it. His caretaker leaned in to assist him. Then he slowly guided George's hand to his mouth. He threw his head back taking in every sip. *The blood of Christ*. This time he let out a long satisfied sigh. Then turning to the man next to him he smiled and patted his midsection.

I was struck by what I had just witnessed. George—in a limited way—savored communion. He delighted in the body of Christ and the cup of salvation. It satisfied him. And he was not afraid to share his joy.

May I do the same at the table of remembrance.

Lord, help me never to take for granted Your body broken for me, Your blood poured out as a sacrifice for me.

Debbi Miller is the executive secretary at Water Street Ministries. She lives with her family in Lititz. She and her family attend Landis Valley Christian Fellowship.

Lord, I Need a Briefcase

"If you know how to give good gifts to your children, how much more will your Father in Heaven give good gifts to those who ask him!" *Matthew 7:11*

We were preparing to move overseas and the paperwork threatening my desk made it look like I had a hampster for a secretary. I needed a briefcase—not a swanky $75 leather case that smelled like Wall Street. I wanted something old and tired and comfortable...something Indiana Jones would have carried into class. Besides, we were broke.

My wife was about to head off to the local thrift store to find what clothes we might need for the kids for the next couple of years.

"Have you ever seen a briefcase there?" I asked.

"Nope, but I have never looked for one either. Come along and look." It sounded like a hot date. I was in.

I walked to the back of the store. A few other people were studying the eclectic treasures in the housewares section. Most of it looked strangely familiar, like being at grandma's house. I walked past her dishes and the macrame plant hangers and the pink Barbie Doll Jeep video cassette rewinder. Then I found it.

It had the look of something that had already seen the world. I glanced around to see if Indy had accidentally left it behind. It was perfect. I reached for the price tag: $10.50. It was a sign.

There was only one problem. The three digit combination was missing. I put it down and walked away.

Then I had a thought. If it were my case, the three digit combo would have been 007. Silly, I told myself. I made another pass and checked to see if anyone was watching. I dialed in the number. Carefully, I pushed the latch closed. Trying to look casual, I then pushed the release. It opened with a click. I think I heard an angel choir.

The cashier rang up my total. "That will be 50 cents." She said.

I paused. I have to be able to sleep with myself. "Actually, it is marked $10.50."

"No." She pointed to a colored tag. "This item is on clearance."

Thank you, Father, for giving good gifts to Your children!

Dwight Kopp and his family live in Maytown. He teaches English at the Milton Hershey School.

You Are the Light of the World

"Let your light shine before men, that they may see your good deeds and praise your Father in heaven." *Matthew 5:16*

We dedicated a cabin at Teen Haven Camp to the memory of an amazing young man named Michael Skinner—a young disciple taken too soon.

The dedication took place during a leadership conference for urban youth called "Illuminate." We spent the weekend learning how to "know the light," "walk in the light," and "be the light." Although unplanned, the memorial for Michael and the time of remembrance had the greatest impact in helping the teens understand the message of the weekend.

Michael was the kind of young man who lit up a room. His smile was enormous, contagious and constant. He took genuine interest in everyone he met and when he spoke with you and listened to you, he made you feel like you were the most important person in the world. Michael embodied Matthew 5:16.

Michael was sixteen when I first met him, and I was struck by his maturity and genuineness. He was excited about God, about serving as a counselor at camp and about his future. But he was also interested in me, and he promised to pray for me. I knew that he would.

His love for Christ and for people was evident everywhere he went. What stood out most to me during both his funeral and the memorial service we had at camp was when people spoke about Michael and his life, they always talked about how Michael helped them see God, feel His love and feel valued. Thinking about Michael's life and the way he lived and loved made each of us want to be more like Jesus.

What better testimony could anyone leave behind?

Father, let Your light so fill me that it would shine to others. Let my life draw others to You.

Jack Crowley is the executive director of Teen Haven.

Requirements

"For all have sinned and fall short of the glory of God, and are justified freely by his grace through the redemption that came by Christ Jesus." *Romans 3:23–24*

An international adoption is quite a journey! My wife and I worked through the process once and are in the middle of our second one. After making your decision to adopt, you complete lots of paperwork for the adoption agency you choose, the U.S. government and the country from which you plan to adopt.

The hardest part of it is putting together what is required for the dossier that we submitted to the country we wished to adopt from! With our paperwork for China we needed twenty "perfect" documents done to exact specifications. No whiteout allowed! These documents included health forms, police clearances, employment letters and background checks that were to be filled out by others. The chance of getting them all done in perfect condition the first time was almost zero. We needed to ask doctors, employers and municipal officials to redo letters and forms because of scribbles, incomplete dates, changes in work situations, or notary expiration dates. Both times we ended up with several frustrated or angry professionals. Our social worker sympathized with us in the process.

This is a reflection of our spiritual lives. It is hard to be perfect! With our paperwork we were saved by the ability to discard a document and redo it, but we cannot go back and undo the mistakes we make in life. Yet God is perfect and His righteous standard is perfection. How do we meet that standard? The answer is that we cannot. We really are in need of a Savior, Jesus Christ, who covers for us!

Lord God, I admit that I am not perfect. In addition to the honest mistakes I make, there are also the times I purposely do the wrong thing out of selfishness. Thank you for providing forgiveness and salvation through Your Son, Jesus Christ!

Brad Sauder attends DOVE Christian Fellowship Westgate, is a small group leader and works as a computer programmer.

Anti-Cell Phone Maniac

"My brothers, show no partiality as you hold the faith in our Lord Jesus Christ, the Lord of glory." *James 2:1 (English Standard Version)*

"All right! Enough with the cell phones! No one wants to hear your personal conversations!" This is what a diner shouted as he positioned himself at the end of the booth motioning with his hands to get our attention. I was part to blame with the phone. A guy to my left answered his and was speaking on it—not very loud—in fact, his voice blended with the din of the room. My phone rang next and I immediately turned it off, but it was right after this that we had the incident. I just sat there thinking how obnoxious this guy was. I thought "He is you're typical New Yorker." If there ever was a person who resembled what we typically think of as a city dweller: cold, selfish, somewhat obnoxious—it was this guy. This was the same fellow who, a few minutes earlier, had almost run into me at the counter. I politely said, "Excuse me," but he never acknowledged that I existed. He just kept walking.

I realize I just crossed a line and have offended some of my friends who either live in or right outside a major city. Unfortunately when we stereotype people we are most times incorrect and it's also wrong thinking. In some circumstances it's called "profiling." That is not always bad especially with the terror threat of our day. But when we do it as in the way I did it, we tend to assume that everyone from that geographical area is the same, resulting in ignoring or maybe mistreating them.

Both Paul and James ended the issue when they declared that we should not be "respecter of persons" (Romans 2:11; James 2:1-13). Peter demonstrated that "God shows no partiality" (Acts 10:34-35) by going to the house of the Gentile and leading him, his family and many others to the Lord. It took the vision of a sheet of unclean animals appearing three times for Peter to get the point.

What will it take for us not to stereotype people?

Lord, thanks for not putting me in a box with other people, but loving me for me. May I love others like You love me.

Dr. Dan Allen is a pastor, writer, conference speaker, radio commentator and Director of Pinebrook Bible Conference, East Stroudsburg.

Needed in the Neighborhood

"The prayer of a righteous man is powerful and effective." *James 5:16*

I love to bake. I enjoy seeing gooey dough turn into a beautiful plate of cookies to share with others. Pulling a pan out of the oven brings joy to me! Several years ago I had a really good reason to bake. A new family moved into our neighborhood so I got out my mixing bowl.

My husband and I walked over to meet the family, carrying plates of goodies. We handed over the sweets and spent some time getting to know them. A strange feeling began to grip me. Something felt wrong! After we went back home, I mentioned how I was feeling to my husband. I felt guilty for feeling negative things after having just met these people. I simply could not shake the sense that something was not right.

With zeal I began to pray for our neighbors and my community. I prayed and prayed some more as the months rolled by. I continued to feel the need for special prayer.

About a year later I heard the news that a crime was committed in another place by one of the family members. They soon disappeared. While I was saddened by the incident, I was grateful that no one in our community came to harm. God's hand of protection was over our street. I pray that each member of that family finds the Lord.

On the National Day of Prayer 2009, I was impressed by one particular point Beth Moore challenged us with. She said our neighbors and our nation need us to pray. They may not be asking us to, but they need us to keep praying. You are so needed in the world today! Only God knows what disasters did not happen because the saints prayed! What blessings were poured out because someone did not give up!

Lord, we ask You for Your grace in our community. May our neighborhoods be safe places for our children and families to grow. May we continue to be the salt and light on our street, in our nation and in the world.

Sarah Sauder enjoys being a mom as well as graphic designer with DOVE Christian Fellowship International.

Do Some Blue Sky Thinking

"Be still in the presence of the Lord, and wait patiently for him to act...." *Psalm 37:7 (New Living Translation)*

I often sit outside on the porch with my 94-year-old mom on quiet summer evenings. Silence is thrust on me. Neither of us are big talkers. So we sit.

Sometimes I read to her, but lately I've opened my eyes and ears to observe the nature around me. I watch the birds flitting from tree to tree. I notice how the leaves of the trees wave as the wind ripples through them. I contemplate the clouds and how they slowly develop and change in the course of an evening. My eyes follow the flight of the bumblebees and the butterflies in the alfalfa field across the road. I've made a conscious act of slowing down on those evenings on the porch. It's not easy. I can think of a hundred things I could be doing.

Years ago, Franklin D. Roosevelt remarked, "Never before have we had so little time in which to do so much." I think he would be shocked to see today's world that is even more obsessed with speed. Sometimes it seems stuck in fast forward. It seems we have lost the ability to let life unfold in its own time.

But we need times that we take a break and have a change of pace. Jesus needed it, so why shouldn't we? There may not be any quiet Judean hillsides for us to retreat to, but we can linger in His presence. Why not do it today? Go outdoors in a quiet space and observe God's creation. Take a deep breath. Look at the clouds. Do some real blue sky thinking! God has a plan, in His timing, for your life and your circumstances today.

You know everything about us, Lord. You know exactly what we need and when we need it. Teach us to slow down and wait on You.

Karen Ruiz is editor of Partnership Publications and frequently tries to do some blue sky thinking.

The Light is Shining On You!

"You are all sons of the light...." *1 Thessalonians 5:5*

One day as I was talking to God and listening for His voice, I pictured some of His children wandering aimlessly around, not quite sure what was going on. Some of them had deep desires to see His kingdom come to those still in darkness. Their desires were at the right place, but they seemed to be discouraged. They were striving in their own efforts. They had many wonderful visions of how God was going to move. It was a good thing, to have vision, but they were trying to make it happen. They had forgotten how to put their full trust in God, relying on His Spirit to accomplish His will. Their shoulders were bowed and their hearts were burdened and overwhelmed.

Then these words came to me for these people: "You are born of the Spirit. His Spirit lives in you. His Spirit is a shining light. It is shining further than you think. Sometimes we go to bed at night and forget to turn off a light in another room. It may be so in the Spirit world—your candle is burning brighter than what you realize. God's Spirit is faithful. He doesn't give up on Himself."

Then I received another picture. I saw a theater stage, the curtain was closed. Behind the curtain there was great activity. People were moving furniture around. Something was happening, but since the curtain was closed we couldn't see what was going on. If God would fully reveal what He was doing through mankind you would be amazed! Your light may be shining brighter than you think. Striving in the flesh will not get you anywhere, but trusting God and resting in His peaceful presence will accomplish much.

It is true that some lamps need their wicks trimmed, so they can shine brighter. If we are willing, He is able to trim our lamps. But it has to be His work in us, and not our own. Can we be fully dependent on Him?

Thank you, Father, for Your faithful Spirit that does not sleep neither slumber. Teach us how to rest in Your Spirit. Give us a revelation of Your faithfulness.

Lydia Anne Miller is a wife and mother of two and attends Newport DOVE Christian Fellowship.

Surprised by God

"Since you are precious and honored in my sight, and because I love you..." *Isaiah 43:4*

Thanksgiving time was again approaching. We had many blessings to remember; a warm house, clothes, friends, food and, yes, turkey. Every year the store where I shop gives a free turkey when a certain amount of groceries are purchased.

I had never taken them up on their offer, but this one year I began thinking about how nice it would be to get a turkey, make several meals and then put some in the freezer. That would certainly help feed our growing teenage sons. So, after some shopping trips, I was delighted to hear the clerk say, "You've won a free turkey." Smug with my sense of accomplishment, I took the turkey home to enjoy.

I had just established a friendship with a new neighbor. As I talked to her that week, she sadly said she had no money for a turkey. For the first time, she was to host both sides of her family for the Thanksgiving meal. Immediately I felt the Holy Spirit prompting, "Give her your turkey." I tried not to listen, but I kept hearing it. After much wrestling, I gave her my turkey, along with some things to add to the meal. I knew I had done the right thing. I felt blessed to have helped.

That was not the end of the story. The next time I was grocery shopping the clerk said, "You've just won a free turkey." I clearly explained that I had already received mine and there must be a mistake. She insisted that I take it. She said, "Well, this must be your lucky day." I left with tears in my eyes, as God seemed to whisper, "You never know the blessings you'll receive in obedience to Me."

Father, thank you for the hugs we receive from You as we go through life, for the blessings received for obedience to You.

Jana Martin lives with her husband Randy and their four sons in Lititz, Pennsylvania. She helps lead worship at Millport Mennonite Church, and leads Mom's in Touch for Bonfield Elementary School in Lititz.

A Thanksgiving Promise

"For the revelation awaits an appointed time; it speaks of the end and will not prove false. Though it linger, wait for it; it will certainly come and will not delay." *Habakkuk 2:3–5*

Our three young adult children made their way home for the Thanksgiving holiday. Just the four of us. Not the 20 or so relatives that we usually hosted. My husband had abandoned our family nine months prior and we were still reeling from the pain.

In the early morning hour I headed out for my usual walk and talk with God. I literally wept as I cried out to Him, saying: "Lord, I know I heard from You that You are going after my husband, Your child, Your lost one who has gone astray and You promised to bring him home. But today is Thanksgiving and I cannot bear this. I am starting to lose my confidence."

Returning home, I picked up my Bible and read the scheduled verses for that day:

"So do not throw away your confidence; it will be richly rewarded. You need to persevere so that when you have done the will of God, you will receive what He has promised. For in just a very little while, He who is coming will come and will not delay (Hebrews 10:35–37)."

As we shared our Thanksgiving blessings around the table later that afternoon, I recounted God's clear word to me from the morning. Our hearts soared with renewed confidence in Him as God moved our eyes off our pain and back on to His promise.

Father, thank you that You meet us right where we are. You comfort us in our sufferings, for You know exactly how we feel. Thank you that You are a promise-keeping God that we can trust. I love You.

Marti Evans is persevering for the promise. She is broker-owner of CUSTOM Real Estate, Inc.

Selfless Service

"Then Jesus said to His disciples, 'If anyone would come after me, he must deny himself and take up his cross and follow me.'"
Matthew 16:24

The further I am from the kitchen the happier I am. However, lately the Holy Spirit has been nudging me to invite someone for lunch or take others a meal. God's promptings challenge me because of my dislike for cooking, and our ever tightening budget. *God, isn't there another way you can use me to bless others, something easy and that I enjoy?*

I was preparing dinner for my husband, making extra food, intending to freeze several portions for other times. As I worked, a conversation with a new church attendee came to my mind…*God I know you want me to reach out to this family, but how?* Suddenly it occurred to me… *this extra meal would be perfect and it wouldn't require additional work for me!*

Immediately I called their business to get their home phone number. *Oh, God you are so good—I love serving You.* What the receptionist said next made my heart sink. "That's great you're making a meal. We always give them gift certificates; it's easier than cooking to accommodate their dietary needs." *Ah…God, I wanted this to be easy. Please let this meal meet their requirements.* However, it wasn't that simple…reluctantly, I went back to the kitchen searching for a recipe to fit their dietary restrictions. As I was preparing their meal, joy overcame my selfish attitude as I realized I had the opportunity to be God's hands and feet by serving them in a tangible way. The meal was delivered and it was graciously received by the family, confirming that God's love was experienced, possibly in a new and much needed way.

Jesus, thank you for making the ultimate sacrifice, providing me with my salvation. Forgive me for wanting it easy when I serve You, thinking of myself first and not of others. Help me follow You even when it's not easy.

Nan Schock serves as a Stephen Minister at Manor Church, Lancaster.

My Daughter, the Mountain Climber

"I will bring forth descendants from Jacob and from Judah those who will possess my mountains…." *Isaiah 65:9*

I read this scripture and knew that God had answered me. I was having a quiet time and had asked God a very important question. "Am I pregnant?" Ladies, maybe you have had this feeling…that a new spirit has arrived on the scene. It is a wonderful secret known only to you and to God.

When our precious daughter was born nine months later, it was obvious that she didn't look quite like our other three children. A chromosome analysis revealed that she was missing a piece of her sixth chromosome. Other children with this deletion had health issues and developmental delays. My husband and I thought that surely our daughter would be the exception. As she got older, however, Ashlyn developed an umbilical hernia and a dislocated right hip. She was also missing her developmental milestones. We had to come to terms with the fact that we had a "special needs" child. Although it was difficult, my faith was never shaken. Because of that very important scripture, I was certain of two things: one, that Ashlyn was not a mistake but a child that God himself had brought forth. Two, that she had a big destiny. The word of the Lord is more real than the circumstances in front of us.

Now Ashlyn is five years old. She talks a little and crawls. She hasn't begun to stand up or walk yet. Yet God said she would possess mountains! I have a friend who has a son with Down's syndrome. He is Ashlyn's age and is walking. But he hasn't begun to talk yet. His parents believe in the many prophecies that their son has received, that he would preach to the nations and be a man appointed by God. Isn't that just like God? To say that a girl who can't walk will be a mountain climber and a boy who can't talk will be a preacher!

God, help me believe that You will do the impossible in my life.

Anne Brandenburg is a mother of six and the wife of Chris, a pastor at Life Center Ministries.

Turn Around

"I can do everything through him who gives me strength."
Philippians 4:13

After graduating from Conrad Weiser High School in Robesonia, Berks County, in 1960, I joined the U.S. Navy to proudly serve my country. Later that same year I got married.

I spent the first 38 years of my life serving the devil. Occasionally I would go to church, and thought I was doing God a favor.

On March 9, 1980, I attended church with my parents and heard a message like I had never heard before. The description of the Man that died for me was so vivid I turned to see just who the pastor was talking about. That Sunday morning I gave my heart and life to Jesus and I have been serving Him ever since.

I prayed for God to use me and make me a blessing. Not too many years ago, He started giving me poems. Many of the poems were written to bless friends of mine that were sick in the hospital. My wife and I have printed two poem books on our computers. Between the two volumes we have handed out over 1,000 books.

It's funny, because in high school, English was not my best subject and poems really bored me. Yet when the Lord changes you He does it the right way! What you loved you now hate and what you hated you now love.

I give all the glory and praise to my Lord Jesus Christ for without Him I am nothing.

Lord, I thank you for the burden You give me for the sick. Now I pray that You give me the wisdom and the knowledge to encourage others to trust in You for their healing. Amen

Kenneth C. Showalter and his wife live in the Ephrata area. They have 3 children, 8 grandchildren, 1 great-grandson, and a greatgranddaughter on the way.

Nothing is Impossible

"If one falls down, his friend can help him up...." *Eccesiastes 4:10*

In July 2009, God gave me an unexpected, unbelievable, incredible vacation. I had barely been out of Lancaster County since the amputation of my leg in 2005, and now here I was driving with a friend 2,880 miles across the United States with the opportunity to visit a dear mentor friend I had not seen in seven years. I would also connect with a friend I had lost contact with for over 23 years. Even though she had moved, the phone number I had was correct, and we were able to share how prayer ministry has impacted our lives. Only God!

While on the west coast, I went hang-gliding over the cliffs of San Diego and the Pacific ocean. I enjoyed the breathtaking view that I felt must be what we will enjoy in heaven! Up there the ocean waves had no sound, the hustle-bustle of life just wasn't apparent and nothing seemed big up there. But the peace was indescribable as the wind blew in my face. It was like I could reach out and touch the clouds. To my delight, I almost was able to touch the top of a palm tree.

It wasn't until we were almost ready to land when it occurred to me that I had just entrusted my life to someone I knew nothing about. I could have plummeted to my death if the operater had not secured the straps properly or the equipment failed! But I knew I had prayed before I made that decision knowing how it feels when you are in God's will— so, I had nothing to fear. Besides, many onlookers were so excited for this one-legged woman, who exclaimed with much enthusiasm, "With God nothing is impossible!"

Thank you Lord for allowing us to help others and for those around us who help us on our journey. You are an awesome God who makes all things possible in our lives.

Darlene Adams is involved in L.O.V.E. Ministry (Letters of Victorious Encouragement), a prison pen pal ministry.

Joshua Brown - Witness of Truth

"Choose you this day whom ye would serve…as for me and my house, we will serve the Lord." Joshua 24:15 (King James Version)

There is a red brick house that sits on a hill near the village of Goshen, southern Lancaster County. In 1760, Joshua Brown, a Quaker farmer and miller, built this home and a mill situated on the Conowingo.

Joshua was a well-known itinerant minister. By this time he had already made two journeys to Virginia, visiting and speaking at Quaker meetinghouses along the way. On his first journey in 1756, Joshua successfully negotiated the release of seven Quaker youths who had been under house arrest for refusing to serve in the militia. He was gratified to find that the young men "had gained the favour of the chief officer, so that he was very pleasant, and discharged them." The chief officer was none other than Colonel George Washington!

Joshua would come to make eleven journeys in all. In addition to Pennsylvania and Virginia, he visited New Jersey, New England, North Carolina and South Carolina. He ministered to Friends in exile during the Revolutionary War (becoming a prisoner himself while in South Carolina). He witnessed against slavery, exhorting Friends not to buy or sell slaves and whoever owned slaves, to free them. However, his focus was always the spiritual life of the Friends who lived on the frontier. Traveling after harvest, he endured the weather and other dangers to minister to families who were often isolated. Throughout, he stayed true to the principles of his faith.

When asked by a non-Quaker if he thought he imposed upon the people, Joshua replied, "I think not, when we appoint meetings, we do not promise to preach; but if we feel our minds engaged to speak, we do it as we find ability. Your preachers preach for money, and are obliged to speak, but we do not."

Father, like Joshua, may we answer Your call to serve You humbly and obediently. Amen.

Marion Baker is the fourth great-granddaughter of Joshua Brown.

Zook's Corner, Lancaster County
Photo by Mark Van Scyoc

December

Charles Finney and the Reading Revival

"For Zion's sake, I will not be silent…" *Isaiah 62:1*

In the winter of 1829-30, the great revivalist Charles Finney came through Reading, Pennsylvania, and recorded some of his experiences in his writings on revival. One of his accounts about his time in Reading reads:

"There were two or more daily newspapers published there at the time. I learned that the editors were drinking men; and were not infrequently carried home, on public occasions, in a state of intoxication. These editors began to give the people religious advice, and to speak against the revival, and the preaching. I asked the people if they did not think that those editors were fulfilling the desires of the devil; if they did not believe the devil desired them to do just what they did? I said, 'If I had a family in the place I would not have such a paper in the house; I should fear to have it under my roof; I should consider it too filthy to be touched with my fingers, and would take the tongs and throw it into the street.' In some way the papers got into the street the next morning, pretty plentifully, and I neither saw nor heard any more of their opposition."

What if we were to be so bold today? Instead of allowing the media to mold and shape the beliefs of our children, our teenagers, and our society, we must rise up with the Word of God on our lips and set the standard for truth in our day. Let us stand on the shoulders of Charles Finney, refuse to be silent, and see our cities transformed by the truth of the gospel that still sets men free!

Father, as it was with the early church and as it was with Charles Finney, fill Your church again with boldness, that we may speak Your Word, with signs and wonders following.

Craig Nanna lives in Reading with his amazing wife Tracie and three kids, and they together pastor Reading DOVE Christian Ministry Center. Craig also serves as the director for a group of pastors and Christian leaders called the Reading Regional Transformation Network.

The Fruit of the Spirit is Joy

"For the joy of the Lord is our strength..." *Nehemiah 8:10*

Sometimes life gets so busy we fail to experience the joy that should be part of that occasion. A friend of my sister had gone through some health issues. So when their 40th wedding anniversary came around, she asked if I would be her event planner from food to decorations, and everything in between. This event was sandwiched in between an upcoming vacation and planning other events at my teahouse.

To say I was joyous during this time was far from the truth. Being selfish, my heart really wasn't in it, and I longed for the opportunity to get away and relax. The whole time I kept thinking, "Why did I agree to this? What was I thinking? How can I be ready for my trip with all that is required to pull off this event?"

When the big day arrived, and I got to see the happiness on their faces, the spirit of joy overwhelmed me. For even though I was focusing on me throughout the planning stages, I was priming the pump so to speak, because I didn't give in to my feelings, but rather persevered. Then when the big day arrived the floodgate of joy was released, and I was so thankful that I had given it my all.

Unknown to us, this joyous occasion was the last special occasion this couple celebrated. A few months later, the health issues that had plagued my sister's friend had returned.

When word came of her passing, I couldn't help but think how good it felt to have brought happiness one last time into their lives. Joy is the fruit of the Spirit. We must learn how to release it.

Lord, teach us to release the spirit of joy each day of our lives. For no matter what we face, we know that Joy cometh in the morning. In Jesus' name, Amen!

Janet Young is owner of a teahouse in Camp Hill.

The Feet in Front of Me

"Come, let us bow down in worship, let us kneel before the Lord our Maker" *Psalm 95:6*

This was a day that I was really worn out. Not unusual for me, as a then mom of two kids under the age of two. But my little baby Christian needed my attention, as he so often did in those early months. He was sitting up on the floor, and I came to him. I didn't know what to do —I didn't have the energy to pick him up, let alone get up myself! So, I stayed on my hands and knees in front of him and rested my head on the floor too. His chubby little feet were right in front of me, so I just started playing "This Little Piggy." That was all he needed to make him smile.

As I was down there, I realized that I was in a bowing position. So I thought about how we worship God. When we worship, we come right before His feet, laying aside everything, bowing with the only energy we have left. And we don't need to even play "This Little Piggy" to make Him smile. (I can't even imagine that, anyway. Can you?) The bowing position suggests that we are weak and sometimes weary before Him, as I was that day on the floor. Our worship is exclaiming that when we are weak, He is strong. Then, He promises to take our weariness. It is another opportunity for Him to prove His power and be glorified. And that is what makes Him smile.

Dear Lord, I am weak and there is nothing I can do on my own. But right now, I bow before You with the offering of my weakness. Please take it and replace it with Your strength to sustain me through this day. Amen.

Tracy Slonaker is a wife, mother of three, and Director of Christian Education at Harvest Fellowship of Colebrookdale.

Honesty is the Best Policy

"Let us therefore come boldly to the throne of grace, that we may obtain mercy and find grace to help in time of need." *Hebrews 4:16*

"Doctor, what time frames are we looking at?"

My question came the day following our daughter's serious auto accident. Bekah lost control on black ice and hit a tree. She suffered a broken arm and orbital bones, brain contusions, and deep facial lacerations. Bob and I were extremely thankful Bekah had survived.

But the doctor's answers stabbed our hopeful expectations. "Based on what I see today, Bekah will be in the hospital two weeks, in-patient rehab for six weeks, and should participate in no sports for one year. She won't return to high school this year."

The reality of his words smashed our dreams. I felt anger rise as I realized Bekah would miss both her senior year and college freshman year of soccer. She wouldn't be captain, and would miss the fun of playing with her long-time friends. "Lord, that's not fair!"

Some well-meaning people suggested that losing a season of soccer was trivial in the grand scheme of things. Intellectually, I agreed. But what did I do with my anger? Deny it? Suppress it?

When Jesus wept with Mary and Martha over their brother's death, He also "groaned in the spirit and was troubled," (even knowing the joyous ending of the story). Jesus apparently was angry at the domination of Satan who brought sorrow and death through sin. So it is possible to react with several emotions towards a traumatic experience; my anger at Bekah's losses did not negate or diminish my gratefulness for her life.

Like Mary and Martha, I ran to the best source possible. Like them, I vented to the Lord. He reminded me that some of our visions, however great or small, "die." He gave me permission to mourn the soccer losses of Bekah's future. The Lord's presence surrounded me, and He listened.

Dear Lord, thank you for allowing us to talk to You honestly and boldly. Thank you for then showering us with Your kindness.

Tamalyn Jo Heim is a new Oma (grandmother) to Isaac who will keep her "honest."

DECEMBER 5

Undeserved Love

"My command is this: Love each other as I have loved you."
John 15:12

I recently had a conversation with a teacher-friend of mine. New to the high school, she was assigned the classes nobody else wanted—the kids with emotional problems and learning disabilities. These are tough kids, and year after year teachers look forward to leaving them behind and moving on to a group of students who are, shall we say, worthwhile investing in?

Ouch. I wonder what Jesus would think of that. I wonder if He'd move on, or if He'd choose to stay right there, pouring His time, resources, wisdom, and love into kids whose behaviors don't warrant it and who can't possibly earn it.

My petty, self-righteous heart is somewhat bothered by the fact that Jesus invested His precious resources into people who didn't deserve it. I'm irritated to find He spent hours listening to "sinners" and went out of His way on numerous occasions to heal and restore the lives of people who hadn't even been following or obeying Him! To put it quite simply, He convicts me. This Jesus would be so much easier to follow if He just loved and served the deserving. Strange. I didn't think so when I was the undeserving one.

Jesus, thank you for Your mercy! Your heart is so much bigger than mine! Help me to follow You in freely investing my time, resources, wisdom and love in the same manner as You.

Jenny Gehman lives in Millersville, where she seeks God regularly concerning her investments.

354

God Stories 5

Remember the Sabbath Day by Keeping it Holy

"You shall work six days, but on the seventh day you shall rest, even during plowing time and harvest you shall rest." *Exodus 34:21*

God reveals a plan for work and rest. He stops His work of creating so He can rest. He invites us to enter into that same time of rest; one day of rest after six days of work. Sounds simple enough, but do we follow through? "If you call the Sabbath a delight, and the Lord's holy day honorable, and if you honor it by not going your own way and not doing as you please...then you will find joy in the Lord (Isaiah 58:13–14)."

"Remember the Sabbath day by keeping it holy (Exodus 20:8)." Do we obey this fourth commandment or miss some of God's delights and blessings by not keeping the Sabbath holy? Does it concern us that the Sabbath has become like every other day of the week—working, shopping, and hurrying to get caught up with unfinished projects? Modern society seduces our attention away from Sabbath rest.

"He who dwells in the shelter of the most high will rest in the shadow of the Almighty. I will say of the Lord, He is my refuge and my fortress, my God in whom I trust (Psalm 91:1–2)."

Rest sounds appealing, but how do we accomplish it? If a job requires work on Sunday, then choose another day for rest. When we find time to meditate on God as our Strength, our Provider, our Guide, and our Redeemer, we will find rest for our body, mind, and soul. The Sabbath is a good day to begin. Sleep restores our bodies. The Sabbath restores our spiritual souls.

May I find the Sabbath a retreat from my hectic week and a joy to honor You, my Lord.

Dona Fisher is chairman of the local National Day of Prayer, president of Change of Pace Bible Studies, and is a freelance writer for Lancaster Sunday Newspaper.

Matters of the Heart

"…For the Lord does not see as man sees, for man looks at the outward appearance, but the Lord looks at the heart." *1 Samuel 16:7*

In the winter of 1980, a classmate introduced me to his friend, my future husband. For me it was love at first sight. For him I'd call it more like a delayed reaction. On our first date, he got sidetracked by doing truck repairs and was two hours late. On our second date, he brought his dogs. Now I'm a dog lover, but these dogs were bad. The small one had missing teeth and chewed glass. The larger one stole a 5 pound roast off of the kitchen counter…from the neighbor's house! He took those dogs everywhere.

By the end of our second date, I learned that his El Camino had no heat. Perhaps the rear window that was missing had something to do with it. When you turned on the defrost, it actually snowed inside and he used an ice scraper to scrape the inside of the windshield. I sat there asking myself, "What do I see in this guy?" As time went by, I had the answer to that question. My future husband had a big heart. He would help anyone and everyone and went out of his way for others. I saw him help a stranger who needed a hot meal. I saw how the success of a man is not measured by wealth.

Jesus always showed His love for others by looking at what was in their hearts and not by appearances. God told Samuel to visit the family of Jesse the Bethlehemite, and there he would find the next king of Israel. Seven of Jesse's sons passed before Samuel, but God didn't choose any of them. He chose the youngest instead, David, who was tending the sheep.

Thank you, God, for giving us Your example of how not to judge a person by their appearance, because we don't know what that person has been through. Thank you for reminding us to treat others how we want to be treated. Amen.

Lisa M. Garvey serves with Hosanna Christian Fellowship in Lititz with the Women's and Prayer Ministries.

Our Refuge and our Strength

"But the Lord has become my fortress, and my God the rock in whom I take refuge." *Psalm 94:22*

My experiences with hospitals have been mostly unpleasant and uncomfortable. A place that people go when they are sick, hurt, struggling with disease, or near death is uncomfortable to me. Hospitals have not had an encouraging or uplifting reputation in my life. That all changed for me when God used a beautiful moment and a young lady named Katelyn who was diagnosed with aplastic anemia.

Katelyn is a young lady who I got to know through TNT Youth Ministry. Katelyn was diagnosed with aplastic anemia, a disease the dramatically lowers the production of blood cells. Katelyn ended up in Hershey Medical Center and was facing chemotherapy and a bone marrow transplant to try to reset her body's production of blood. For a healthy and very active young lady this was going to be a very difficult season in life.

Mike Wenger, executive director of TNT Youth Ministry, and I went to visit Katelyn. Mike brought his guitar along because we knew that Katelyn loved to sing worship songs. It was difficult to encourage a young lady facing a season of IVs, medication, a bone marrow transplant, and the effects of aggressive chemotherapy, but worshiping God has a way of bringing hope to the hopeless.

As we began to sing together we could feel the Holy Spirit begin to bring healing and hope to her spirit. We cried and sang together for almost an hour. I sensed that God was really in this situation even though there were struggles ahead; He used this moment to bring strength and courage.

That was several months ago, and we are thankful to God that Katelyn has made it through the chemotherapy and the bone marrow transplant. She has been allowed to go home and her blood levels are steadily getting back to normal.

Father, thank you for being our strength when our circumstances seem hopeless.

Grant Gehman serves as the director of TNT Youth Ministry in Ephrata.

My Ebenezer

"Samuel took a stone and set it up...He named it Ebenezer, saying, 'Thus far has the Lord helped us.'" *1 Samuel 7:12*

The surgeon's words cut sharply into my reality: "There is a fifty-fifty chance that your tumor is malignant!" In the days that followed, I planned for the worst, while praying for the best. What a joy to hear the word "benign" through the haze of recovery from anesthesia!

Now a five-inch permanently etched scar is a reminder of this life-changing event that propelled me, and my husband, closer to God and each other. Decisions we made following my surgery have allowed us to simplify our lives and refocus our priorities.

1 Samuel 7 describes a momentous event in the life of the Israelites. Philistines threatened to attack the vulnerable Israelites. Their priest, Samuel, cried to the Lord who intervened by sending thunder. As a result, the panicked Philistines lost the battle with the Israelites. It was then that Samuel set up his Ebenezer stone as a reminder of God's help.

How could the Israelites forget what God had done when they saw that stone monument? We, too, can set up "Ebenezer stones" to remind us of God's work in our lives.

Dear Lord, help us to never forget the ways You've worked in our lives in the past.

Leona Myer, with her husband Everett, serves on the pastoral elder team at Hosanna! A Fellowship of Christians, in Lititz.

Hugs and Kisses

"Jesus said to him, 'You shall love the Lord your God with all your heart, with all your soul, and with all your mind.'" *Matthew 22:37*

I've seen the sign in several furniture and craft stores: Always Kiss Me Good Night. I would add a sequel: Give Me a Hug Every Morning.

For a single woman living alone that would seem to be useless advice. However it has very special meaning for me.

I don't remember how the conversation started or what we had been discussing, but God telling me to blow Him a kiss still resonates in my heart. I'll admit I didn't obey immediately—twelve Amish passengers would have wondered if their taxi driver was crazy. But once they were delivered and I was on a quiet back road with only a few cows and an inquisitive mule for an audience, I kissed my fingers and tilted my head back to blow it heavenward.

And heard God chuckle and say, "Again."

The same press of the Spirit I sometimes experience during worship rested on my chest. I felt silly blowing God kisses but what did that matter if it delighted Abba? With the Spirit's coaching, the hugs started a few weeks later. Stretching my arms skyward, I locked my hands to form an "O." Hugs and kisses for my beloved, morning and night.

Holy Spirit, teach me to love God with all my imagination.

Ruth Morris is a member of Worship Center. She is a special projects writer for several parachurch ministries.

Confirmation

"Lord, you have assigned me my portion and my cup; you have made my lot secure...You have made known to me the path of life; you will fill me with joy in your presence...." *Psalm 16:5, 11*

If you've read any of John Ortberg's books, you know how he can put a humorous spin on situations that can outright "get us down." For instance, in his book *God is Closer Than You Think*, he likens our daily search for God to *Where's Waldo?* On some days, God seems very real to us. But on other days He can seem so very far away. "Where *are* you God? I *need* you!"

During one of my recent weekend-warrior stints, I performed a half-gainer off a slippery backyard retaining wall, precipitating the need for an MRI of my knee. Anxious to get going on whatever process was necessary to promote healing, I pleaded with God to please just speed things up so that I could take my upcoming overseas trip.

The following days showed such marked improvement that I was almost embarrassed to hobble through the door of the imaging center. My request for classical music brought a cheerful, "Beethoven then, with ocean waves in the background," from the technician, and I was immediately filled with the strains of that beautiful old hymn, *Joyful, Joyful We Adore You!* (Henry van Dyke 1907). Precious Lord, what a beautifully unexpected confirmation of your concern for me!

So where's God? Everywhere! Even when we don't feel His presence, He's there guiding and directing not just the daily order of our lives, but working through those who attend to our temporary needs. Beautiful confirmations that He's on the job *24-7*. Thank you, Lord!

Dear Lord, how I adore You! Thank you for taking care of all those little details that give me so much encouragement. "Ever singing, march we onward, victors in the midst of strife; joyful music leads us sunward in the triumph song of life." Amen!

Janet Medrow is the assistant to the director at the National Christian Conference Center in Valley Forge. She also serves as a deacon at Great Valley Presbyterian Church in Malvern.

No Longer a Grasshopper

"…But the Lord is with us." *Numbers 14:9*

The workplace is filled with talented, well-educated people with impressive work experiences and all the qualifications for success.

Sometimes I feel like a grasshopper in the eyes of the many people I interact with in my job as a writer and editor. I can identify with the feelings of the spies who checked out the land God promised them. In Numbers 14, the story is told of how the spies reported, "Sure it's a great place to live, but we can never live there. The land is inhabited by giants so big that we are like grasshoppers in their eyes."

Sometimes I feel like a grasshopper, insignificant to handle the massive workload before me. I feel overwhelmed by the creativity and knowledge my job demands. I wish that I could feel smart, confident and in control at all times.

But those negative feelings I battle are bothering me less and less because God showed me that feelings aren't the truth. If God is always with me—just like He promises, then it doesn't matter what I face. It doesn't matter if I feel confident or not. I can say like Joshua and Caleb who maintained when they checked out the land, "It's a great land and God will give it to us because He is with us. Do not be afraid of the inhabitants of the land."

My job isn't to check out the workplace competition. It isn't to compare myself with their credentials. It isn't to compete against them.

My job is to keep my eyes on Him. It means that I diligently pursue my work, perfect it and work hard, but my ultimate trust is in God who empowers me.

Lord, so what if I feel like a grasshopper. The truth is that Your strength causes me to succeed—even in the workplace.

Lou Ann Good is retired, but this is from the personal journal she kept while employed as a newspaper editor.

Thirst Quenched!

"...Whatever you did for one of the least of these brothers of mine, you did for me." *Matthew 24:40*

Working with people who have many needs and have been abused can be exhausting and frustrating at times. However, sometimes there are moments of humor and joy. I'll never forget this story:

William was an older hard-of-hearing man with slight mental retardation. He was a pleasant fellow and loved talking to people. He was placed in an institution in the early 1960s. He progressively lost his hearing until he became totally deaf. Unfortunately, he was also a diabetic and became totally blind as well. In spite of being both deaf and blind, William was still eager to learn Braille and loved to have visitors. William preferred using the British two-handed alphabet, because it was easier for him to feel with his hands. I remember working with him in the dining hall. William didn't learn Braille very well, but he sure loved having someone to talk to! He still used his voice to talk to those around him, but it was in a high volume, since he couldn't hear himself.

One day, some staff from the Deaf Education Department decided to treat William to a meal at a posh restaurant. They took him to a fine restaurant, with specially folded napkins; fine linen table cloths—the works! William was quite excited, but still had not mastered all the social graces for such an occasion. He didn't know what to order, so the staff decided to take a chance and order something for him in preparation for his meal. They figured he would enjoy orange juice with his meal.

Upon tasting the orange juice, he exclaimed in a very loud voice: "Oh! Orange juice! That's what they give us over in the Mental Hospital to clean our bowels out!" Needless to say, the staff volunteers wanted to sink under the floor! Aren't you glad that God has a sense of humor?

Lord we know You have said that those who will receive the Father's blessing at the final judgment are those who helped others in need— the hungry, the thirsty, the unclothed, the sick...help us to reach those people with joy.

Jim Schneck is a free-lance interpreter for the Deaf, an advocate for the multi-disabled and and a doctoral student.

Coins and Nails

"May the words of my mouth and the meditation of my heart be pleasing in your sight, O Lord, my Rock and my Redeemer." *Psalm 19:14*

Taking a walk through various neighborhoods a few times a week, it is not unusual to discover a half dozen or more coins that have been dropped in the roadway. It's no matter that generally only one is collected at a time, or how small an amount, finding an unexpected gift can serve to brighten a day. At the same time, it is not unusual to discover a half dozen or more nails of all sizes, potentially ready to do damage.

Each discovery reminds me of the potentials related to my own actions of the day. I can say or do something positive, no matter how large or small, that may serve as a brightener to someone's day, or I can say or do something negative, again no matter how large or small, that has a possibility of causing some real damage.

Lord, help me to be cognizant of my words and actions, so that they may serve to become a gift in someone's day. Amen.

Casey Jones, who resides in Parkesburg, is an advocate for development of comprehensive marriage and family ministries, including ministries to the hurting in churches. He is developer of a Transformation Initiative for Building Healthy Communities through Healthy Families.

The Journey is as Important as the Destination

"May our Lord Jesus Christ himself and God our Father, who has loved us and given us everlasting comfort and hope...encourage your hearts and strengthen you in every good deed and word."
2 Thessalonians 2:16–17

Sometimes we are faced with challenges. As my husband, Jimmy, and I have aged, we have had concerns for our youngest daughter, Shelly, who is mentally challenged. In her forties, Shelly is a blessing to our household, church, the Special Olympics, and her present ministry job. Over the years our protective hands have been on her life.

This has been especially hard for Jimmy. He has been her father, coach, boss, and protector...but now he has to let her go.

Shelly interviewed at the local hospital but was not hired. So her dad encouraged her to volunteer at the job she wanted: dishwashing. For the next year Shelly faithfully washed dishes, never missing her shift even though she had already worked eight hours at her present job. We knew her challenges would make finding another job difficult, but we believed if they had the opportunity to see her work and her attitude, she might have a chance.

One year later, Shelly was hired in the dish department.

She shared her journey at church: "I decided to do a great job in the kitchen like starting the dishwasher and loading it. I learned how to roll the silverware up in a napkin. I swept the kitchen floor. I wanted to show them I could do it and would be faithful and patient. I believed that my faithfulness would show them I would make a good employee. I wanted them to know that I don't give up and I am loyal."

Dear Father, help us to trust You and to do all we can to overcome obstacles and to make our dreams live. Amen.

Anne Pierson has been married to Jimmy for forty-nine years and is the mother of two girls, has three granddaughters and numerous foster children.

"Croc Chet" Class

"Surprise us with love at daybreak; then we'll skip and dance all the day long." *Psalm 90:14 (The Message)*

I enjoy knitting and crocheting, so when asked to teach an elective, I suggested a needlework class. However, I got ruffled at my list of students: three girls and five boys. What? I knew a couple of them and thought they were looking for a goof-off class. Later I received a revised list. All the girls pulled out to go to choir. Thinking I could scare off those who didn't want to work, I issued a list of requirements and passed them out a week before the class. Nobody budged.

As the first day approached I prayed and prepared myself for what I just "knew" was going to be a tough haul. I walked in and sure enough no one had their materials. As I got ready to lower the boom, I saw their faces. They wanted to learn. They were serious.

I passed out some yarn and crochet hooks which they promptly dubbed "croc chet" hooks. After a few tries at a slip stitch their manly macho, "how hard can this possibly be?" melted. It took one class to get the slip stitch and to learn to chain.

They teased each other and laughed and worked desperately hard to master their fingers and yarn. It soon became my favorite class. They wanted to know if they were better than the girls last year, and I had to admit they were. What they lacked in skill they made up for in tenacity.

So, okay, I know God had lessons: facing one's fears, walking through doors that don't look right and can't possibly be God. The scripture, "He knows the plans He has for us, plans for good and not for evil, to give me a future and a hope" seems far too extreme for a crochet class, or is it? Don't we learn through the simple to trust in the complex? He wants to bless me with joy and to change my vision to see light instead of shadows around the bend.

Lord, thank you for Your lessons that are ever so gentle in hindsight. Thank you for prodding me and being patient with my mumblings and fears. For You have said that You are with me wherever I go.

Christina Ricker is a victorious warrior, wife, mom and nana.

God's Tattoos

"See, I have inscribed you on the palms of My hands..." *Isaiah 49:16*

I was raised in the West—Texas, that is. I will always remember my parents and kin folks telling us kids how disgusting and ugly tattoos were and that once you got one they were there forever. In light of that, I'm not particularly a fan of tattoos—on myself, that is.

But there is one tattoo I truly love, and it's *my* name written by God on His hand—forever!

If you know Christ as Savior, your name is there, too. And if you don't, then you can know your name is there by believing Jesus died for your sins and confessing Him as your personal Savior and repenting of all your sins and asking God into your heart.

Father God, thank you for forgiveness and Your love for me. You wrote my name on Your hand. I love that tattoo!

Alton Alexander attends Ephrata Church of the Nazarene.

God's Tinkering

"For those God foreknew he also predestined to be conformed to the likeness of his Son...." *Romans 8:29*

Henry Ford, as the story is told, hired an electrical wizard to repair one of his huge electrical motors. Charlie Steinmetz came, found the problem, repaired it, and sent Mr. Ford a bill for $10,000.00. Henry Ford could not imagine such a large expense for "a little bit of tinkering." Surely Charlie placed too many zeros on his invoice. Mr. Steinmetz's response to Henry was simple: $10.00 for "tinkering" and $9,990.00 for "knowing where to tinker."

In order for God to conform us to His image it takes a bit of tinkering. I imagine it to be something like the Holy Spirit crawling down into the sewers of our soul to remove that which does not honor Him in order to rebuild and conform us to that which does honor Him. While all of us desire change to happen instantly, so much of being conformed takes a lifetime.

We all have a past, but when we came to Jesus, the cross made the difference between us and our histories. Jesus became a curse for us so that we could become redeemed from the curse (Galatians 3:13). The cross separated us from "the empty way of life handed down to [us]" (1 Peter 1:18). And, we were made alive, our sins forgiven, taken away and nailed to the cross (Colossians 2:13-14). Jesus is the great Counselor.

Ask the Holy Spirit, the One whom Jesus sent, to continue to conform your life today—He knows exactly where to tinker.

Father, continue to conform me to Your image so that I might reflect Your Son to someone today. In Jesus' name. Amen.

Steve Prokopchak helps provide oversight and direction for DOVE Christian Fellowship International's network of churches.

God Knows Best

"Delight yourself in the Lord, and he will give you the desires of your heart." *Psalm 37:4*

Last year, I wrote about how disappointed my husband and I were because we didn't get the house we wanted. And my husband, Shawn, didn't get the job he wanted. Little did we know at the time that God had better plans for us.

About five months after we found out that we didn't get the house or job, the Lord opened up another house for us to buy! And we bought the house a month before the economy went into a bad recession. It's also in a good school district, which will be a blessing for our son. Now we are officially first-time home buyers!

And the Lord opened up another job for Shawn right down the road from where we live! So now he can walk to work, which saves us on gas money. And the job even pays more then the previous one, which is a double blessing!

My husband and I are truly grateful. We were able to see why the Lord said no and had us wait. However that may not always be the case. We may never know why God says no until we get to heaven. Maybe you are facing God's no right now in your own life. You're wondering why the Lord is having you wait. My hope and prayer is that my story will encourage you and remind you that God truly does know best.

Dear Heavenly Father, thank you for the times that You have us wait on You. Help us to remember that You know what is best for us and will always provide for our needs and even our wants at times. Amen.

Jenn Paules is a part-time DJ for WJTL, FM 90.3, an ESL instructor, but more importantly a full-time wife and mother.

$150 Squirrel's Nest

"And wheresoever the children of men dwell, the beasts of the field and the fowls of the heaven hath he given into thine hand, and hath made thee ruler over them all." *Daniel 2:38 (King James Version)*

About ten years ago, my children and I moved into our house on Stone Run Drive. We are surrounded by trees, birds, squirrels, chipmunks—we love it.

My son once left a three-foot rag on the picnic table and that evening at supper we were entertained by the squirrels trying to heave that extra long nest-lining fifty feet up a pine tree to their nest. The cloth got stuck and the squirrels had to give up on that priceless piece of lining. We didn't give up though. The next day, we hoisted my youngest son up the tree to retrieve the fabric. We cut the fabric into three-inch squares and spread them beneath the tree. By evening, the squirrels had their new lining nicely in place.

Each year, the squirrels entertain us with babies that play outside our kitchen window while we eat dinner. They also took a liking to my front porch swing. On many occasions we find the squirrels cuddled between the pillows and taking a nap.

One day last September I arrived home from work and was speechless at the scene I found. The cushion and pillows on my swing had been shredded—quite literally whole chunks of fabric were missing and the stuffing was pulled out.

I realized immediately that the squirrels were again lining their winter nest, but this time they used my $150 hand-quilted swing cushion. I wanted to cry!

As I recovered from my loss, I recalled the verses that speak of how God expects us to help take care of all the creatures in creation. I'm not sure He meant for us to line their nest with quilts, but He did create them to come up with those ideas on their own.

Precious Father, thank you for the joy that Your creation brings. Help us always to see the value in even the tiniest creation.

Lisa Hildebrand works for Susquehanna Valley Pregnancy Services and ministers as a teacher and speaker in local churches.

Mourning into Dancing

"You have turned for me my mourning into dancing; you have loosed my sackcloth and girded me with gladness…" *Psalms 30:11*

What an amazing picture these few words paint! It is clear that the writer has known grief, but the sorrow that once engulfed him has been replaced with joy. No simple task, but certainly not too difficult for our faithful God!

No one can avoid grief. It's "par for the course." Life is full of unexpected loss and uninvited sadness. We all suffer in some way, but that's not the end of the story!

Anyone who has been afflicted in any way or has navigated the murky waters of depression due to loss knows how hopeless one can feel. The idea of going from that place to being able to break out into a dance of delight seems almost foolish or perhaps even cruel. But there is nothing foolish or cruel about the way He loves us.

In some of my most challenging times, He has graciously come to my rescue, again and again. Surely, He has carried my grief and my sorrows just as Isaiah 53:4 promises. Jesus, the man of sorrows, the One who is well acquainted with grief, has faithfully come alongside me in my difficulties and turned my "mourning into dancing!"

How wonderful it is that our God is not put off by our misery, like others often are. And with tender thoroughness, He removes even the reminder of our heartache, by carefully wrapping us in His gladness! We are released into a cheerful celebration of his care and clothed in glorious contentment.

Thank You, Lord, for carrying me through so many painful seasons. Your everlasting arms have been a great comfort to my soul. I praise You that you wrap me with Your goodness and grace. Your joy is indeed my strength!

Kathi Wilson and her husband Mark, co-authors of *Tired of Playing Church* and co-founders of Body Life Ministries, are members of Ephrata Community Church.

Adore Him

"Come, follow me," Jesus said, "and I will make you fishers of men." *Matthew 4:19*

If you knew me well, you would not be surprised that I start listening to Christmas music in September. And if you *really* knew me, you would understand that I sing these songs rather loudly as I drive. So, God got my attention with words to the carol, "Oh Come All Ye Faithful."

For some reason, I began to sing, "Oh come let us BEHOLD him," instead of, "Oh come let us ADORE him." What was I thinking? And then it really hit me.

Two things. Number one: Obviously, God is not calling us to behold, but adore Jesus. When you behold, you can just walk by and say, "That's nice," before you continue on your way. We behold items in store windows all the time, but we do not necessarily commit to buying them. When you adore, you stop in your tracks, stare, and say, "I gotta have that!"

Number two: The song does not say, "Stand around and notice Jesus." There is an action attached. Come. In order to come, you need to leave behind what you are doing and go to Him. It is a commitment. It cannot be multi-tasked with your job. Peter put his net down to follow Jesus; he did not bring it along. There is no part way. There is no squeezing Him in. If you are totally committed to Jesus, you will squeeze everything else around Him! The wise men got up and risked their lives to come to Jesus. What do you need to drop for Him?

Dear Lord, please show me what I have before You. Give me discipline to drop it, and to come and adore you. I love You. Amen.

Tracy Slonaker is happily married mother of three and Director of Christian Education at Harvest Fellowship of Colebrookdale.

And What Would You Like for Christmas?

"...And be thankful." *Colossians 3:15*

My father, a pastor for many years in Michigan, once had a most interesting thing happen to him. While Christmas shopping one December day at a Sears store, he was passing through a corridor that led from the main store to the automotive department. There, sitting off to the side, he saw the store's Santa Claus eating his lunch. While passing my dad, he heard his name called. It was Santa—a member of the church he pastored!

When asked if he had any interesting stories, this man told my dad of one particular event. He said he had been playing Santa for years, each year listening as the usual flood of kids asked for everything under the sun. Then, one day, a little boy came up and sat on his lap. When asked what he wanted for Christmas, he said, "My Daddy doesn't have much money and he sure would like to have a new pair of pants, my mother doesn't have a nice dress, and she sure would like to have one, and my little sister doesn't have a dolly and she sure would like to have a little dolly."

With that, the boy stopped talking. This man then said to the little boy, "And what would *you* like for Christmas?"

The boy looked up at him and said, "Please Sir, if you have a little toy left over, I sure would like to have one. I've never had a toy."

My dad's friend then told my dad how he excused himself, went into the back room and cried.

Dear Father, You have been so good, so kind, and so generous to us. As a nation, we have been incredibly blessed. And, as Your people, our bounty is almost without limits. May we have thankful hearts. Bless those who have so little and use Your people to point them to You. In Jesus' name. Amen.

Doug Winne is senior pastor of the Lancaster Evangelical Free Church in Lititz.

Applause!

"He who was seated on the throne said, 'I am making everything new!'" *Revelation 21:5*

I was desperately searching for what to do for a Christmas Eve Service. As hard as I thought, nothing was coming. Then, I did what Christians do when they realize *why* they're stuck…I prayed and waited on God. A few days later, God gave me a vision…*Applause!* I heard applause and I saw a man being welcomed home. It was the applause of heaven!

For months I'd been working on a story about a down-and-out man *"adopted"* by a church. But, there was always something missing…Applause! Then, I remembered reading Max Lucado's book, *The Applause of Heaven.* And, I remembered Jesus' words, "Well done, good and faithful servant…come and share your master's happiness!" I realized what my story was missing...focus. The focus needed to be on the transformational work of the Lord. Suddenly I had a story from God, and a Christmas Eve play. But, little did I know how important it would be to stay focused on that vision from God.

It seemed like everything that could possibly derail a play happened. Cast problems…director problems…personal problems. But God kept bringing that vision to my mind…Applause! Every time it seemed that the whole thing was about to implode, God would bring that vision back to mind.

Despite all the problems, the cast became those characters and God used the play to bless people in ways that was amazing. Afterwards, people were saying things like, *"You told the story of my life…that was me!"* *"That was the story of my father's life."* One man, in tears, couldn't even finish what he was trying say. Sometimes, the story we try to tell is ours. But, only God's story can transform and define people's lives.

God, thank you for the salvation that Your love has made possible for all of us down-and-outs who desperately need to belong to Your eternal family of Christ.

Dave Klingensmith is pastor of worship and youth at Sandy Hill Community Church in Coatesville.

Celebrate His Coming Every Day

"For to us a child is born, to us a son is given, and the government will be on his shoulders. And he will be called Wonderful Counselor, Mighty God, Everlasting Father, Prince of Peace." *Isaiah 9:6*

Why do we celebrate Christmas only one day of the year? While it may be fun sharing gifts with one another, is our focus truly on the one that the prophets of old declared, "One was coming who would pay the price of sin for mankind." It was supposed to be an unusual event, but most people didn't fully comprehend what all this meant. Even His own mother struggled to understand how she would carry a child conceived by the Spirit, instead of an earthly father. Yet to her amazement, this child grew within and was one day born into this world.

He was and is the "Great I Am." Much was born to us that day. The redemptive power of Christ was given to us. Through the giving of this child, the Father's love was revealed to us. There was now an everlasting light that would pierce the darkness—through this light, hope was brought to the hopeless.

Then why not celebrate the birth of our Savior every day of the year! I grew up in a home that did not exchange or give gifts during Christmastime. However, one Christmas morning, when I was twelve years old, I came downstairs to the kitchen to see the table set. There was an orange, a few nuts and a piece of candy on each plate. I was delighted. It was not the gift that blessed me, but the attitude of my father's heart wanting to bless his children.

There are many different ways to share His love. It could be a hug, a word of encouragement, or a note. A small blessing could mean the world to another. Make an effort to celebrate His coming every day. Every day is special in God's eyes.

Father, thank you for giving us Your Son. Give us a revelation that we might experience Your joy every day. We want to celebrate the coming of Your Son, morning, noon and night, every day of every year!

Lydia Anne Miller is a wife and mother of two and attends Newport DOVE Christian Fellowship.

An Angel's Timely Appearance

"Go ye into all the world, and preach the gospel to every creature."
Mark 16:15 (King James Version)

With the advent of the interstate highways, it is possible to travel seventy miles in one hour and not truly see anything. As I prayer walked seventy miles through the western part of West Virginia along the North Bend Trail Rail, I saw more than some people do in a lifetime. I also heard the voice of the people telling their own "God Stories"—something you do not hear while driving on a busy highway.

Near the village of Cornwallis as I sat down by a gravel road to rest my feet, a voice startled me. An older gentleman was standing behind me. Soon we were chatting about God and America. Then Roy gave a testimony about when he was in the hospital and saw and was spoken to by an angel.

Roy's heart had three arteries with 95 percent blockage. The doctor informed him that he needed open-heart surgery. Later an angel in the form of man came to his bedside to say that he was sent from God and that Roy did not need open-heart surgery. When the doctor came to see Roy four days later, Roy was smiling and appeared to be in much better condition. Roy told him that his God informed him that he did not need open-heart surgery. The doctor was so taken by Roy's testimony that he performed angioplasty instead. God's healing power was so evident that day that the doctor and all the nurses that performed the operation came to the Lord. Roy is a seventy-six-year-old man who does not keep his God a secret. Roy would have witnessed to me if I were not a Christian. Roy knows that he serves an awesome God.

Father, may we please have the boldness to share Your light by witnessing to others about our faith in Your son, Jesus.

Jim Shaner is a board member of Chester County Women's Services Medical and founder of One Nation Under God–Walk Across America.

Finishing Strong

"Therefore, since we are surrounded by such a great cloud of witnesses, let us throw off everything that hinders and the sin that so easily entangles, and let us run with perseverance the race marked out for us." *Hebrews 12:1*

This year marks the twentieth year that I will be a Christian. Twenty years, wow! That's more than half the years I've been alive. It's hard to believe that just a few short blocks up the street is the exact place where I gave my life to Christ with my good friend Jim looking on.

I often think about Jim since he passed away about a year ago. He taught me so much about God and the importance of studying the Bible. He also taught me the importance of always being ready to give an answer for why I believe. He died on Good Friday of last year of a massive heart attack in his study. I wonder sometimes if he can see me in heaven. I just want him to know that I'm doing my best to pass on some of the same things he passed on to me. That I'm carrying his torch and I'll keep on carrying it till the day the Lord calls me home. Hopefully by then someone will be ready to take the torch from me.

Jim was a man who did his best to live out his faith and because he was not afraid to do so, he played a big part in my coming to Christ. He was a living example to me as to why we must continue to live out our faith for all the world to see. This is why we must press on and do our best to finish strong. Because there are others out there who are searching for truth, others who are lost, and others who are looking for God. Can they find him in you?

Help us God to finish strong until the day You call us home. Amen.

Rob Heverling is a youth leader at Mount Aetna Bible Church in Myerstown.

The Really Real Thing

"…He has also set eternity in the hearts of men…." *Ecclesiastes 3:11*

Every Christmas our family, like many others in the church, orders poinsettias to help decorate the sanctuary for the season. After the Christmas Eve service everyone takes their poinsettias home. Since we were going to visit my mom in Ohio the next day, we decided to take one to her. So, we packed it up in the car with all the rest of our bags, gifts and luggage, and gave it to her when we arrived. She placed it on a table in the living room and watered it regularly. A few weeks later, after we were back home, I was talking with her on the phone and she told me of her surprise at how nice the poinsettia had stayed (she attributed this to putting ice cubes in it instead of actual water). But eventually, when *none* of the leaves fell off, her curiosity was aroused. A closer inspection revealed that the poinsettia she had been watering all these weeks was artificial. I had picked up the wrong one!

It made me think of how watering artificial plants is similar to us when we focus exclusively on temporal things rather than the eternal. It's not the *really* real thing. Although the scripture tells us that God has made everything beautiful in its time, he has also set eternity in the hearts of men. That mark of eternity whispers to us that we are made for something other than this world. Something more. Something real.

Father, I pray You will help us learn how to look beyond the present, to reach for the higher goal, and let the mark of eternity guide us in all we do in our brief stay here on earth.

Becky Toews leads the women's ministry at New Covenant Christian Church. This is an excerpt from her new book, *Virgin Snow: Leaving Your Mark in the World.*

What Really Matters

"But store up for yourselves treasures in heaven, where moth and rust do not destroy, and where thieves do not break in and steal. For where your treasure is, there your heart will be also."
Matthew 6:20–21

I stared in disbelief at the news article. A significant business construction project that I had developed, sold, and overseen less than ten years before was being totally disbanded. The intricate plans and buildings we worked hard in developing were now likely to sit empty. I had poured my all into that project. I recalled the huge celebration of my peers when the project was signed. This was followed by countless job meetings, endless travel, thousands of details, stress in managing costs, and facilitating a nail biting schedule with a host of contractors. When completed, it was truly a hallmark project. Now only a few years later it was being totally disbanded. How can this be?

Talk about shaping perspective. My pride and joy was checked as I found myself needing to inwardly grieve as I read the disheartening news release. It is so easy to lose focus or misplace perspective in the pursuit of life, isn't it? Thankfully, as a believer, my heart and identity is not in earthly things where moth and rust destroy.

The Lord quietly reminded me afresh of what really matters in life. It is not the things we build, the masterpieces we attach our name to, nor the credentials in our résumé. How quickly these fade and fall away, especially in the ever-changing world we live in today.

What really matters are the things that will last, our eternal treasures. To look at the life of Jesus will provide a perspective of heavenly treasures. Do our day-timers, checkbooks, and ambitions reflect this eternal perspective?

Lord, may my day-timer and personal goals today give evidence of living with an eternal perspective rooted in Jesus Christ.

Brian E. Martin serves as lead pastor at Weaverland Mennonite Church in East Earl. He and his wife Shirley have two married and two young adult children, and one grandchild.

Finishing Well

"Altogether, Enoch lived 365 years. Enoch walked with God; then he was no more, because God took him away." *Genesis 5:23–24*

When I got into my office, I noticed that the light was blinking on my answering machine. I pushed the *play* button and heard the voice of a woman asking me to please call her back as she was trying to make a connection with a church in Ephrata.

Returning the call, I reached Betty. She was ninety years old and living in a local retirement home. One of the nurses that cared for her was from Ephrata and going through a very difficult time. Betty thought that we may be able to help her. As we talked, I was blessed and challenged by Betty's joy and passion for the Lord. It was refreshing, and the "fragrance" of Jesus was everywhere. As our conversation came to a close, she said, "I pray that God will give me one more day to intercede for the lost and share the good news with them."

Many years ago, at a pastors' conference, I was reminded of all the men and women in scripture who wholeheartedly served God for a period of time but at the end of their lives were not serving Him. At that conference I made a commitment to finish well. After all, it is not how we begin the race but how we finish that counts.

Betty was an example to me of one who was finishing well. Even though she experienced some difficult things throughout life, she did not become bitter or resentful but is experiencing the joy of the Lord and pointing others to Him.

Lord, forgive me for the times I have allowed my passion for You to wane. Help me to return to my first love and restore my passion for You. Amen.

Kevin Horning serves as pastor of New Life Fellowship in Ephrata.

The Open Door

"Here I am! I stand at the door and knock. If anyone hears my voice and opens the door, I will come in and eat with him, and he with me."
Revelation 3:20

It was New Year's Eve and my wife was on call for the recovery room. I was trying to content myself with some reading, and what was on TV did not interest me. I was trying to think of something to salvage the evening. I had received a phone call several days before, requesting that I visit a person who had attended our church as a youth but had left for a different kind of life. He was now very ill and his mother and children were concerned for his salvation. I discussed visiting him with my wife. She thought it might be beyond her thirty-minute limit from the hospital, but we decided to check if it suited for us to visit.

I called and learned that the man was not feeling well and was not receiving visitors that day. I said I would try the next day, but the woman asked for my name. When I told her, she said he had talked about me and that she'll check if he would be open for a visit. He agreed that I should come.

When we met him, he was on oxygen and had labored breathing. He was glad to see me and we talked about the past and his physical condition. I talked with him about much water going over the dam and would he be willing to recommit his life to the Lord? With tears in his eyes, he acknowledged how he had walked away from God and had sinned. We prayed together as God met us there and a peace and joy filled the room.

The next morning we received a phone call saying he was taken to Hospice overnight. Within an hour another call told us that the Lord had called him home.

Praise God for opening doors for peace to be made and for calling us to minister for Him. Amen.

Glenn Hoover and his wife, Ginny, serve on the leadership team at Carpenter Community Church.

Index

A Celebration of Partnership

The following regional networks within South Central Pennsylvania partnered in publishing this devotional. We invite you to contact them to learn more about how God is at work to bring transformation in your local region.

The Regional Church of Lancaster County

Keith Yoder, Chair, and Lisa Hosler, Assistant Chair
Box 311, Leola, PA 17540
Phone: (717) 625-3034   www.theregionalchurch.com

We are a network of Christian congregational, marketplace, and ministry leaders dedicated to the growth of God's Kingdom in Lancaster County through relational partnership.

To attain spiritual and social transformation of Lancaster County, we actively cultivate partnerships to:

PRAY: fill the region with continual united prayer and worship
WITNESS: communicate the gospel of Jesus Christ to every person in each local community and culture group
LOVE: mobilize initiatives to transform our communities with the love of God
PROTECT: promote biblical unity, reconcile relationships, and provide spiritual discernment for the well-being of the Church.

Many partnerships; one mission: Lancaster County transformed by the gospel of Jesus Christ.

Reading Regional Transformation Network

Craig Nanna, Director
P.O. Box 8188, Reading, PA 19603
Phone: (610) 371-8386   Email: craignanna@readingdove.org

Reading House of Prayer

Chad Eberly, Director
Phone: (610) 373-9900 Email: ChadE@rhop.net   www.rhop.net

Uniting leaders together in strategic kingdom relationships for the purpose of transformation in the Reading region. Our priorities include advancing the kingdom of God in the Reading region through relationship, the unity of the body of Christ, the house of prayer, and strategic initiatives that will produce transformation.

Transforming Ministries: Coatesville Regional

Bill Shaw, Executive Director
643 East Lincoln Highway, P.O. Box 29, Coatesville, PA 19320
Phone: (610) 384-5393   www.QuietRevolution.org

A catalyst in the movement for church unity and community transformation. Generated out of humility and united prayer the mission of LTM is to feature the Lordship of Jesus by being a conduit for the development of trusting cross cultural relationships and incubator of collaborative ministry initiatives.

Lebanon Valley Prayer Network

Stephen J. Sabol, Executive Director
825 North Seventh Street, Lebanon, PA 17046
Phone: (717) 273-9258

This Network exists to lay a foundation of worship and intercessory prayer for the purpose of birthing transformation in the Lebanon Valley.

Lebanon 222

Jay McCumber, Director
515 Cumberland Street, Lebanon, PA 17042
Phone: (717) 279-5683

The Lebanon 222 Team exists to discern and implement God's heart for the Lebanon Valley.

Capital Region Pastors' Network

Dave Hess, President
P. O. Box 9, Camp Hill, PA 17001-0009
Phone: 717.909.1906   Email: c.reg.pastors@pa.net

We are a network of pastors in the Capital Region of Pennsylvania committed to Christ and to developing relationships among pastors, rooted in prayer, which lead to partnerships in ministry bearing the fruit of revival.

For more copies of this book

Visit www.theregionalchurch.com